T0135879

Bibliographic information published by the Deutsche Nationalbibliothek

The Deutsche Nationalbibliothek lists this publication in the Deutsche
Nationalbibliografie; detailed bibliographic data are available
in the Internet at http://dnb.d-nb.de .

ISBN 978-3-8325-2361-9

Logos Verlag Berlin GmbH
Comeniushof, Gubener Str. 47,
D-10243 Berlin
Tel.: +49 (0)30 42 85 10 90
Fax: +49 (0)30 42 85 10 92
INTERNET: http://www.logos-verlag.de

Nelson Baloian, Wolfram Luther, Dirk Söffker,
Yoshiyori Urano (Eds.)

Interface and Interaction Design for Learning and Simulation Environments

International DAAD-PhD Summer Academy at the University of
Duisburg-Essen, Duisburg, July 20 to August 7, 2009

Revised Contributions

Volume Editors

Nelson Baloian
Department of Computer Science – Universidad de Chile
Blanco Encalada 2120, Santiago 6511224, Chile
E-mail: nbaloian@dcc.uchile.cl

Wolfram Luther
University of Duisburg-Essen,
Chair of Scientific Computing, Computer Graphics, and Image Processing
Lotharstraße 65, 47048 Duisburg, Germany
E-mail: luther@inf.uni-due.de

Dirk Söffker
University of Duisburg-Essen,
Chair of Dynamics and Control
Lotharstraße 1, 47048 Duisburg, Germany
E-mail: dirk.soeffker@uni-due.de

Yoshiyori Urano
Graduate School of Global Information and Telecommunication Studies
Waseda University
Honjo-Campus, Japan
E-mail: urano@waseda.jp

ACM Subject Classification (1998): H.1.2, H.5.2, H.5.3.

Preface

The goal of three international DAAD Summer Academies was to bring together highly motivated young researchers at the PhD level with their professors and internationally renowned experts in the emerging interdisciplinary fields of human-machine interaction and computer supported cooperative work. Additionally, the organizers hoped to extend the bi-national PhD-net programme recently launched by the German Academic Exchange Service (DAAD) to the three Universities of Chile, Duisburg-Essen, Germany, and Waseda in Tokyo, Japan.

During a three-week period at the end of July and the beginning of August 2009, thirty-two participants took part in the DAAD Summer Academy organized by the department of Computer Science and Applied Cognitive Science at Duisburg. This publication gathers the original material presented by the lecturers along with brief introductions and explanations. This collection shows the state of the art in the fields of human-machine interactions in different application scenarios, modeling, analyzing and evaluating groupware systems and cognitive technical systems, ubiquitous and mobile learning environments, including reviews of the development of the scientific fields involved, and new ideas and research directions. The Human-Machine Interaction in Networked Systems series will be continued at the University of Waseda focusing on collaborative learning interactions in communities of practice and learning in February 2010.

Acknowledgments

The organizers of the international PhD Summer Academy 2009 in Duisburg would like to express their deep gratitude to all participating lecturers. Without their contributions neither the Summer Academy nor this book would have been possible. Special thanks are due to the German Academic Exchange Service (DAAD) for funding three consecutive Summer Academies in Santiago, Duisburg, and Tokyo.

CONTENTS

From Action to Intelligent Interaction: Cognitive Architectures realizing Flexible Behavior

Dirk Söffker

Chair of Dynamics and Control, University of Duisburg-Essen, D-47048 Duisburg

1 From Action to Intelligent Interaction: Motivation

Motivation and Outline

Classical control approaches realize fast, realiable, and calculated behavior. Depending on the underlying model quality or related system knowledge used during design process technical applications can be improved, new solutions be implemented etc. Instead of automated solutions human-based solutions may be not reliable, but ensure up to now another quality of flexible and adaptive behavior, especially the human ability to deal with unknown situations, to learn from interaction, and from own experiences is unique. The task for future applications is: how can combined Human-Machine-Systems assisted or replaced by technical cognition, resp. how Cognitive Technical Systems can be used to improve technical and/or HMS-based applications?

2 What is the common aspect between Human-Machine-Interaction, between Information Science and Control, and between todays cognitive approaches and former ideas of cybernetics?

Control: the hard and the soft view / Feedback / SISO / MIMO

The idea of feedback to improve the dynamical behavior of the outputs of technical solutions as well as of complex systems (in general) is not new. The general idea of feedback introduced by Wiener in the 40ties of the 20th century fixes to systems in general, whereby the similiar idea introduced by Schmidt at the 'Technische Hochschule Berline-Charlottenburg' fixes to technical applications. The later extended ideas introducing the term closed-loop as well as the idea of algorithm looks different but realizes the same principal idea but from todays view with different objects. Based on some axioms and definitions like 'system', 'causality', very easily feedback loops can be realized. The engineers task of realizing system theoretic goals like stability, observability, contrallability, robustness etc. leads to different approaches focussing to technical control of

Single Input - Single Output (SISO) as well as Multi Input - Multi Output (MIMO) systems. The common aspect of the known technical approaches is that the design of the implemented feedback rule is usually rule-based or model-based, nevertheless the rule as well as the model-based feedback is designed in advance.

3   What is interaction?

Interaction / Human-Machine-Interaction I-VI / Interaction

Interaction can be defined as the ongoing causal exchange of two units individually to each other. The units (understand as systems) are acting autonomously, so also humans can be understand as systems. Besides technical system-system interaction and social science-oriented human-human interaction, possible combinations also include human-system interaction, which is considered here. Descriptions of human-human interaction are usually based on description techniques using linguistic terms, while technical system-system interaction can be described by formalized, typically qualitative and/or quantitative mathematics-based approaches. But how can human-machine interaction be described? Details and a list of further reading are given in [1].

The interaction itself is examined with respect to clustering, analysis of human errors and formalization. It was observed that the formalization is strongly related to the internal structure of the sequences, whereby this structure is related to the logic of the action sequence. This observation forms the core of the situation-operator model extended and developed by the author. In contrast to previous publications about situations and/or states and actions, this examination [1] leads to the internal structuring of situations and requirements related to the modeling of actions, including the one defined as situation-operator sequence or modeling (SOM). Other examples of the HMI class under consideration are the pilot-aircraft and the operator-power plant relationship.

The typical feature of the HMI-systems to be considered here are

- the complexity of the technical system to be controlled,
- the spatial distinction between the guiding operator and the system,
- the high grade of automatic or autonomous subsystems to be guided by the operator, and
- the guiding, observing, and/or monitoring character of the human operators work.

The 'closed loop' concept of control science as a metaphor shows the principal structure of the interaction, whereby, in contrast to technical control loops, the human-system interaction closed loop cannot be described by mathematical equations or by technical/physical values. Furthermore, the question arises of how the higher goals of technical control loops, such as stability, robustness, observability and controllability, can be examined within this context. To solve the question about the suitable description of human-machine interactions, it is necessary to determine what information is observable from the scenes that can be used for measuring within the modeling context. But what is a measurement? Within this context, spoken words and visible actions on the part of the human as well as displayed parameters and observable behavior on the part of the machine that can be measured or monitored are denoted as measurements. Furthermore, knowledge is available about the context of actions.

4 The Situation-Operator-Model modeling technique

Qualitative Modeling I-VI

The SOM-approach in detail is introduced in [1], updated and detailed in [3,4], and within this context already detailed in the previous summer academy contribution [5].

The description of complex systems using a Situation-Operator model allows

- the mixture of different types of (variable) quantities (the relations R can be different ones within the situation S),
- the integration of logical and numerical quantities (by different characteristics C), and
- the description of real-world problems using a mixture of a complex set of descriptions (variables).

Operators are used to model the system changes (changes of situations). This defines the events of the change of the considered part of the real world, the system. Operators and situations are closely connected due to the identity (partial or complete) of the characteristics of the situations and the explicit assumptions of the operators. This includes the situation consisting of passive operators (internal causal relation: because), whereby the change is carried out by active operators (external causal relation: to). The change in the considered world results as a sequence of actions modeled by operators. It should be noted that operators correspond to situations. Both are used not only for structural representation of the system's organization but also for internal representation and storage of human operators and intelligent systems. They are the core/background of all the higher organized internal (cognitive) functions and procedures of intelligent systems, like learning, planning, and also of the proposed supervision concept. Furthermore, it becomes clear that learning results from a loop between estimated behavior (using cognitive structures with elements of the mental model for such purposes as planning) and the observed behavior of the environment, which-in the case of non-agreement with the prediction-provides good reasons to reflect on the assumed behavior and its elements, which is called learning. This loop also makes clear i) that learning without feedback (or without environment) is not possible and ii) that different points, elements and facts are necessary for successful learning processes, including previous knowledge, available cognitive functions (like dealing with mental elements and planning procedures), the possibility of suitable environment reaction observation and also the ability to observe and remark differences between postulated and observed behavior. These differences can be easily detailed and used to structure the learning process as well as possible difficulties within this complex loop. The author discusses in detail several student theses regarding a) classification of human errors, b) modeling of human learning, c) reconstruction of mental models from interviews, d) reconstruction of mental models from observed and monitored human behavior during disasters and e) classification of dynamic group decisions in [1].

The resulting cognitive architecture describing human cognitives procedures starting with perception as a process mainly defined by previous knowledge and structuring abilities, detailing situation awareness as the individual process of situated understanding, interpreting, and cognitively working with the percepted input in combination with the already known and experienced knowledge.

5 Modeling and models of human cognition and cognitive architectures

Models of human cognition, Comparison of the modeling approaches

Based on Strubes definition of cognition [6] also technical systems can be defined as cognitive if they are able to act on the base of knowledge resp. using a knowledge representation level. The related tasks using cognitive functions and procedures [2] allow the system the act and to interact with its environment. From this point of view depending on the abilities of the representation level Cognitive Technical Systems can play roles as controller, intelligent interface, supervisor etc.

Cacciabue [2] introduced criteria to compare models of human cognition. Human cognition in general includes cognitive functions and cognitive procedures, whereby cognitive functions include the phenomenological observable aspects of human learning, human reasoning and planning. Cognitive procedures relate the functions with the memory and so forth. The criteria developed by Cacciabue [4] are PIPE, AoR, and KB, denoting respectively perception, interpretation, planning and execution, allocation of resources, and knowledge base. Unfortunately it is not clear in which way these aspects of human models are able to detail all possible aspects of human cognition modeling as well as the implementation aspects of human models for programming. The models are discussed in detail by Cacciabue[4].

6 Elements realizing Cognitive Technical Systems (CTS)

Implementation aspects realizing CTS / Ongoing CTS projects of SRS I-V

Technical systems usually are connected with the environment with sensors and actuators, so physical variables of different qualities has to be measured. Preparing the data to information, prefilters has to be built, realizing complexity reduction. Obviously the prefilters has to be pre-programmed or skilled to fullfil the task. Up to now the training of prefilters has to done be supervisors. Independing from this it should be noted that substantiated knowledge may be not free of errors and also has possibly to be refined or updated.

If the representations level is fixed (by the approach or the task) the related algorithmic elements realizing cognitive functions and procedures can be implemented. Especially within virtual or synthetic environments the principal aspects of cognition can be studied by simulation. Here especially the aspects of learning as well as refining of learned aspects are of interest.

The refining process of the underlying model structure can also be done by mathematical approaches, like statistical smoothing etc. The updated model can therefore be used during the learning and updating process. In case of assistance systems the internal model can first be skilled, than used for supervision, and later used for realizing autonomous behavior, due to the aspect that the model represents after adaption/learning from the interaction the partners behavior by copying its behavior.

A fundamental question is about the point how many knowledge should be included into the Cognitive Technical System by the developer skilling filters or preprogramming task specific aspects. Also aspects about how much of which kind of relations can be learned from the system itself. For robust control of unknown dynamical SISO systems a Cognitive Technical System also should be able to learn from the interaction. Usually the problem is solved by system and parameter identification procedures (to realize a model representing the system). Otherwise the controller as interaction partner is able to identify the systems behavior during interaction, so future controller systems also may have the ability to learn. If no knowlegde can be assumed also the automatic structuring and training of the prefilters has to be realized.

Assumed that Cogntive Technical Systems are able to learn, to act situated and individually, a series of additonal aspects of the realiability and the safety of algorithms, architectures has to be discussed.

7 Recommended literature of the author (and others) detailing the contribution

1. Söffker D: Systemtheoretische Modellbildung der wissensgeleiteten Mensch-Maschine-Interaktion. Logos Wissenschaftsverlag, Berlin, 2003.
2. Cacciabue PC: Modelling and Simulation of Human Behavior in System Control. Springer, London, 1998.
3. Söffker, D.: Interaction of Intelligent and Autonomous Systems - Part I: Qualitative Structuring of Interactions. MCMDS-Mathematical and Computer Modelling of Dynamical Systems, Vol. 14. No. 4, 2008, pp. 303-318.
4. Ahle, E.; Söffker, D.: Interaction of Intelligent and Autonomous Systems - Part II: Realisation of Cognitive Technical Systems. MCMDS-Mathematical and Computer Modelling of Dynamical Systems, Vol. 14. No. 4, 2008, pp. 319-339.

5. Baloian, N.; Luther, W.; Söffker, D.; Urano, Y. (Eds.): Multimodal human-machine interaction in different application scenarios. Readings of the Summer Academy, Santiago de Chile, 2008, Logos Wissenschaftsverlag, Berlin, 2009.

6. Strube, G.; Habel, C.; Konieczny, L.; Hemforth, B.: Handbuch der Künstlichen Intelligenz. Oldenbourg Wissenschaftsverlag, 4th. Edition, 2004, Chapter 2: Kognition, pp. 1972.

©

From Action to Intelligent Interaction: Cognitive Architectures realizing Flexible Behavior

Dirk Söffker

Contact: soeffker@uni-due.de
Website: www.srs.uni-due.de

Chair of Dynamics and Control
University of Duisburg-Essen

UNIVERSITÄT DUISBURG ESSEN

Söffker: From Action to Intelligent Interaction: Cognitive Architectures ...
© for all figures/illustrations by SRS U DuE

Outline

- Motivation
- From control to autonomous behavior: modeling of interaction
  - SISO/MIMO
  - HMS
  - Cognitive behavior
- Cognitive architectures: organization of knowledge for interaction
  - Principal aspects
  - Key features designing cognitive architectures
- Ongoing applications
- Summary and future work

UNIVERSITÄT DUISBURG ESSEN

Söffker: From Action to Intelligent Interaction: Cognitive Architectures ...
© for all figures/illustrations by SRS U DuE

2

Motivation I

Control realizes fast, realiable, and calculated behavior

- Improves interaction and dynamical behavior of technical systems
- Model-based control allows analytical and numerical calculation
- But: needs models > theoretical/exp. modeling

Humans realize flexible and adaptive behavior

- Ability to deal with unknown situations
- Ability to learn from interaction and from own experiences
- But: restricted realibility

Improving/assisting/'replacing' HMS by technical realized cognition

UNIVERSITÄT DUISBURG ESSEN

Söffker: From Action to Intelligent Interaction: Cognitive Architectures ...
© for all figures/illustrations by SRS U DuE

1

Control: the hard view and the soft view

- Cybernetics (Wiener) and Regelkreislehre (Schmidt) (40ties of the 20th century)

	Control	Algorithm
Basic idea:	Realizing feedback	Realizing calculations
Modern view:	Design the dynamic properties	Design the (dynamic) algorithm
Core:	Design the feedback to realize I/O mapping	Design the algorithm to realize I/O mapping
	Object: signals	Object: data (Data type (> variables)

- The human controller realizes knowledge-guided interaction:
  - Are we able to model this human behavior?
  - How can the interaction be described?

UNIVERSITÄT DUISBURG ESSEN

Söffker: From Action to Intelligent Interaction: Cognitive Architectures ...
© for all figures/illustrations by SRS U DuE

3

Idea of feedback

Disturbance
Plant
Controller
Control value
Reference value

Terms:
- **System** > plant
- **Feedback** > controller
- **Interaction:** Dynamics of the closed loop

Task of the Engineer:
Design of the feedback
> Improve dynamics
> Realization of 'higher' goals

Higher Goals:
- Stability
- Improved dynamics
- Robustness
- ...
- Automatic control

4

Söffker: From Action to Intelligent Interaction: Cognitive Architectures …
© for all figures/illustrations by SRS U DuE.

UNIVERSITÄT DUISBURG ESSEN

SISO / Technical control: Facts

System / Plant:	Technical, one input, one output I/O-relation fixed
Feedback / Controller:	Mechanical, fluidic, electrical one input, one output, I/O-rel. fixed
Goal / Aim:	Dynamics, Stability, Robustness
'Who's' designing the feedback?	Humans, in advance
Characterstics System/Controller || Assumptions:	I/O-structure fixed / values: physical tuning (< tuning rules)
Scient. period:	40ties/50ties/60ties 20th century

5

Söffker: From Action to Intelligent Interaction: Cognitive Architectures …
© for all figures/illustrations by SRS U DuE.

UNIVERSITÄT DUISBURG ESSEN

MIMO I

Typical description for (linear) MIMO-systems:
> System of ODEs 1. order (linear, const. coefficients)

$$
\begin{bmatrix} \dot{x}_1 \\ \dot{x}_i \\ \dot{x}_n \end{bmatrix} = \begin{bmatrix} a_{11} \cdots a_{1n} \\ a_{i1} \cdots a_{ii} \cdots a_{in} \\ a_{n1} \cdots a_{ni} \cdots a_{nn} \end{bmatrix} \begin{bmatrix} x_1 \\ x_i \\ x_n \end{bmatrix} + \begin{bmatrix} b_1 \\ b_i \\ b_n \end{bmatrix} u, \quad y = Cx
$$

- Complex dynamics and complex couplings are expressed using ODEs
- Some values are measurable

6

Söffker: From Action to Intelligent Interaction: Cognitive Architectures …
© for all figures/illustrations by SRS U DuE.

UNIVERSITÄT DUISBURG ESSEN

Example:

Control of an inverse, elastic pendulum

7

Söffker: From Action to Intelligent Interaction: Cognitive Architectures …
© for all figures/illustrations by SRS U DuE.

UNIVERSITÄT DUISBURG ESSEN

MIMO: Facts

System / Plant:	Mathematical description, MIMO I/O-relation fixed
Feedback / Controller:	Design by mathematical algorithms realizing problem equivalent goals
Goal / Aims:	Analysis, synthesis of dynamic properties
'Who's' designing the feedback?	Human, in advance
Characteristics of system/controller Assumptions:	I/O-structure fixed, values are represented by mathematical expressions (signals, functions) realizing 'higher' goals
Scientific 'period':	60ties/70ties/80ties 20th century

Söffker: From Action to Intelligent Interaction: Cognitive Architectures ...
© for all figures/illustrations by SRS U DuE

UNIVERSITÄT DUISBURG ESSEN — 8

Interaction

In the minimum two ‚systems' are interacting.

Two-way reaction between players or systems

System – System
Human – Human
Human – System

> **Human-Machine-Interaction**
> **Human-Machine-System**

What is interaction?
How can the interaction be described?

Söffker: From Action to Intelligent Interaction: Cognitive Architectures ...
© for all figures/illustrations by SRS U DuE

UNIVERSITÄT DUISBURG ESSEN — 9

Human-Machine-Interaction I

Example:
Supervision and
Control of
Railway Traffic,

here:
Hagen Electronic
Operating Center of the
Deutsche Bahn AG

Söffker: From Action to Intelligent Interaction: Cognitive Architectures ...
© for all figures/illustrations by SRS U DuE

UNIVERSITÄT DUISBURG ESSEN — 10

Human-Machine-Interaction IV

Abstraction and
aggregation lead to a
strong reduction of
interaction elements

(Gielg (Diploma Thesis), Söffker, 1998)

Söffker: From Action to Intelligent Interaction: Cognitive Architectures ...
© for all figures/illustrations by SRS U DuE

UNIVERSITÄT DUISBURG ESSEN — 11

-10-

Human-Machine-Interaction V

Grafische Darstellung der Handlungssequenz:

Hypothese / Plan:

Tatsächlicher Verlauf:

(Gielg (Diploma Thesis), Söffker, 1998)

Söffker: From Action to Intelligent Interaction: Cognitive Architectures …
© for all figures/illustrations by SRS U DuE

12

Human-Machine-Interaction VI (and assumptions)

Causality ⇔ from the cause to the effect

i) final chain
ii) inner connections

Which is the adequate description? (techn./physic. values > information)

Higher goals: - stability / dynamics - robustness - observability
- controllability -> automatic control

Söffker: From Action to Intelligent Interaction: Cognitive Architectures …
© for all figures/illustrations by SRS U DuE

13

Qualitative Modeling Approach I
(structural variable systems)

Situation:

The term situation describes a fixed problem constellation and denotes the considered system.

The situation consists of an inner structure, which also allows the integration of time-variant values.

The graphical representation is realized by characteristic (C) and inner relations (R). Different detailed graphical representations are possible.

(Söffker, 1998f, 2001, 2003)

Söffker: From Action to Intelligent Interaction: Cognitive Architectures …
© for all figures/illustrations by SRS U DuE

14

Qualitative Modeling II
(structural variable systems)

Operator:

Operators are used to represent functional connections of real world facts. The connection can be passive (constitutional) or active ('ability to change something'). Operators 'represent/model outer world facts'.

The function of an operator is denoted with (F), as 'input' the explicit and implicit assumption for realization of F (eA, IA) are used.

For detailed modeling known techniques will be used.
The SOM-technique is working as a meta-modeling approach.

: Function / (Charakteristic)
: Assumption
: Explicit assumption
: Implicit assumption
: comment

(Söffker, 1998f, 2001, 2003)

Söffker: From Action to Intelligent Interaction: Cognitive Architectures …
© for all figures/illustrations by SRS U DuE

15

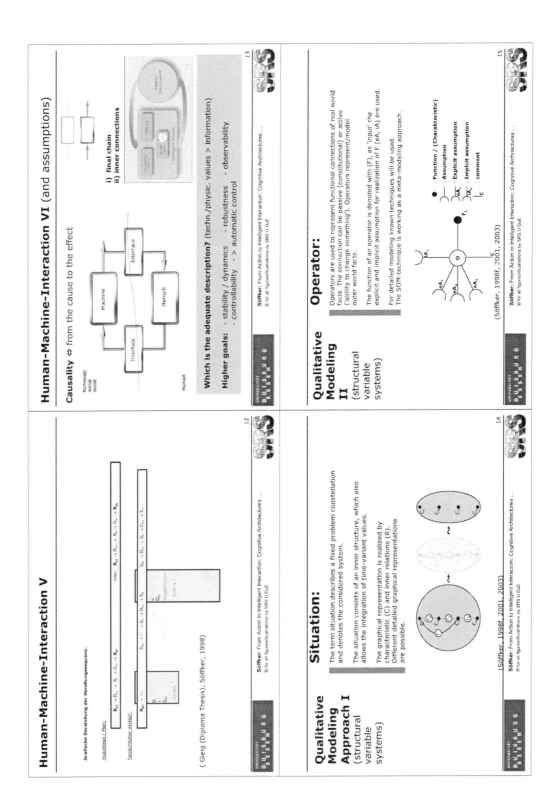

Qualitative Modeling III

(structural variable systems ⇔ cognitive systems ⇔ e.g. HMS)

Start S_1
'Actual'

Goal S_2
'Desired'

$S_1 ; S_2 ; (O_1, O_2, O_3)$

Describtion on the base of assumed facts about the real world

Necessary:
- Model of the 'world' > Human > 'Human interaction'
- Controllability
- Observability

Qualitative Modeling IV

(structural variable systems ⇔ cognitive systems ⇔ HMS)

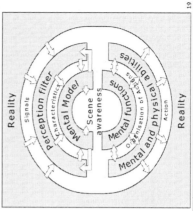

Research Work (SRM, U Wuppertal):
- Classification of human errors, 1998-2001
- Modeling of human learning (of computer gamers), 1997-2001
- Reconstruction of mental models from interviews, 1999-2001
- Desaster reconstruction (BirgenAir Desaster), 1997
- Classification of dynamical group decisions, 2000-2001
  (> Diploma Theses SRM, U Wuppertal; Habilitation Söffker 2001)

Qualitative Modeling V

Qualitative net-oriented approach allows structural analysis

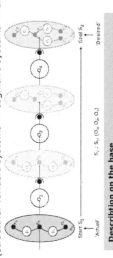

Qualitative Modeling VI

Resulting structure representing the the I/O-behavior

Human-Machine-Systems: Facts

System / plant:	**Qualitative/quantitative describtion** / **I/O-relation variable**
Feedback / Controller:	**Human realizes the interaction** situative, problem equivalent, goal orientiert
Goal / Aim:	**Stabilizing the interaction, realizing goals**
'Who's' designing the feedback?	**regular:** 'designer' **anomal:** the interacting human
Feedback / Controller |Assumptions:	**I/O-relation usually fixed/planned** in anomal cases: learning, concluding, acting: **flexible reaction**
Scientific period:	-

What is cognition? I

Definition:
(Strube, Max-Planck Institute for biological cybernetics, 1995)

- Cognition decouples the inputs and the outputs of systems (may be also of animals or humans),
- allows the anticipation of intended actions as well as the storage of experiences, and
- is not related only to humans or animals.

Relations to systemtheoretic view of dynamical systems:

⬆ I/O-system, adaptive, defined (S-R-/rule-/knowledge-based)

⬆ Cognitive systems are interacting with others (environment, systems).

Cognition can extend the engineering solutions of control, supervision, and assistance. **Why?**
Flexibility to adapt behavior, to act situated appears as key.

What is cognition? II

What makes cognition interesting for engineers? An example:

> basic ideas of AI/behavior-based approaches
> automatic carpet cleaning

I: Class. behavior-based	II: map-based	III: > ‚map'-matching problem <

Resulting idea I: Adaptive modeling, learning abilities or task-oriented situation interpretation may lead to situated ‚understanding' and flexible reaction

---

What is cognition? III

Example II:

> it seems to be possible
to deal with complex systems/complex models
(hybrid / qualitative)

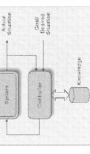

Different levels of model/signal quant.:
A: Equation-based PDE/ODE/DAE
  - scalar/vector-based math. description
B: ….
C: „System' behavior unknown/unstruct.
  - hybrid / complex set of variables

What is cognition? IIIb

Example II:

> Replacing the interacting system

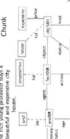

Resulting idea II: Model- and related I/O-description must be choosen problemequivalent; in general: **hybrid hierarchical**

24

Why is cognition also for engineers interesting?

Combination of ideas:

I:	Suitable problem description	⟷	Modeling level > Hybrid hierarchical
II:	Saving and preparing of models an experiences	⟷	Modeling and Memory) > Cognitive features
III:	Goal- and task-oriented use of models and methods	⟷	Realizing learning, planning, ar reasoning in the context of - task and - actual situations.

to realize flexible and situated automatic feedback to affect systems behavior and to reach given goals (Söffker, 2001)

Cognition may be the base for a new kind of control.

25

How to compare cognitive architectures?

Criteria to compare cognitive architectures (Cacciabue, 1998):

PIPE
(Perception, Interpretation, Planning, Execution): cognitive functions

AoR
(Allocation of Resources)
- Interaction between Memory and Knowledge Base

KB
(Knowledge Base / Memory)
- '... denotes the work between KB and Memory ...'

Additional criteria to compare cognitive approaches (Söffker 2001; Ahle, Söffker 2008):

> Modeling and mapping outside world to internal representations
> Formalized homogenious approach

26

Known approaches I

ACT-R (70ties f as ACT*; Anderson, Lebiere, 1998)

- LISP-based semantic net description technique to describe facts with chunks

>> Goal: Knowledge structuring

Fact
The rich young professor buys a beautiful and expensive city house.

Chunk

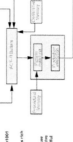

(Anderson, Lebiere: ACT-R 5 Tutorial, 2004)

27

Known approaches II

EPIC (Kieras, 90ties)

>> Realizes the results on human perceptual/motor performance, cognitive modeling techniques, and task analysis methodology

(Kieras, U Michigan, EPIC Report 05/1995)

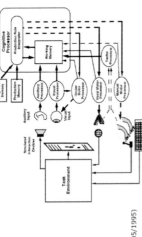

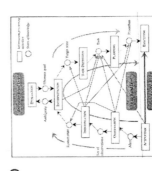

Known approaches III

SHEL (Edwards, 1972)

- States the interaction between Software (Rules), Hardware (Machines), Liveware (Humans), and Environment

SOAR (80ties f; Rosenbloom et al. 1998)

- Problem solution based on equivalent descriptions
- Representation of knowledge in production rules, in objects
- Learning based on neuro-psychological ideas (of chunks)

Known approaches IV

STEP-LADDER (Rasmussen, 1990)

- Identifies qualitatively cognitive functions
>> Repeats R. 3-level concept

(from Cacciabue, 1998)

Known approaches V

FALLIBLE MACHINE (Reason, 1990)

- Complex internal connections
- structuring of the KB
>> Distinction between focal and peripherical memory

KB = Knowledge Base
PWM = Peripheral Working Memory
FWM = Focal Working Memory
FG = Frequency Gambling
SM = Similarity Matching
DS = Direct Search

(from Cacciabue, 1998)

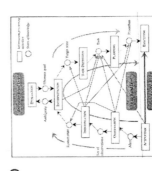

29

30

31

Key features of cognitives approaches I

Requirements/Questions:

- Taskoriented implementation of 3-level approach (skill-based/rule-based/knowledge-base)
  - **Cognitive-Technical-Systems have to include hierarchical implemented knowledge representation (KR) approach.**
- Connection between cognitive functions and modeling approach
  - **KR-approach must allow the realization of all cognitive features.**
  - **Cognitive features must be able to deal with the used KR-approach.**

Söffker: From Action to Intelligent Interaction: Cognitive Architectures ...
© for all figures/illustrations by SRS U DuE — 33

Realized CTS at SRS I

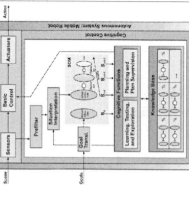

Situative reaction must be flexible for interaction with unknown Environments.

(Ahle, Söffker, 2005)

Söffker: From Action to Intelligent Interaction: Cognitive Architectures ...
© for all figures/illustrations by SRS U DuE

Known approaches VI

COCOM (Hollnagel, 1993)

- Details cognitive functions and procedures and their relations
- Explains perception firstly

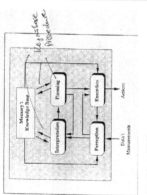

(Cacciabue, 1998)

Söffker: From Action to Intelligent Interaction: Cognitive Architectures ...
© for all figures/illustrations by SRS U DuE — 32

Key features of cognitives approaches II

- Connection between KB and cognitive functions
  - „Operation system' necessary to
    - realize perception/interpretation organization,
    - handle the I/O-relation and
    to realize cognitive functions and procedures
    - refine experienced knowledge structures.

Cognitive architectures realizes the
- organization of I/O-relation (from perception to execution),
- coordination of different levels of behaviors, and
- processing of cognitive functions and procedures.

Cognitive architectures deal with
- task related, problem specific knowledge representations.

No KR or no ability to realize cognitive features
> No cognition

Söffker: From Action to Intelligent Interaction: Cognitive Architectures ...
© for all figures/illustrations by SRS U DuE

Realized CTS at SRS II

Concept of a Situative, Flexible Supervision Module

Advantages:

Logic of human actions is formalizable and can be 'supervised'.

Complex scenes can be described.

Consistent model-based approach

(Ahle, Söffker 2009)

	Real world	Scene	Action
Sensory level	Sensors	Sensors	Sensors

SOM

Replaceable part
Basic/operator library
- Blinking right
- Sheer out right
- Breaking

Meta-operator library
- Quick lane change
- Slow lane change
- Normal lane change

Error classification
- Friction
- Rigidity
- Side- and wideeffects

Processing level:
Setting up situation — Setting up operator — Setting up meta-operator — Checking for errors

Checking assumptions — Checking for goal — Goal trans-formation

Analysis level:
Information to driver — Goal of the driver

Söffker: From Action to Intelligent Interaction: Cognitive Architectures ...
© for all figures/illustrations by SRS U DuE

Implementation aspects realizing CTS I

From sensors raw data to structured information: From signals to information, how?

- Skilled/programmed prefilter to realize 'complexity reduction' - includes task-related knowledge

Using important, detailed by variable facts and relations: How to refine models?

- Constants inside knowledge structures are fixed and combined with variables to be defined by interaction

37

Söffker: From Action to Intelligent Interaction: Cognitive Architectures ...
© for all figures/illustrations by SRS U DuE

Implementation aspects realizing CTS II

Realization of prefilters

- Automatic definition of signal feature combinations describing systems states

State m
State c
State 2
State 1 of human classified training data

A number of m states → Feature filter → Vectors of n features for m states → Regression → Distributions and Membership functions

© SRS 2009

The distribution and the regression of the n features used to distinguish m states build the system model.

38

Söffker: From Action to Intelligent Interaction: Cognitive Architectures ...
© for all figures/illustrations by SRS U DuE

Ongoing CTS projects of SRS I:

- **Simulation of cognition / SOM2 / Map SOM to CPN**
  Dipl.-Ing. D. Gamrad

  > Synthetic worlds   > no prefilters necessary
  > World partially unknown   > learning nessesary
  > **Realization of cognitive features**
  > **Covering and implementation of SOM in suitable languages**
  > **Cognitive architecture building> simulation of cognition**

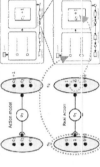

39

Söffker: From Action to Intelligent Interaction: Cognitive Architectures ...
© for all figures/illustrations by SRS U DuE

Ongoing CTS projects of SRS II:

- **Cognitive-based supervision and assistance**
  X. Fu, M.Sc.

  > Real world application   > **prefilters necessary**
  > Logic of action is given   > **knowledge structure is fixed**
                              > **KB refinement nessary**

  > Supervision by checking consistency of interaction
  > Assistance vs. autonomy   > **Decisions/Judgements**

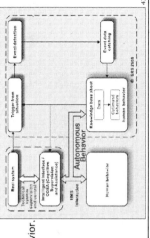

Söffker: From Action to Intelligent Interaction: Cognitive Architectures ...
© for all figures/illustrations by SRS U DuE

UNIVERSITÄT DUISBURG ESSEN

40

Ongoing CTS projects of SRS IIc:

- **Cognitive-based supervision and assistance**
  X. Fu, M.Sc.

  Interface will allow
  - personalization,
  - supervision, and
  - autonomous behavior.

  Refinement of the model by learning of variable elements

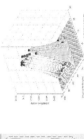

Söffker: From Action to Intelligent Interaction: Cognitive Architectures ...
© for all figures/illustrations by SRS U DuE

UNIVERSITÄT DUISBURG ESSEN

41

Ongoing CTS projects of SRS IId:

- **Cognitive-based supervision and assistance**
  X. Fu, M.Sc.

  Interface will allow
  - personalization,
  - supervision, and
  - autonomous behavior.

  Cognitive supervision on the base of actual models

Söffker: From Action to Intelligent Interaction: Cognitive Architectures ...
© for all figures/illustrations by SRS U DuE

UNIVERSITÄT DUISBURG ESSEN

42

Ongoing CTS projects of SRS IIe:

- **Cognitive-based supervision and assistance**
  X. Fu, M.Sc.

  Interface will allow
  - personalization,
  - supervision, and
  - autonomous behavior.

  Supervision allows also switching to autonomous behavior in cases of emergency

Söffker: From Action to Intelligent Interaction: Cognitive Architectures ...
© for all figures/illustrations by SRS U DuE

UNIVERSITÄT DUISBURG ESSEN

43

Ongoing CTS projects of SRS III:

- **Robust control of complete unknown nonlinear systems**
  F. Zhang, M.Eng.

> Numerical model
> (to represent the system)

> **KB unknown**
> **KB is explored by interaction of controller-system**
> **KB is graphically represented.**
> Knowledge about stability is implictly used.

> Knowledge structure unknown, constant knowledge (stability) is used.

> Learning is only possible by analyzing the interaction.
> **Control trials are choosing by simulation optimization based on actual KB.**

Söffker: From Action to Intelligent Interaction: Cognitive Architectures ...
© for all figures/illustrations by SRS U DuE

44

Ongoing CTS projects of SRS IV:

- **Multi-sensor/multi-information fusion for process supervision based on skilled or automatically defined prefilters**
  Hammoud Al-Joumaa, B.Sc.
  Loui Al-Shrouf, M. Sc.

> Real world, real classified data

> **Definition of prefilters**
> **Automatic definition of prefilters**

Söffker: From Action to Intelligent Interaction: Cognitive Architectures ...
© for all figures/illustrations by SRS U DuE

45

Summary and future work

Summary

- Cognition features may improve controllers behavior by the implemented flexibility (situated and knowledge-based; learning abilities)

- Main aspects are:
  - KB/Information structuring and the combination with cognitive features and functions > E. description || Cognitive architecture
  Keys are:
  - Task-oriented KB structuring
  - Task-oriented cognitive features

Future work > Next steps

- All-in-One-approach

- Optimization of learning/adaption approaches

Söffker: From Action to Intelligent Interaction: Cognitive Architectures ...
© for all figures/illustrations by SRS U DuE

46

Thank you for your attention!

From Action to Intelligent Interaction:
Cognitive Architectures realizing flexible Behavior

Dirk Söffker

Head of Chair of Dynamics and Control (SRS)
Engineering Faculty
University of Duisburg-Essen

Lotharstr. 1-21, 47057 Duisburg, GERMANY

E-mail: soeffker@uni-due.de
Web: www.srs.uni-due.de

Tel.:   0049 203 379 – 3429
Fax: 0049 203 379 – 3027

Any questions?

Söffker: From Action to Intelligent Interaction: Cognitive Architectures ...
© for all figures/illustrations by SRS U DuE

47

Modeling and Analysis of Interaction for the Realization of Cognitive Technical Systems

Dennis Gamrad, Dirk Söffker

University of Duisburg-Essen, Chair of Dynamics and Control
{dennis.gamrad, soeffker}@uni-due.de

1 Modeling of human interaction behavior

Modeling process of ..., From the real world to ..., From the model to ... I-II, From the simulation to ..., Example: Detection of the human error rigidity

The contribution presents an approach for the automated analysis of Human-Machine-Interaction [1] and its implementation as representational level for a cognitive architecture [2]. As a basis of the approach, the interaction between a human operator and a technical system is formalized using a Situation-Operator-Modeling (SOM) approach [3]. The implementation of a SOM-based model of interactions is realized using high-level Petri Nets [4, 5]. From the Petri Net model a full state space can be generated, which contains all possible situations of the system. The state space is analyzed by formal query functions, e.g. to detect human errors [6], which are formulated in a generic manner.

2 Cognitive architecture and learning from interaction

Cognitive architecture, Architecture of ..., Implementation of ..., Action model ..., Modeling of perception, Learning, Learning of operator's ... I-II, Learning of relations, Learning of meta operators

The cognitive functions planning, perception, and learning as well as the interaction with the environment and the suitable representation of knowledge are strongly connected to each other. The proposed cognitive architecture provides a unique and homogeneous SOM-based representational level for all cognitive functions. Furthermore, the whole information processing is based on the same methodical background. Additionally, the architecture allows the integration of different AI methods for planning, learning, etc. As a special feature, several instances of the architecture can be combined.

Due to the fact that the environment is usually not static and partially unknown, a cognitive system has to be able to learn from interaction with the environment. By the cognitive function learning, it is able to extend and refine its mental model to improve its performance successively with respect to a given task. In the proposed architecture, the operators as well as the structure of the situation can be learned. For the learning of operators two different approaches are implemented, the learning of experiences (effects of an operator to a special situation) from the interaction and the learning of the operator's function and assumptions (effects of an operator to situations in general). Finally, learning of the situation's structure results from a generalization of the operator's assumptions.

Beside the learning of experiences and operators' functions and assumptions, the sample size of the assumptions and the effort of operators related to the needed time or energy can be learned, too. Furthermore, a sequence of operators can be combined to a meta operator. They can be used as a representation of successful plans or frequently performed action sequences.

3 Example of application / experimental results

Application to ..., Arcade game: ..., Modeling of interaction, Simulation and ...

As an example of application, the proposed cognitive architecture is connected to an arcade game [7] and has to learn its interaction rules. In the arcade game an agent interacts with a grid-based environment. The environment consists of different kinds of fields and the agent can perform the four moving actions `up', `down', `left', and `right'. The functions and assumptions of the operators are modeled in the action model to enable goal directed behavior by the generation of plans. However, the mental model has not to be fully realized, since the system learns from interaction.

The simulation results show that the mental model of the proposed cognitive architecture is refined in a suitable way to realize goal-directed behavior. The mental model is used to enable planning and interaction with the environment, the differences between internal representation and outside world are detected, and learning improves the performance of the system.

References

1. Gamrad, D., Oberheid, H., Söffker, D: Automated Detection of Human Errors based on Multiple Partial State Spaces. MATHMOD 2009 - 6th Vienna International Conference on Mathematical Modelling, 651 – 659 (2009).
2. Gamrad, D., Söffker, D: Simulation of Learning and Planning by a Novel Architecture for Cognitive Technical Systems. 2009 IEEE International Conference on Systems, Man, and Cybernetics (2009).
3. Söffker, D.: Systemtheoretic Modeling of the knowledge-guided Human-Machine-Interaction (In German). Habilitation Thesis, Univ. of Wuppertal (2001), published at Logos Wissenschaftsverlag, Berlin (2003).
4. Jensen, K.: Coloured Petri Nets. Basic Concepts, Analysis Methods and Practical Use. Vol. 1-3, Springer-Verlag (1997).
5. Kummer, O.: Referenznetze. Logos Wissenschaftsverlag, Berlin (2002).
6. Dörner, D.: The Logic of Failure: Recognizing and Avoiding Error in Complex Situations. Perseus Publishing (1997).
7. Rocks'n'Diamonds, http://www.artsoft.org/rocksndiamonds/, Artsoft Entertainment (2004).

Modeling and Analysis of Interaction for the Realization of Cognitive Technical Systems

Dennis Gamrad and Dirk Söffker

Contact: dennis.gamrad@uni-due.de
Website: www.srs.uni-due.de

Chair of Dynamics and Control
University of Duisburg-Essen

Motivation I

Autonomous technical systems

- Localize and plan actions by themselves
- Refine and use domain specific models of the environment

Cognitive systems

- Unknown environments and situations
- Learn from interaction with the environment
- Flexible behavior

➤ Cognitive Technical Systems

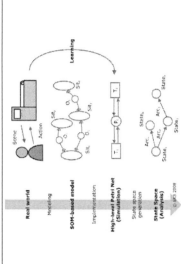

Gamrad, Söffker: Modeling and Analysis of Interaction for the Realization of Cognitive T…
© for all figures/illustrations by SRS U DuE

Motivation II

Cognitive Technical Systems

- Interdisciplinary field
- Inspired by human cognition
- Interaction with the environment
- Cognitive functions

Mental model

- Representation of outside world
- Structuring of knowledge

➤ Knowledge representation as key feature of cognitive systems

➤ Situation-Operator-Modeling (SOM) approach

Gamrad, Söffker: Modeling and Analysis of Interaction for the Realization of Cognitive T…
© for all figures/illustrations by SRS U DuE

Modeling process of human interaction behavior

Real world

Modeling

SOM-based model

Implementation

High-level Petri Net (Simulation)

State space generation

State Space (Analysis)

Learning

Gamrad, Söffker: Modeling and Analysis of Interaction for the Realization of Cognitive T…
© for all figures/illustrations by SRS U DuE

From the real world to the model

Real world   ...

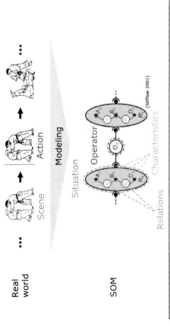

Scene   Action   ...

Modeling

Situation

SOM

Operator

Characteristics

Relations

[Söffker 2001]

4

From the model to the simulation I

SOM-based models and high-level Petri Nets consist of passive und active elements.

[Söffker 2001]

5

From the model to the simulation II

High-level Petri Nets (HPNs)

- Established software tools
- Graphical modeling
- Simulation and analysis
- Standardized analysis methods

Renew for Reference Nets

- Nets and Java objects as tokens
- Flexible modeling
- No automatic state space generation

State space generation within the model

6

From the simulation to the analysis

Automated generation of action spaces

- Effects of all operators related to an initial situation
- Effects of all operators related to the new situations
- Experiences storing effects of the operators

Representation as experiences

- Initial situation, operator, final situation
- Stored in an object-oriented database
- Query functions for graph analysis

7

Example: Detection of the human error rigidity

Definition according to Dörner's classification

- External effects and disturbances change situation.
- Strategy is not changed so planned goal can not be reached.

Formalization for state space analysis

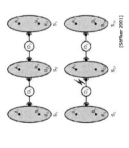

[Söffker 2001]

- Action of the user is not directed to a final goal situation.
- User action was directed to a previous user goal situation.

Gamrad, Söffker: Modeling and Analysis of Interaction for the Realization of Cognitive T...
© for all figures/illustrations by SRS U DuE

8

Cognitve architecture

Environment

Gamrad, Söffker: Modeling and Analysis of Interaction for the Realization of Cognitive T...
© for all figures/illustrations by SRS U DuE

9

Architecture of cognitive architectures

Hierarchical planning

- Different grades of abstraction
- Different action spaces
- Depending on the current situation
- Problem-relevant encapsulation

Combination of several instances

- Parallel or hierarchical
- Different mental models
- Reduction of complexity

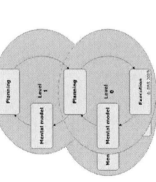

Gamrad, Söffker: Modeling and Analysis of Interaction for the Realization of Cognitive T...
© for all figures/illustrations by SRS U DuE

10

Implementation of interaction modeling

Situations for information processing

- Java objects as token in the Petri net
- List of the class 'Characteristic'
- Indirectly linked to the relations

Operators in the action model

- Sequence of operator nets
- List of the class 'AssumptionList'
- Function nets representing effects

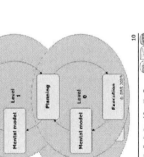

Gamrad, Söffker: Modeling and Analysis of Interaction for the Realization of Cognitive T...
© for all figures/illustrations by SRS U DuE

11

Action model → mental action space → planning

Generation of a mental action space

* From general to special knowledge
* Experience representing the effects of an operator to a certain situation
* Partial or complete graph

➡ Also generation of experiences from interaction

Planning

* Different weightings (security, energy, time, etc.)
* Algorithms for graph search

➡ Plan represented by a list of experiences

Gamrad, Söffker: Modeling and Analysis of Interaction for the Realization of Cognitive T...
© for all figures/illustrations by SRS U DuE.

Modeling of perception

Virtual characteristics

Measured characteristics

SRS 2009

Perception model

* Relations represented by operator nets
* Linked through assumption to situations

Perception module

* Situations from the sensing module
* Interpretation of measured characteristics
* Application of several relations

➡ Virtual characteristics added to a situation

Gamrad, Söffker: Modeling and Analysis of Interaction for the Realization of Cognitive T...
© for all figures/illustrations by SRS U DuE.

Learning

Mental model

Perception model (Operator nets)	
Action model (Operator nets)	
Mental action space (Experiences) © SRS 2009	

Filter

Meta operators

Generalization

Information ← Data

Real world (Actions and scenes)

Interaction

Gamrad, Söffker: Modeling and Analysis of Interaction for the Realization of Cognitive T...
© for all figures/illustrations by SRS U DuE.

Learning of operator's function and assumptions I

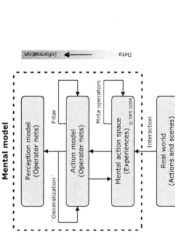

From experiences to action model

* From special to general representation
* Generation of operator nets
* For all characteristics
* Assumptions from initial situation
* Function from differences between initial and final situation
* Connection to operator net sequences

➡ Filter to reduce operator's assumptions to the relevant ones

Gamrad, Söffker: Modeling and Analysis of Interaction for the Realization of Cognitive T...
© for all figures/illustrations by SRS U DuE.

Learning of operator's function and assumptions II

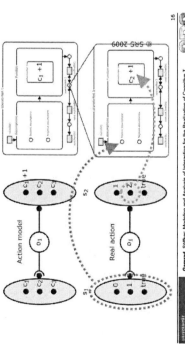

Gamrad, Söffker: Modeling and Analysis of Interaction for the Realization of Cognitive T...
© for all figures/illustrations by SRS U DuE

16

Learning of relations

'Generalization' of knowledge

* Interpretation of operator's assumptions
* Generation of virtual characteristics
* Previous assumptions replaced by new virtual characteristics
* Operator nets added to perception model

Example: Threshold function

* Several assumptions reduced to one parameter
* Gaps closed by hypotheses

⬆ Integration of different AI methods

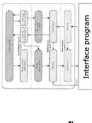

Characteristic c_1 (integer)

Detected assumptions: Threshold:
1 2 3 4 5 6 7 8 9 10 (11)   11

Gamrad, Söffker: Modeling and Analysis of Interaction for the Realization of Cognitive T...
© for all figures/illustrations by SRS U DuE

17

Learning of meta operators

Representation of meta operators

* Experience on a higher hierarchical level
* Combination of several simple experiences

Learning from interaction

* Frequently performed actions
* Successful plans
* Paths without alternatives

⬆ Reduction of the mental action space

⬆ Faster state space analysis

Gamrad, Söffker: Modeling and Analysis of Interaction for the Realization of Cognitive T...
© for all figures/illustrations by SRS U DuE

18

Application to technical systems

Communication between architecture and hardware

* Sensing and execution modules
* Interface program
* Communication protocols (e.g., TCP/IP)

Configuration of the cognitive architecture

* Measured characteristics
* Possible operators
* Initial knowledge

⬆ Programming of system's behavior by initial knowledge

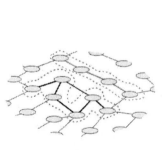

Interface program

Gamrad, Söffker: Modeling and Analysis of Interaction for the Realization of Cognitive T...
© for all figures/illustrations by SRS U DuE

19

Arcade game: Rocks'n'Diamonds

User controlled agent

Hostile monster agents

Emerald

Exit door

Advantages
- Simple handling
- Custom levels and elements
- Replaceable by technical processes

Tasks of the human operator
- Picking up a certain number of emeralds or diamonds
- Entering the exit door

Gamrad, Söffker: Modeling and Analysis of Interaction for the Realization of Cognitive T...
© for all figures/illustrations by SRS U DuE

20

Modeling of interaction

x position (integer)
y position (integer)
environment (set of situations)
vitality (decision)
type of upper field (string)
type of right field (string)
type of lower field (string)
type of left field (string)
...

Initial perception model
- All fields and their types as input
- Agent's position, collected points, etc.
- Types of the surrounded fields

Initial action model
- Four moving actions for the directions
- One waiting operator for every action of the hostile agents

Incomplete action model refined during interaction

Gamrad, Söffker: Modeling and Analysis of Interaction for the Realization of Cognitive T...
© for all figures/illustrations by SRS U DuE

21

Simulation and experimental results

Learning from interaction
- Incomplete/wrong mental model
- Differences between assumed and real outside world

Refining the mental model

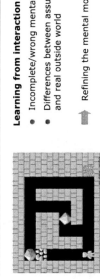

Gamrad, Söffker: Modeling and Analysis of Interaction for the Realization of Cognitive T...
© for all figures/illustrations by SRS U DuE

22

Summary and future work

Summary
- Modeling of human interaction behavior
- Architecture for Cognitive Technical Systems
- Learning of an arcade game

Application to different fields, like mobile robotics, assistance systems, etc.

Future work
- Further development of the learning modules
- Application to a real technical system (mobile robot)

Gamrad, Söffker: Modeling and Analysis of Interaction for the Realization of Cognitive T...
© for all figures/illustrations by SRS U DuE

23

Incentives in Arrival Management:
Agents' Interests vs. Designers' Expectations

Hendrik Oberheid[1] and Dirk Söffker[2]

[1]Institute of Flight Guidance, German Aerospace Center (DLR),
D-38108 Braunschweig,
[2]Chair of Dynamics and Control, University of Duisburg-Essen,
D-47057 Duisburg

1 Introduction

The contribution deals with the validation of planning mechanisms for arrival management in air traffic control, focusing on the compatibility of participating agents' interests with designers's expectations. Future arrival management is expected to feature increasing interaction and data exchange between the aircraft and ground systems. Part of the planning made by systems on the ground, will be based explicitly on user (i.e. aircraft) inputs and preferences. If the new interaction protocols and planning mechanisms are not designed properly, the self-interested behavior of individual aircraft can run counter to the realization of a high global system efficiency. In this work, a model-based approach using a Coloured Petri Net (CPN) Model [1] is used to analyze the incentive-compatibility of two alternative sequence planning mechanism for merging aircraft during approach. It is shown that for one system variant individual agents' interests contradict some of the system designers' behavioral expectations, while for a second variant incentives and expectations are better aligned.

2 Arrival Management

Arrival Management - today and in future (slide 1)

Aim of the arrival management process in general is to provide an optimal (safe and efficient) scheduling, guidance, and control of arrival traffic to an airport. Four subproblems have to be solved:

1. *Sequencing*, i.e. establishing a favorable arrival sequence (sequence of aircraft) according to a number of optimization criteria,
2. *Metering* that is to calculate for each individual aircraft the target times over (TTO) certain points (fixes) of the respective arrival route,
3. *Trajectory generation*, which means finding an efficient and conflict free route for each aircraft from its current position to the runway threshold, and also
4. *Clearance generation*, that is, to provide detailed instructions to the controller with regard to the specific clearances which should be given to an aircraft in order to lead it along the route as planned.

At large airports, more and more automation support is introduced to support the controller with these tasks and optimize the traffic planning (see changes, slide 1). Notably, future procedures and mechanisms for arrival management are likely to feature a much closer integration of the respective actors and planning systems in the air and on the ground as it is the case today [2,3]. A direct coupling and data exchange will be established between the ground-based arrival management system AMAN and the Flight Management Systm (FMS) on board of the aircraft via a digital datalink. The trajectory will then no longer be commanded unilaterally to the aircraft by the air traffic controller. Rather the trajectory will be the result of some kind of bidirectional negotiation between air and ground, and take user (aircraft) preferences and performance data explicitly into account.

In the optimal case, the coordination and negation allows much more fuel and noise efficient trajectories to be realized. However, it also includes the risk that some actors might use their degrees of freedom for strategic actions and selfish behavior, and that actors might hold back certain information in order to optimize their position in a globally undesirable manner.

3   Model-Based Analysis of Incentives

Modeling and Validation Approach (slide 2)

To investigate if undesirable manipulations have to be expected, the contribution proposes a model-based approach to analyze agents' behavioral incentives in the distributed planning process (slide 2).

The core of the approach is based on

- the formalization of the relevant decision context by appropriate modeling tools and
- the application of mathematical solution concepts (decision theoretic criteria) to reason about agents incentives

and possibly predict actors behavior. After the analysis of rational behavior and incentives within the system, the results are compared to the behavioral expectations of the system designer. These can usually be drawn from a more informal (hermeneutic) actor role analysis of the design documents (e.g. use cases). If rational behavior and behavioral expectations by design can be shown to contradict, recommendations for the modification of the design should be derived.

4   Sequence Planning for a Merging Point

Arrival Management - Example Protocol (slide 3)
Rating Functions for Sequence Quality Evaluation (slide 4)
Simulation Scenario (slide 5)

In this contribution the analysis approach is exemplified on a sequence planning mechanism for merging arrival streams during approach (slide 3). Core of the mechanism is that the approaching aircraft submit an Earliest Time of Arrival (ETA) for the Merging Point (MP) to a ground-based Arrival Manager. Based on this Earliest Time of Arrival, the Arrival Manager computes a favorable sequence and Target Times (TTAs) to guarantee a safe separation (min 75s) when overflying MP. The Target times are then realized autonomously by the aircraft.

In order to decide which potential aircraft sequence is most favorable, the arrival management system uses a set of rating functions (slide 4). In this example a first rating function *QEarlyEta* is considered to evaluate how close the target times of (TTAs) come to the earliest times (ETAs) given by the aircraft. A second rating function type evaluates the stability of the planned sequence with regard to the last planning cycle. Of this stability rating function, two alternative versions QTTAStabiliy and QPOSStability were compared and considered in the presentation. While QTTAStability rates stability based on stable aircraft target times, QPOSStabiliy rates the stability based on aircraft positions.

On slide 5, the specific operational context and traffic situation to be investigated is introduced. A key point is, that while the aircraft approach the merging point MP, disturbances of a weather and wind change affect the Earliest Times of Arrival of different aircraft. The modified times have to be submitted to the planning system. Aircraft may have an interest, however of submitting the new ETA sooner or later (delay information), as due to the stability function the planning system's response depends on the order of incoming ETAs.

5 Validation Objectives

The important designers' expectations towards aircraft behavior when dealing with the sequence planning system are:

- Aircraft should correct their ETA as soon as possible.
- Deliberate delays of update are undesirable for planning - but difficult to detect.

The model-based validation should support the decision

- if aircraft timing of submitting ETAs impacts the outcome,
- if timely submission is in agents's own best interest,
- if timely submission is rewarded by the planning system, and
- if the planning system can be manipulated.

6 Agent Strategies and Outcomes

Best Case, Average and Worst Case Outcomes (slide 6)
TTA_stability - Expected Position depends on... (slide 7)
POS_stability - Expected Position depends on... (slide 8)

On slide 6, results from an individual simulation with the above scenario and mechanism are given. In the graph, for a specific aircraft D, the best case, average case and worst case outcomes in terms of the position in the sequence are pointed out. It can be observed that the achieved position for aircraft D depends on the setting of the planning system (weighting of stability vs. optimization), but also on the timing of its own submission as well as the timing of other aircraft. Thus the timing of the result can have a significant impact on the aircrafts achieved utility.

On the slides 7 and 8, aggregated results from large set of simulations with randomized initial traffic situations (initial ETA) and weather effects (ETA shifts) are shown. The results show that the expected position in the sequence for four aircraft A,B,C,D depend on a) if the shift was favorable (new ETA earlier) or unfavorable (new ETA later) and b) the timing of the aircraft submission with respect to the others.

The results on slide 7 demonstrate that when the rating function TTA_stability is used, submitting earlier ETAs instantaneously is in the aircrafts' interest, but holding back information on later ETAs also improves the expectations. The latter result is in conflict with the designers' expectations.

On the other hand, the results on slide 8 show that for rating function POS_stability, submitting earlier ETAs instantaneously improves the expectations, but for the submission of later ETAs timing does generally not affect the expectations. This rating function is better suited to align the incentives for agents with the interests of the system designer.

7 Conclusions

The contribution argues that new planning mechanism in air traffic management demand new methods to investigate incentives for cooperation or competition. Results from a CPN model of sequence planning are used to reason about potential agent behavior. This behavior is checked against the designers' expectations in order to destinguish between more or less favorable system variants. The presented analysis approach supports incentive-compatible designs and will be used on an extended range of rating functions and scenarios as an input into the design of currently developed arrival management systems.

References

1. Jensen, K., Kristensen, L.M., Wells, L.: Coloured Petri Nets and CPN Tools for Modelling and Validation of Concurrent Systems. Software Tools for Technology Transfer (STTT) **9**(3-4) (2007) 213–254
2. Korn, B., Helmke, H., Kuenz, A.: 4D Trajectory Managment in the Extended TMA: Coupling AMAN and 4D FMS for Optimized Approach Trajectories. In: 25th International Congress of the Aeronautical Sciences, Hamburg, Germany (2006)
3. Oberheid, H.O., Söffker, D.: Designing for cooperation - mechanisms and procedures for air-ground integrated arrivalmanagement. In: IEEE International Conference on Systems, Man and Cybernetics, Montreal, Canada (2007) 253–259

Arrival Management - today and in future

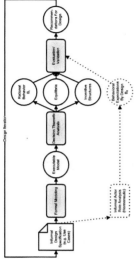

Arrival Management

Today
1. Voice Radio communication
2. Vector-based guidance
3. Unidirectional command flow ground->aircraft
4. Non-deterministic planning through human controller
5. Aircraft/Crew with limited situation awareness

Future
1. Datalink communication
2. Trajectory-based guidance
3. Bidirectional negotiation process, 4D-trajectory (space & time) contract between aircraft and ground
4. Largely deterministic planning through automated AMAN
5. Aircraft with improved situation awareness (CDTI)

Yes?

NO

Strategic behavior/optimization through individual aircraft?

Cooperative Arrival Management in Air Traffic Control
Oberheid, Söffker - Slide 8

Modeling and Validation Approach

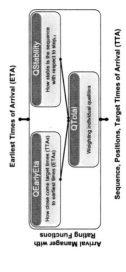

Rational Behavior B_i
Equilibria
Incentive Structures

Formal Modeling — Executable Model — Decision Theoretic Analysis — Evaluation/ Validation — Recommendations For Design

Informal Design Specification (e.g. Use Cases)

Informal Actor Role Analysis (Hermeneutic)

'Behavioral' Expectations By Design B_d

Design Iteration

Model-based approach and decision theory to validate…

↗ …if agents' incentives are compatible with designers' expectations
↗ …if emergent behavior is compatible with system design goal

Cooperative Arrival Management in Air Traffic Control
Oberheid, Söffker - Slide 9

Arrival Management – Example Protocol

Focus on sequence planning task

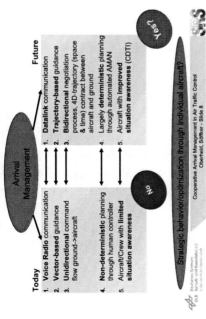

Agent n: Aircraft

Agent 1: Arrival Manager

Earliest Time of Arrival for Merging Point
Position (POS), Target Time (TTA)

Merging situation

Aircraft input
↗ Earliest Time of Arrival (ETA)

Arrival manager output
↗ Position in sequence (POS)
↗ Target Time of Arrival (TTA)

Cooperative Arrival Management in Air Traffic Control
Oberheid, Söffker - Slide 10

Rating Functions for Sequence Quality Evaluation

Earliest Times of Arrival (ETA)

Arrival Manager with Rating Functions

QEarlyEta — How close come target times (TTAs) to earliest times (ETAs)

QStability — How stable is the sequence with respect to step$_{t-1}$

QTotal — Weighting individual qualities

Sequence, Positions, Target Times of Arrival (TTA)

↗ Rating functions decide which candidate sequence is selected.
↗ Weighting balances adaptivity vs. stability.

Cooperative Arrival Management in Air Traffic Control
Oberheid, Söffker - Slide 11

Simulation Scenario

Initial situation
- 4 aircraft merging to common waypoint MP
- Earliest Times of Arrival (ETAs) submitted
- Initial sequence A→B→C→D

Scenario event
- Wind change (north to south)
- A and B delayed, C and D accelerated
- Earliest Times of Arrival (ETAs) have to be corrected.

Agents' choice
- Correction of ETA mandatory but...
...timing of submission of corrected ETAs is free!

Reaction of arrival manager (AMAN)
- Depends on order of incoming ETAs

Cooperative Arrival Management in Air Traffic Control
Oberheid, Söffker - Slide 15

Best Case, Average, and Worst Outcomes

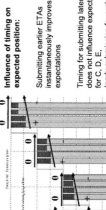

Aircraft D

Bar chart indicates sequence positions
- Best case POS (green)
- Average POS (blue)
- Worst POS (red)

Observation
- POS depends on timing.
- POS depends on ratio $r = w_s/w_e$.
- POS depends on other aircraft.

Depending on timing, aircraft D can be scheduled POS 1 to 4!

Cooperative Arrival Management in Air Traffic Control
Oberheid, Söffker - Slide 17

TTA_stability - Expected Position depends on...

- Initial sequence (A→B→C→D)
- Direction of ETA-shift for this aircraft
(red: new ETA later, green: new ETA earlier)
- Timing of ETA-shift submission (No 1., 2., 3., or 4.)

Influence of timing on expected position:

Submitting earlier ETAs instantaneously improves expectations

Holding back information on later ETA improves expectations!

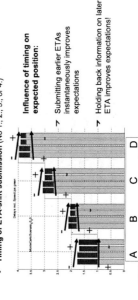

Cooperative Arrival Management in Air Traffic Control
Oberheid, Söffker - Slide 23

POS_Stability - Expected Position depends on...

- Initial sequence (A→B→C→D)
- Direction of ETA-shift for this aircraft
(red: new ETA later, green: new ETA earlier)
- Timing of ETA-shift submission (No 1., 2., 3., or 4.)

Influence of timing on expected position:

Submitting earlier ETAs instantaneously improves expectations

Timing for submitting later ETAs does not influence expectations for C, D, E,
(early submission favorable for A)

Cooperative Arrival Management in Air Traffic Control
Oberheid, Söffker - Slide 25

Towards Risk Analysis to enable Safe Service Robotics

Philipp Ertle[1], Dirk Söffker[2]

[1] University of Applied Sciences, Ravensburg-Weingarten, ZAFH Autonome Mobile
Serviceroboter, philipp.ertle@hs-weingarten.de
[2] University of Duisburg-Essen, Chair of Dynamics and Control, Duisburg, Germany
soeffker@uni-due.de

Service robots shall provide services to humans and this in close interaction and distance with humans [1]. From these basic conditions some implications are following, especially with respect to the required consideration of safety aspects. An extension of actual methods is needed, which is explained briefly in the sequel.

Well known industrial robots are closely related to service robots but differ at least in the set of minimal requirements: 1) Spatial separation is unreasonable, due to the need of direct interaction with humans. 2) Tasks should be less repeatable, than rather adapted to the environment. 3) Additionally one has to deal with an unmodified, complex, and open environment to enable mobility- and manipulation capabilities.

It seems to be impossible to meet these requirements with conventional programmed tasks - it seems to be necessary to apply learning and autonomous decision capabilities because these are helpful to generate desired emergent behavior [2]. Thus, there are two fundamental reasons why advanced methods of monitoring the operation state are necessary [3,4]: changing and initial unknown conditions of an open environment and changing systems due to autonomous adaptation on changing conditions. Incomplete initial knowledge of conditions already implicates continuous surveillance. Continuous surveillance of safety aspects implicates continuous comparison of actual risks with tolerable risks, because a system is considered as safe when risks do not exceed tolerable risks [5]. This situation-based understanding of dynamic risk [3] possibly may enable the system itself to detect and therefore to avoid unsafe states via feedback of risk values and triggering of protective functionalities.

Thus, the required basic steps are the description of the system's architecture with surveillance and conservative adaptation capabilities on the one hand and on the other hand the elaboration of methods for determining and quantifying the dynamic risks and tolerable risks. Future research work will address these topics.

References

1. Schraft, R., Schmierer, G.: Service robots. AK Peters Ltd., Natick, MA (2000)
2. Haun, M.: Handbuch Robotik. Springer, Berlin Heidelberg (2007)
3. Wardziński, A.: Safety Argument Strategies for Autonomous Vehicles. In Computer Safety, Reliability and Security, 277-290 (2008)
4. Alexander, R.D., Herbert, N.J., Kelly, T.P.: Structuring Safety Cases for Autonomous Systems. In 3rd IET International Conference on System Safety (2008)
5. IEC 61508: Functional safety of electrical/electronic/programmable electronic safety-related systems. Beuth-Verlag, Berlin

Overview

- What are service robots?
- What is safety?
- Why do we need surveillance during operation?
- Why do we need cognitive systems therefore?
- Summary and outlook

Fujitsu "enon"

Erle, Söffker: Towards Risk Analysis to Enable Safe Service Robotics
© for all figures/illustrations by SRS U DuE

-0-

The domain of service robots (SR)

- SR have to provide services to humans, therefore...
  - a spatial separation due to human robot interaction is impossible,
  - often multiple and more complex tasks are required and
  - need for mobility results.
- Action has to be performed in unstructured, human environment.
- SR systems can not be specified completely in advance.

→ Different safety challenges

Erle, Söffker: Towards Risk Analysis to Enable Safe Service Robotics
© for all figures/illustrations by SRS U DuE

-1-

Safety vs. security and how it may be concretized

- Security: Protect robot against misuse, i.e.
- Safety: Protect environment from harm through robot.
- What is safe?
  Safe = "Freedom from unacceptable risk of harm" [K. Grote und E.K. Antonsson, 2009]
- Safe = risk lower than tolerable risk
  → One needs to determine the risk

→ But: Functions can not be fully specified, especially when systems are able to learn.

tolerable risk

Safe | hazard

Risk

0

Erle, Söffker: Towards Risk Analysis to Enable Safe Service Robotics
© for all figures/illustrations by SRS U DuE

-2-

Surveillance of the operation mode

- The system changes during operation time.
- Risk analysis can not be worked out completely during development process.
- Need for continuous evaluation.
- "Online Risk Analysis" for mobile autonomous robots.
- Conservative attitude towards determination of risk: risk=1
- Reduction of Risk by applying principles: generalization to deal with unknown situations.
- Challenges are: $risk_t = f (Situation\ S_t)$
  $risk_{t1} = f (Situation\ S_t, action\ A_t)$

Erle, Söffker: Towards Risk Analysis to Enable Safe Service Robotics
© for all figures/illustrations by SRS U DuE

-3-

Structuring the safety topic

- Definition of risk:

  Risk = Probability * Consequence

Risk

Physical risk	Logical risk
Movement is generally hazardous through...	Manipulation of environment: Risk potential through...
...cinematic energy.	...objects for human.
...potential energy.	...combination of objects.

Thoughts about a framework

- A service robot should act human like / perform human abilities.
- Evolutionary answer to enable such abilities are cognitive structures.
- Need for flexible interface to all available information.
- Need for extracting abstract information out of environment.
- Need for extraction of task specific information.
- Need for associate information to knowledge.
- Need for storage of knowledge due to learning processes.
- Need for prediction of action.

→ Cognitive approaches are able to satisfy these requirements.

Summary and Outlook

- Implementation of Service robots need for
  - Autonomy to deal with unpredictable situations and
  - Learning capabilities to enable complex tasks.
- Safety should be guaranteed in every case.
- Implementation of a online risk analysis is supposed.

- How available architectures should be modified.
- How risk can be determined quantitatively, also the tolerable risk.
- How risk analysis methods can be formulated.

Thank you for your attention!

**Towards Risk Analysis
to Enable Safe Service Robotics**

Philipp Ertle
University of Duisburg-Essen
Chair of Dynamics and Control (SRS) and
University of Applied Sciences Ravensburg-Weingarten
ZAFH - Centre of Collaborative Research
Doggenriedstraße, 88250 Weingarten, GERMANY
E-mail: philipp.ertle@hs-weingarten.de
Web: www.srs.uni-due.de
Tel.: 0049 751 501 - 9835

Any questions?

Cognitive-Based Driving Supervision and Assistance

Xingguang Fu, Dirk Söffker

University of Duisburg Essen, Chair of Dynamics and Control
{xingguang.fu, soeffker}@uni-due.de

1 The underlying structure of interaction logic: Situation-Operator-Modeling

The underlying structure of..., Overall concept of ..., Cognitive-based supervision: main concept

The contribution is denoted to a modeling approach for cognitive-based driving supervision and assistance [1]. The proposed method is implemented using data from experimental environments [2]. As underlying structure of the action logic, the Situation-Operator-Modeling approach [3, 4] is used to represent the interaction between human driver, vehicles, and the environment. The core of the approach is the assumption that changes in the parts of the real world to be considered are understood as a sequence of effects or changes. The items scenes and actions of the real world are used to model these changes. The item scene denotes a problemfixed moment in time but independent from time, and it is modeled by situations. The item operator denotes the action changing the scenes.

Situations and operators are related to each other and therefore can also be used to relate the assumed structure of the real world to the structure of the database - called the mental model -of an intelligent system. The concept of cognitive supervision and assistance [5] can be divided into 4 levels: Sensory-, Processing-, Analysis-, and Information level, within which the driving events can be detected and saved in the knowledge base by supervising the interaction between the driver and the vehicle.

2 Implementation of the cognitive supervision for lane-changing manoeuvers

Experimental environments I-II, Implementation within ..., Representation of ..., Representation of the driving process I-II, ..., Establishment of ..., Selection of ..., Programming-based implementation

The driving data are collected from both the Dynamic Driving Simulator® and the experimental vehicle ViewCar® in the German Aerospace Center (DLR), Braunschweig, Germany. Driving scenes and actions can be represented by situations and operators established using a combined visualization of recorded video and sensor data. Due to the fact that some characteristics building the situations can not be directly caught from raw data, a number of prefilters are necessary for the model to calculate or refine the data to get the correct parameters for the characteristics. The 7 basic characteristics for the lane-changing manoeuvres include *actual lane, velocity, indicator signal set, passing lane exists, actual lane free, lane changing possible,* and *acceleration possible.* Similarly, the operators can be detected by comparing the sensor values from the main actuators of the vehicle, such as the steering wheel, the gas/brake pedal, and the indicator set signals.

The implementation of this model is realized by a Java-Application, which enables the UDP-based communication between sensor system and a user interface. With the integrated prefilters and operator library, the application can provide online processing with raw sensor measurements from the database as input. The results of the analysis are fed back directly to the user interface, which displays the interpreted characteristics, operators matching the actual situation with respect to the assumptions, and the actual operator of the driver. The consistency between the possible operators and actual operator are always checked, and a warning message will be given to the driver if any contradiction has been detected.

3 Personalization/ Individualization of the driver model

Framework and Individualization I-II, Building the personalized knowledge-base I-II

Driver drives differently. They differ in their driving styles, how fast driving on the highway, how hard to press the gas pedal for accelerating, and how far to keep when they are following a vehicle [6]. One direction that could improve the driving supervision and assistance is focused on the personalization or individualization according to the different driving styles. These driving styles representing the individual driver patterns can be described by a number of driver models, which are acquired by supervised off/on-line training process. The typical parameters of the individual driving styles from each driver are learned and classified into more detailed categories and saved in a individual knowledge base of driver behaviors during the training process, so that the driving safety of a specific driver can be supervised by comparing his/her behaviors with the normal patterns.

The driving process includes a number of maneuvers. According to the SOM approach they can be considered as a series of scenes and actions modeled by interconnected situations and operators. The individual driving behaviors appear in typical maneuvers such as driving into/off the highway, following patterns, overtaking scenarios, and lane changing maneuvers. The modeling of personalization process is built by catching the related measurements when the corresponding maneuver or events occurred and recording into the individual knowledge base about driver's behaviors.

An example of this proposal is illustrated by a highway driving algorithm consists of non-individual and individual elements, which is described by the "event distribution" based on Multivariate Normal Distribution (MND) method. The results of the tests show that a more accurate decision-boundary should be derived in order to optimize the personalized driver model, so that the controlling of the vehicle can be taken by the personalized assistance systems autonomously without changing the styles of the driver.

References

1. Fu, X.: Analysis and Modeling of a Driver-Vehicle-Interaction. Master thesis, Chair of Dynamics and Control, University of Duisburg-Essen, Duisburg, Germany, July 2008.
2. Fu, X., Gamrad, D., Mosebach, H.; Lemmer, K., and Söffker, D.: Modeling and implementation of cognitive-based supervision and assistance. Proc. 6th Vienna Conference on Mathematical Modeling on Dynamical Systems MATHMOD 2009, Vienna, Austria, 2009.
3. Söffker, D.: Modeling the Human-Machine Interaction: Relations between Human Planing, Cognition, Mental Representation and Action. In: Biswas, G.; McIlraith, S.: Hybrid Systems and AI: Modeling Analysis and Control of Discrete plus Continous Systems. Technical Report SS-99-04 Knowledge System Lab, Stanford University, California. Paper from the AAAI 1999 Spring Symposium, Stanford University, California, March 22-24, 1999.
4. Söffker, D.: Interaction of Intelligent and Autonomous Systems - Part I: Qualitative Structuring of Interactions. MCMDS-Mathematical and Computer Modelling of Dynamical Systems, 14(4): pp.303-318, 2008.
5. Ahle, E. and Söffker, D, "Interaction of Intelligent and Autonomous Systems - Part II: Realization of Cognitive Technical Systems," MCMDS-Mathematical and Computer Modelling of Dynamical Systems, 14(4): pp.319-339, 2008.
6. Ohta, H.: Individual differences in driving distance headway. Proceedings of Vision in Vehicles IV Conference, Amsterdam, Elsevier, pp. 91-100, 1993.

Cognitive-Based Driving Supervision and Assistance

Xingguang Fu, Dirk Söffker

E-mail: xingguang.fu@uni-due.de
Web: www.srs.uni-due.de

Chair of Dynamics and Control
University of Duisburg-Essen

Outline

- The underlying structure of interaction logic: SOM approach
- Concept of cognitive supervision and assistance
- Implementation within an experimental environment
- Framework and individualization
- Building the individualized/personalized knowledge-base
- Summary and outlook

Motivation

- Requirements for driving assistance systems: safety and comfort
- New research direction: Cognitive assistance system
- Background and advantages of Cognitive Technical Systems:
  - → Based on representations of interaction logic
  - → Ability for supervision and autonomous behavior in parallel
  - → Fast, precise, and self-rectifiable
- New focus: Individualization/Personalization
  - → Supervising and learning from the driver
  - → Guidance of the vehicle

The underlying structure of action logic: Situation-Operator-Modeling approach

- The world can be understood as a sequence of scenes and actions modeled by situations and operators.
- The internal structuring of SOM allows the representation of
  i) systems and
  ii) interaction in an open environment.

(a) Situation and operator [Söffker 2001]

(b) Operators changing situations [Söffker 2001]

Overall concept of cognitive supervision and assistance

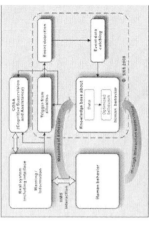

- Sensory level: perceive scenes and actions from the real world

- Processing level: set up hybrid situation vectors and select operators

- Analysis level: check the consistency and errors

- Information level: inform the driver with warnings

Concept of automated supervision

Fu, Söffker: Cognitive-based Driving Supervision and Assistance

© for all figures/illustrations by SRS U DuE

-4-

Cognitive-based supervision: main concept

How to realize the main concept for driving supervision and assistance?

Fu, Söffker: Cognitive-based Driving Supervision and Assistance

© for all figures/illustrations by SRS U DuE

-5-

Experimental environments I: ViewCar©

Experimental vehicle: ViewCar® by DLR (German Aerospace Center)

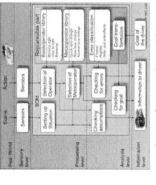

Measuring devices and the ViewCar©

Video samples from different views

Fu, Söffker: Cognitive-based Driving Supervision and Assistance

© for all figures/illustrations by SRS U DuE

-6-

Experimental environments II: SimCar©

Simulation environment – Net-based and coupled with SRS

Precise measurement from environment (distances,....)

Raw data

Dynamic driving simulator – SimCar© (DLR)

Simulation data construct

Fu, Söffker: Cognitive-based Driving Supervision and Assistance

© for all figures/illustrations by SRS U DuE

-7-

Representation of the driving environment: building technical situation awareness of vehicles

Typical scenes of highway driving: lane-changing maneuver

left — 3

middle — 2

right — 1

Sn, Sbl, Sb, Str, Sr, Srr

Data sample:
Acceleration, velocities, yaw rate, distances, lateral deviation, indicator set, etc.

Fu, Söffker: Cognitive-based Driving Supervision and Assistance

© for all figures/illustrations by SRS U DuE

UNIVERSITÄT DUISBURG ESSEN

- 9 -

Representation of the driving process II

Interpretating the scenes and building situations and operators

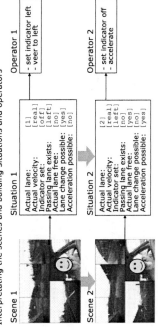

Scene 1

Situation 1
Actual lane: [1]
Actual velocity: [real]
Indicator set: [off]
Passing lane exists: [left]
Actual lane free: [no]
Lane change possible: [yes]
Acceleration possible: [no]

Operator 1
- set indicator left
- veer to left

Scene 2

Situation 2
Actual lane: [2]
Actual velocity: [real]
Indicator set: [left]
Passing lane exists: [no]
Actual lane free: [yes]
Lane change possible: [no]
Acceleration possible: [yes]

Operator 2
- set indicator off
- accelerate

Fu, Söffker: Cognitive-based Driving Supervision and Assistance

© for all figures/illustrations by SRS U DuE

UNIVERSITÄT DUISBURG ESSEN

- 11 -

Implementation within an experimental environment

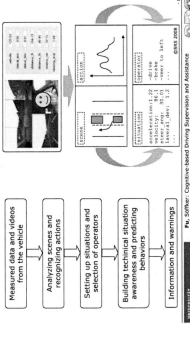

Measured data and videos from the vehicle

Analyzing scenes and recognizing actions

Setting up situations and selection of operators

Building techinical situation awareness and predicting behaviors

Information and warnings

scene

action

situation
acceleration:1.22
velocity: 86.1
steer_ang: 30.01
lateral_dev: 1.2 ...

operator:
-drive
-brake
-veer to left
...

©SRS 2008

Fu, Söffker: Cognitive-based Driving Supervision and Assistance

© for all figures/illustrations by SRS U DuE

UNIVERSITÄT DUISBURG ESSEN

- 8 -

Representation of the driving process I

Synchronization of measurements

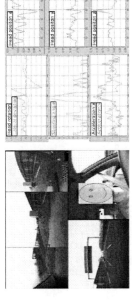

Recorded driving videos

Sampled data

Head position

Head orientation

Steering angle

Acceleration

Fu, Söffker: Cognitive-based Driving Supervision and Assistance

© for all figures/illustrations by SRS U DuE

UNIVERSITÄT DUISBURG ESSEN

- 10 -

Establishment of situations based on characteristics

Construction of pre-filters by extracting parameters of characteristics

Sensor data	Pre-filter for data compression	Situation	Characteristics

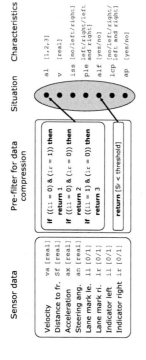

Sensor data:
- Velocity va [real]
- Distance to fr. sf [real]
- Acceleration ax [real]
- Steering ang. an [real]
- Lane mark le. ll [0/1]
- Lane mark ri. lr [0/1]
- Indicator left il [0/1]
- Indicator right ir [0/1]

Pre-filter for data compression:

```
if ((ll = 0) & (lr = 1)) then
   return 1
if ((ll = 0) & (lr = 0)) then
   return 2
if ((ll = 1) & (lr = 0)) then
   return 3

return [Sf < threshold]
```

Characteristics:
- al [1,2,3]
- v [real]
- iss [no/left/right]
- ple [left/right/left and right]
- alf [yes/no]
- lcp [no/left/right/ left and right]
- ap [yes/no]

Fu, Söffker: Cognitive-based Driving Supervision and Assistance
© for all figures/illustrations by SRS U DuE
UNIVERSITÄT DUISBURG ESSEN

Selection of operators according to actions

Setting up the actual operator by comparing the signal combination with the basic operator library

Sensor data:
- Indicator set signal x_{is}
- Steering wheel signal x_{sw}
- Throttle pedal signal x_{tp}
- Brake pedal signal x_{bp}

→ Operator selection module → O_a Actual operator

Basic operator library:
- drive O_{b1}
- accelerate O_{b2}
- decelerate O_{b3}
- brake O_{b4}
- set indicator left on O_{b5}
- set indicator right on O_{b6}
- set indicator off O_{b7}
- veer to left O_{b8}
- veer to right O_{b9}

Fu, Söffker: Cognitive-based Driving Supervision and Assistance
© for all figures/illustrations by SRS U DuE

Programming-based implementation

Realization of the model by a Java-application

Data receiving → Data compression → Comparison with basic operators → Actual operator; Characteristics recognition → Actual situation; Checking assumptions → Warning message

Fu, Söffker: Cognitive-based Driving Supervision and Assistance
© for all figures/illustrations by SRS U DuE

Framework and Individualization I: algorithms

General driving regulations

Sensors
Video cameras
GPS
Generalized knowledge-base

Constants of individual drivers

Ratios
Thresholds
Variables
Individualized/Personalized knowledge-base

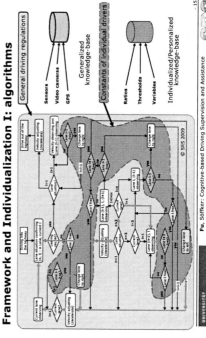

© SRS 2009

Fu, Söffker: Cognitive-based Driving Supervision and Assistance
© for all figures/illustrations by SRS U DuE
UNIVERSITÄT DUISBURG ESSEN

Framework and Individualization II: passing maneuver

Sheer off

Right lane free
Right lane free

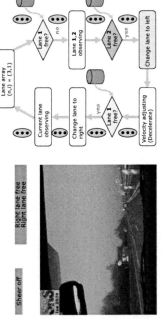

Lane array (n,i) = (3,1) — Lane 1 free? — no — Lane 1.2 observing — Lane 2 free? — yes — Change lane to left
Current lane observing — Change lane to right — yes — Lane 1 free? — Velocity adjusting (Decelerate)

Building the personalized knowledge-base I

Example scenarios: passing maneuver

- Step 1: Analyzing the event distribution based on measured/triggered data
- Step 2: Defining driver's individual features by calculating borders

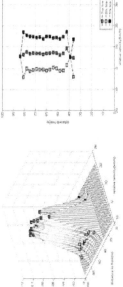

Building the personalized knowledge-base II

Simulation and distribution analysis: passing maneuver

- The individualized driving behavior can be learned by using observed/realized distribution analysis.
- The personalized knowledge-base describes the individualization of a single driver.
- The personalized knowledge-base can be used for supervision.

Summary and Outlook

- Implementation of an automated cognitive-based supervision concept
  → Detailed in theory and realized with experimental environments
  → Establishment of situations and characteristics allows
    ▪ technical situation awareness
  → Detection of human actions and comparision with dependent situations allows
    ▪ consistency check of the underlying interaction logic
  → Building the personalized knowledge-base by distribution analysis
  → Algorithms allow to take over the guidance of the vehicle
- Outlook
  → Analysis of more complex driving environments
  → Improve the personalization of the knowledge-base
  → Integration of the cognitive-based supervision program into a real driving assistance system

Human Bone-Modeling and Reconstruction using Superquadric Shapes

R. Cuypers

Department of Computational and Cognitive Science, University of Duisburg-Essen

cuypers@inf.uni-due.de

Abstract. The focus of this talk is the development of an interactive concept for semi-automated and automated 3d bone reconstruction and measurement in operational planning using superquadric shapes (SQs). For this task, it combines methods from different engineering disciplines as graphical interface design, geometrical analysis and orthopaedic kinematical simulation. Finally, the quality of the measurement procedure is tested using human and adequate animal bone data.

Keywords: Graphical interface construction, superquadrics, 3D modeling, biomedical engineering

1 Operational Planning

- The rise of computer based operational planning systems resulted in a significant improvement of the quality of orthopaedic therapy.

- The planning of the insertion of bone implants requires the manipulation of 3D-reconstructed bone shapes.

- Therefore, we need models and interfaces that enable the surgeon to efficiently and effectively control the involved processes.

- Topics: Bone preparation, implant positioning, features measurement.

2 Superquadrics

- Family of geometrical shapes, that are defined by the implicit equation

$$F(x,y,z) \equiv \left[\left(\frac{x}{a_1} \right)^{\frac{2}{\varepsilon_2}} + \left(\frac{y}{a_2} \right)^{\frac{2}{\varepsilon_2}} \right]^{\frac{\varepsilon_2}{\varepsilon_1}} + \left(\frac{z}{a_3} \right)^{\frac{2}{\varepsilon_1}} = 1$$

- Parameters
  - (x, y, z): Position of point

- o (a_1, a_2, a_3): Scaling
- o (e_1, e_2): Roundness
- o Furthermore, there are origin and orientation
- o Extended models also offer deformations like bending, tapering etc.

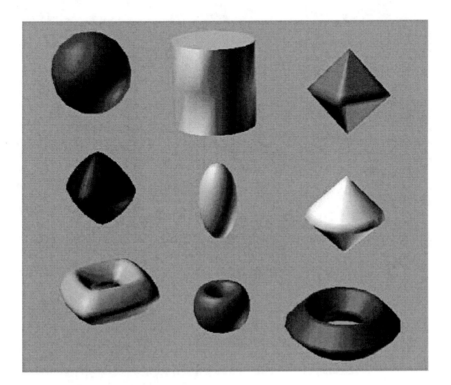

Figure 1: Overview of superquadric shapes

- Advantages of superquadrics:

  - o High descriptive power with few parameters
  - o Well-behaved inside-outside function
  - o Easily extensible using deformations
  - o Can produce more complex models by coupling multiple SQs
  - o Simple enough for fast user-interaction

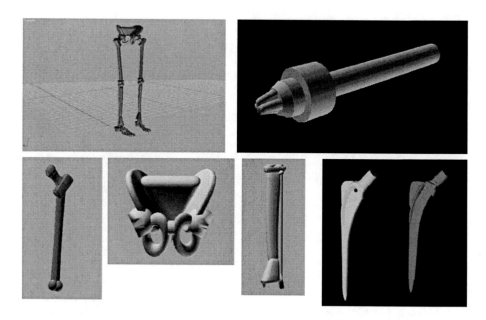

Figure 2: Overview of bones/implants/tools reconstructed using superquadrics

3   3D Surface Reconstruction

- Preprocessing stage prepares bone data to provide additional data that helps with decomposition and improve surface quality.
    - Mesh surface reconstruction (primitives)
    - Mesh smoothing
    - Extraction of global and local surface features (connectivity, curvature, etc.)

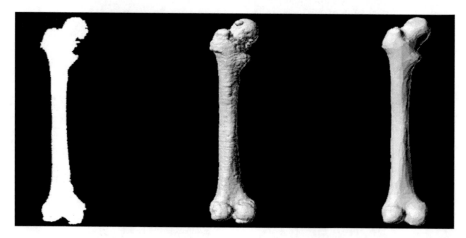

Figure 3: Original (left), reconstructed (middle) and smoothed bone data (right).

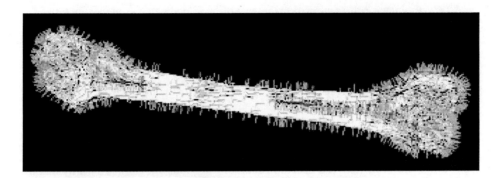

Figure 4: Extraction of local bone geometry features.

4 System Overview

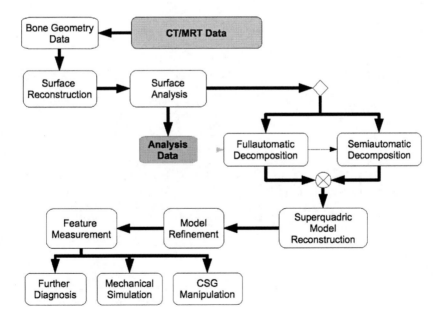

Figure 5: Overview of the system workflow.

5   Semiautomated Decomposition using Selection Tool

- Problem: Fully automatic recovery of bone geometry produces dissatisfying results
- Reason: Most shape decomposition algorithms are generic and dissect the bone disadvantageously
- Intuitive manual decomposition by humans may be very different
- Conclusion: The user needs a way to interact with the recovery process

- Further reasons for bad recovery results:
    - o Bad Input data (holes, outliers, wrong area of interest)
    - o Unknown target shape conditions
- What we want: The decomposition of the points should be in a way that the parts can be easily approximated by the superquadric model
- What we need: A selection tool, that is at least as powerful as the superquadric model.

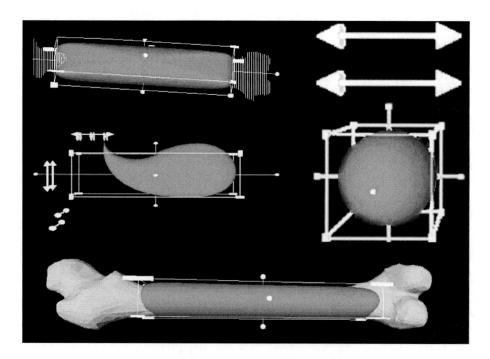

Figure 6: Overview superquadric-based selection tool

- Features:
    - o Points can be interactively selected by superquadric shapes using the mouse
    - o Selection of point groups with a superquadric-based template.

6 Automated Decomposition of Bone Geometry

- For comparison with the semi-automatic method and for convenience.
- Supports decomposition using different surface attributes (curvature, connectivity etc.) and previous knowledge of the bone.
- Can be used to support the semi-automatic process using the selection tool as well as the fitting process.

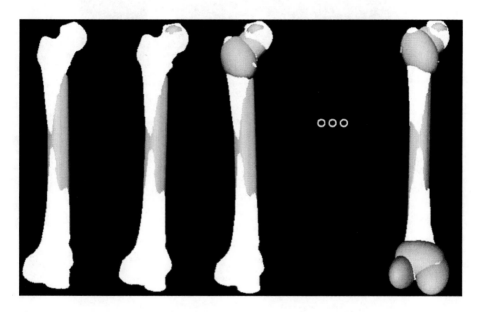

Figure 7: Reconstructed superquadric model (automated method)

7 Bone Recovery using Superquadric Fitting

- Fit SQs to the individual bone parts using nonlinear-optimization methods.
- Extraction of features from sq model.

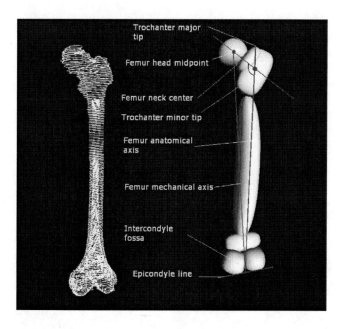

Figure 8: Reconstructed and measured superquadric model.

8 Fracture Interpolation

- A fractured bone is split into multiple components.
- Components of the same part will still yield similar superquadrics nevertheless.
- Superquadric fitting is used to reconnect the components and quantify the error.
- „Bone History" allows for the recognition of deformations.

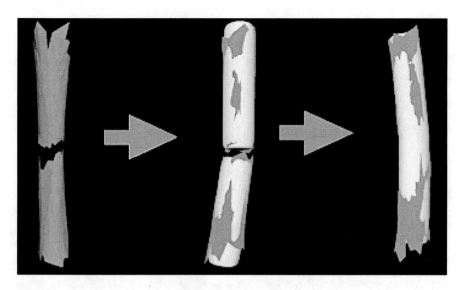

Figure 9: Interpolated fracture of bone components

9 Smooth Surface-Blending using Cuffs

- Blending between adjacent superquadrics may be very steep.
- Solution: Add additional superquadrics to the screen for smooth transition.
- This effectively comes down to fitting a superquadric to multiple others.

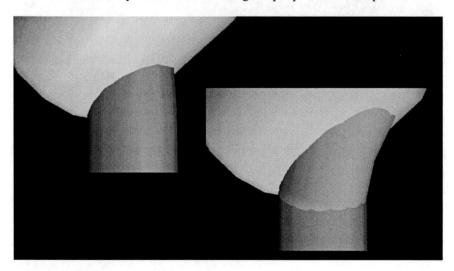

Figure 10: Blended superquadrics using cuffs

10 Verification

The quality of reconstruction is verified using human bones or adequate replacements, like pig bones (for certain cases).

Advantages of pig bones:

- Shape similar to human bones (for femur, pelvis and some others).
- Easily available compared to human bones .
- Since the bones are laid-open, an optical ray-based scanning device can be used which gives away surface information for free.

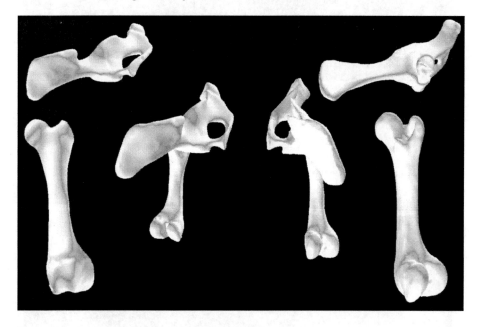

Figure 11: A sample of prepared pig bones

11 Other Applications

- Bone Feature comparison
- Bone sample generation.
- Training scenario data.
- Stem Fitting for THA planning.
- Mechanical simulation.

12 Future Improvements

- Further extension of the selection tool (more geometric types).
- More components of the lower kinematical system
- Operational support for more surgical procedures.
- Conceptualization of similarity measure between bones and implants for Fuzzy search in a database.

13 References

G. Alefeld & J. Herzberger, *Introduction to interval computations.* (New York: Academic Press, 1993).

A. H. Barr, Superquadrics and angle-preserving transformations. *IEEE Computer Graphics and Applications, 1*:1, 1981, 11–23.

L. Chevalier, F. Jaillet & A. Baskurt, Segmentation and superquadric modeling of 3D objects. In *Journal of Winter School of Computer Graphics, WSCG'03, 11*:2, Feb. 2003, 232–239.

R. Cuypers, Z. Tang, W. Luther, J. Pauli Efficient and Accurate Femur Reconstruction using Model-based Segmentation and Superquadric Shapes, *Proceedings Telehealth and Assistive Technologies ~ TeleHealth/AT 2008,* Baltimore USA, ACTA Press, 2008, 99-104.

E. Dyllong & C. Grimm, A modified reliable distance algorithm for octree-encoded objects, *PAMM, 7*: 1, 2008, 4010015-4010016.

E. Dyllong & C. Grimm, A reliable extended octree representation of CSG objects with an adaptive subdivision depth, *Lecture Notes in Computer Science, 4967,* 2008, 1341–1350.

E. Hameiri & I. Shimshoni, Estimating the principal curvatures and the Darboux frame from real 3-D range data, *Systems, Man, and Cybernetics, Part B: Cybernetics, IEEE Transactions on* , 33(4),, Aug. 2003, 626-637.

B. Heidari, F. Madeh Khaksar & D. FitzPatrick , Automatic landmark detection on epicondyles of distal femur in x-ray images, *4th European Conference of the International Federation for Medical and Biological Engineering,* 2009, 533–536.

A. Jaklič, A. Leonardis & F. Solina, *Segmentation and recovery of superquadrics.* Vol. 20 of *Computational Imaging and Vision.* Kluwer, (Dordrecht, 2000).

T. Ju, F. Losasso, S. Schaefer & J. Warren, Dual contouring of hermite data. In *Proceedings of the 29th Annual Conference on Computer Graphics and interactive*

Techniques (San Antonio, Texas, July 23 - 26, 2002). SIGGRAPH '02. ACM, New York, NY, 2002, 339-346.

M. Kang, Hip joint center location by fitting conchoid shape to the acetabular rim region of MR images, *Engineering in Medicine and Biology Society. IEMBS '04. 26th Annual International Conference of the IEEE*, 6, 2004, 4477-4480.

P. Lindstrom & G.Turk, Evaluation of Memory-less Simplification, *IEEE Transactions on Visualization and Computer Graphics*, 5(2), 1999
    http://www.gvu.gatech.edu/people/peter.lindstrom/papers/tvcg99/tvcg99.pdf

William E. Lorensen & Harvey E. Cline, Marching Cubes: A high resolution 3D surface construction algorithm. In: *Computer Graphics*, 21 (4), July 1987, 163-169.

D. Metaxas & D. DeCarlo, Shape evolution with structural and topological changes using blending. *IEEE transactions. Pattern Recognition and Machine Intelligence, 20*:11, Nov 1998, 1186–1205.

A. Rohatgi, Virtual Material Deposit and 3D Volume Preserving Smoothing. *www.anilrohatgi.com/docs/VirtualMaterialDeposit.pdf*

J. C. Russ, *The image processing handbook,* 3rd ed., (CRC Press, Boca Raton, FL, 1999).

H. Samet, *The design and analysis of spatial data structures.* Reading, (MA: Addison-Wesley Publishing Company, 1990).

G. Zheng & X. Dong, Automatic reconstruction of a patient-specific surface model of a proximal femur from calibrated x-ray images via Bayesian filters. *ICIC (1) 2007*, 1094–1102.

Cooperative Construction of Cryptographic Protocols Modeling and Analysis

B. Weyers, W. Luther

University of Duisburg-Essen
Department of Computational and Cognitive Sciences, Lotharstr. 65
47057 Duisburg, Germany
{weyers, luther}@inf.uni-due.de

Abstract. The focus of this talk is the development of a framework for the cooperative genera-tion of user interfaces based on visual languages, meaning construction with concept graphs, and cooperative Petri net construction. Our approach combines the methods and results of different research areas to develop a framework that uses various extensions of Petri nets to model parts of the action logic and presents recent applications to the cooperative construction of concept keyboards.

Keywords: Cooperative interface construction, visual language, Petri net–based action logic

1 Process and Real Life

- Petri net (PN)–based implementation of a procedural process model
- Situation-operator-model–based automatic supervision of the human-machine interaction
- Control unit of a nuclear plant (KSG/GfS Simulator Center Essen, Germany)

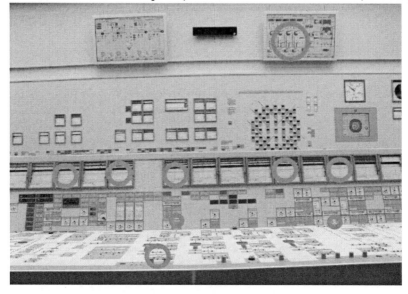

Fig. 1. Typical system interface (H. Boussairi, Diploma thesis, Duisburg 2008)

2. Input/Output Interfaces

- Display information to describe
    - o Possible actions (together with complementary information).
    - o The actual situation.
    - o Information about the process simulation.
- Collect user actions and input parameter.
- User interface as an iconic system
    - o Use iconic system as a structured set of related icons in a spatial arrangement to launch actions.
    - o Alternatively, use an iconic sentence (action sentence) to describe the situation or action.

3 Use of Petri Nets in Human-Computer Interaction

- Before design phase
- Modeling of human activities (since 1990)
    - o Places in the PN represent the actions carried out by the user, whereas the transitions represent the reactions from the user interface.
- Validation of interactive systems [1]
- Modeling cognitive activity
    - o Recognition of (ab)normal situations
- Colored Petri nets for ergonomic task analysis and modeling (adaptive systems) [2, 3]
- Interactive Cooperative Object formalism (ICO)

4 Formal Description of the Action Logic

- Describe the action logic (AL) using a nested PN
    - o Use several PN extensions to model real word processes, hybrid, stochastic, timed PN.
    - o Add conditions, colors, self-executable and nested transitions.
    - o Use nested transitions to model subtasks by "calling a subnet".
- PN: <N, P, T, A, SP, EP, M>
    - o N is the name of the net
    - o P is a finite set of *places*: $p_1, p_2, \ldots, p_n$
    - o T is a finite set of *transitions*: : $t_1, t_2, \ldots, t_m$
    - o A is a finite set of *oriented arcs* between P and T (T and P)
    - o SP is the set of *start places* (a subset of P); EP is the *end place*
    - o $M : P \rightarrow [0, 1]$ is called a *marking function* for the P

5 Colored Petri Nets

User adapted dialogues can be represented by "coloring" the marking function of the PN

- M: P→ Γ, where Γ is a set of token colors denoting distinct contexts of system use, set elements have simple or structured data types.
- Fusion places allow synchronization of several places with the same token sets.
- Transitions contain program code, guard functions or time delays.
- Unidirectional and bidirectional edges with complex logical constructs (conditions) are allowed (colored marking propagation rules).

6 Decomposition of Petri Nets and Cooperation

- Forms of cooperation
  o Games with stringent roles
  o Protocols
  o Free dialogue forms
- Decomposition algorithms for PN reflecting the roles
- Decomposition for interfaces

7 Petri Net Transformations

- Real world scenario of cooperative work [4]
- PN decomposition in parts corresponding to different workers
- Union of PNs via common interface
- Distributed or stepwise modeling
- Rule-based net transformation
- r(L,R) : Identify L in a net and replace by R
- Union : allows development of the subnets independently of one another
  o A union of two nets followed by a parallel transformation of the united nets yields the same result as two transformations of the original two nets followed by a union of the two transformed nets.
- Benefits: Formal model validation
  o Validation by simulation
  o Correctness
  o Completeness
  o Non-ambiguity
  o Usability

8 Dialog Model

DM = <PN, LP, PhP> [3]
- PN is a Petri net.
- LP is its *logical projection as a* couple $<LP_p, LP_t>$, where LP_p is a logical projection of places and LP_t is a logical projection of transitions.
- The logical projection of places LP_p is a function that associates to each place of the PN a description of information displayed. $LP_p : P \rightarrow I$ (meaning) The logical projection of transitions LP_t is a function that associates to each transition of the PN a description of the task performed: $LP_t : T \rightarrow G$ (meaning of operation)
- The physical projection of places PhP_p is a function that associates to each information item in LP_p its screen layout D: $PhP_p : I \rightarrow D$ (image generated by using a visual language)
- The physical projection of transitions PhP_t is a function that associates to each task in LP the action that the user has to perform to achieve it: $PhP_t : G \rightarrow A$ (this should be the representation of the task).

9 What We Want

- Define the visual language, meaning and layout of the icons actors, objects, actions
- User group generates the interaction logic via an appropriate visual language
  - Construct the visual information I describing the situation according to the mental process model and produce a layout.
  - Choose an appropriate action A depending on the task and the human experience.
- The system interprets I and A and maps it to the places and transitions of the AL-PN or constructs a corresponding subnet from scratch.
- Effectiveness and correctness can be checked by gluing the subnets and simulating the process or by identifying the subnet in the global PN.

10 Inverse Mapping

We must construct
- the inverse application of the physical projection $<PhP_p, PhP_t>$ and the logical projection $<LP_p, LP_t>$.

It is necessary to create the marking and the information content in the places
Interesting aspects
- Redesigning the interface is correlated with PN transformations
- Fusing or breaking down actions by folding and unfolding subnets

11 Visual Languages

Several approaches to visual languages (VL)
- Formal grammars
- Public information systems
- Messages oriented (different categories)
  - Process and object icons
  - Iconic sentences with terminal symbols (EBNF)
- Syntactic analysis of visual language (spatial parsing) is the analysis of the spatial arrangement of icons in an iconic sentence to determine the underlying syntactic structure.
- Semantic analysis of visual language (spatial interpretation) is the interpretation of an iconic sentence to determine its underlying meaning.
- The result of the syntactic analysis of an iconic sentence is a parsing tree, which can be described by an iconic system with the head icon representing the entire iconic sentence.

Visual communication has the ability, through symbolism, to enable a person to interpret meanings hidden deep in visual images (paintings, photographs, film or television). Only visual media have the ability to give form to abstract ideas. (Jacques Hugo, 2005, http://www.usabilitynews.com/news/article2585.asp)

Problems to solve:
- Inherent ambiguity (of icons)
- Spatial parsing (ambiguity of direction)
- Capture of realistic images vs. non-realistic, non-figurative visual representations.

12 Sound Patterns

- Conventional association between phonetic patterns and their word meanings
- Sound patterns are based on encoding schemes with phonetic and syntactic structure of human language
- Different ways in which sound can encode meaning [5]
- Prosody is a major channel
  - makes speech more impressive than writing
  - encodes emotional information
  - shares its major elements with music: intensity, melody, articulation and rhythm
- Songs: language serves as a carrier medium for melodic sounds
- Strong role of cultural imprint in the constitution of (subjective) meaning interpretation of musical meaning [6]

13 Understanding Visual Languages

Mental model
- Elementary signs/icons
- Interactive signs, actor signs, object signs, controller signs, layout signs, ghost signs
- Complex signs
- Common knowledge of visual codes and conventions

From the designer's perspective:
- the coding characteristics of the medium
- the principles of visual communication
- the user's needs, knowledge and perception of the visual codes used

From the user's perspective:
- perceptual, cognitive and discriminatory skills and the knowledge of the codes and conventions of visual communication in the particular medium

Elementary computer-based signs are organized in either concurrent or sequential chains. These chains can be described as chains of dancing steps, i.e., as units of connected syntagmatic and paradigmatic movements in time and space [7].

14 Levels of Meaning

Denotative meaning

The *logical, cognitive or denotative content* of the image, for example a graph which depicts a process over a certain period.

Connotative meaning

The *connotative* or *associative meaning* is found in explicit or implicit links established by the structuring of visual or cognitive elements. For example, the juxtaposition of graphical elements on the screen let the user form an association between the elements.

Stylistic meaning

Stylistic meaning may be contained in the image in the form or style of its presentation, often combined with a brand name or a product.

Affective meaning

Feelings or attitudes can be communicated or implied by affective language usage or the facial expressions of depicted individuals.

15 Formal Specification

- Chomsky hierarchy $G = (N,T,S,R)$ is a type 2 grammar if all productions $r \in R$ have the form
  - $r : A \rightarrow \psi$ (containing terminal and nonterminal symbols from T and N, S denoting the start symbol)
- Icon: $(X_{meaning}, X_{image})$
- Iconic system quintuple: G (VL, VP, S, x_o, R)
- VL is a set of logical objects; VP is a set of physical objects.
- S is a finite, nonempty set of icon names.
- x_o is an element in S, denoting the head icon name.
- R is a mapping from S into $2^{VL \cup S} \times VP$, denoting icon rules.

Elementary icon:

If $X_m \cap S$ is empty. X_m is subset of VL, so that x is of the form ({labels}, image). The labels could denote names of objects/procedures; the elementary icon can be an object icon, a process icon, or an operator icon.

There are special elementary icons. An *image icon* is one where X_m is empty, so x is of the form ({ }, image). A *label icon* is one where the physical part is null, so x is of the form ({labels}, $\varnothing$). Finally, a null icon is of the form ({ }, $\varnothing$).

Complex icon:

If $X_m \cap S$ is not empty. A complex icon indicates other icons and defines icon relations. There are the following types:

- Composite icon: if $X_m \cap VL$ is not empty. The icon x is of the form ({OP, y_1, y_2, ..., y_p }, image), where y_1, y_2, ..., y_p are subicons or logical objects, and "OP" is an *iconic operator* which operates on the subicons y_1, y_2, ..., y_p to create a new icon. The location attributes of the subicons will determine the order in applying the iconic operator.
- Structural icon: if $X_m \cap VL$ is empty. The icon x is of the form ({y_1, y_2, ..., y_p}, image). In other words, x is related to y_1, y_2, ..., y_p , but the mechanism for composing x from y_1, y_2, ..., y_p is unspecified.

Functions:

- $X = ICON(X_m, X_i)$ create an icon X with logical part X_m and physical part X_i
- X display contents of icon X (X_m, X_i)
- VL(X) display logical part of X called X_m
- VP(X) display physical part of X called X_i
- mat(X_m) materialization of logical part X_m
  X_i as physical part X_i ; mat: $2^{VL \cup S} \rightarrow 2^{VP}$
- dmat(X_i) dematerialization of physical part X_i
  X_m as logical part X_m dmat : $2^{VP} \rightarrow 2^{VL \cup S}$

Direct manipulation interface:

- Create icon (Xmeaning, Ximage)

- Display content and parts of content
- Define physical and logical operators on icons
  - o Image processing operators
  - o Logical operations in knowledge bases
  - o Combination by superposition and concept merge
  - o Indexing
  - o Clustering
  - o Similarity
- Operators work on the logical and physical parts of an icon

(cp. Chang [8])

16 Meaning Construction – Conceptual Graph

Idea: Specification of the logical part of an icon
- A conceptual graph CG is a finite, connected, bipartite graph.
- Nodes represent concepts or conceptual relations.
- A conceptual relation has one or more edges linked to concepts; thus, a relation can be monadic, dyadic or *n*-adic.
- The smallest CG is a single concept.
- The meaning of an elementary icon is described by a CG.
- Different meanings for the same icon image

Notation:
- [CONCEPT] $\rightarrow$ (RELATION) $\rightarrow$ [CONCEPT] , or
  [CONCEPT] — (RELATION) $\rightarrow$ [CONCEPT]
               (RELATION) $\rightarrow$ [CONCEPT] (for multiple arcs)
- Conceptual graph for ARROW (Arrows signifying movements of new objects):
  ARROW, d_arrow; u_arrow; r_arrow,
  "movement of new objects", EVENT,,
      [EVENT = INSERTION] —
      (THEME) $\rightarrow$ [OBJECT]
      (event.GO) $\rightarrow$ [PATH =P.1] $\rightarrow$ (path.TO) $\rightarrow$ [PLACE]
      with the conceptual graphs
      [OBJECT = LINE] and [PLACE = ROW].

17 Further Concepts

- Attributed graphs
  COCOViLa Grigorenko 2005, http://www.cs.ioc.ee/cocovila/docs.php
- Visual graphs as models for semi-abstract visual syntax
  Erwig, http://web.engr.oregonstate.edu/~erwig/papers/abstracts.html
- Spatial reasoning

-63-

http://www.cs.rug.nl/~aiellom/publications/aielloPHDThesis.pdf
- Visual Model Editor for Collaborative semantic Modeling
  Richter et al., http://www.formatex.org/micte2009/book/603-607.pdf
- FreeStyler
  Hoppe et al., http://www.collide.info

18 Applications

Focus on interaction logic via concept keyboards (CK):

- ConKAV (Middleton, Kraft, Putzer 2004–2006) [11]
- CoBo (Selvanadurajan, Kováčová, Weyers 2006–2007)[11]
- CoBoCC [9]
- dSdR [10]

Fig. 2. Implementing the Needham-Schroeder Protocol (NSP) with CoBo (Andrea Kováčová, Diploma thesis, Duisburg 2007)

(See also the contributions: Algorithm Visualization Using Concept Keyboards, Co-operative Visualization of Cryptographic Protocols Using Concept Keyboards in [11])

19 Meaning Construction

A sends his name and an encoded cryptogram with timestamp t_A, name of the partner B and symmetric key K_{AB} provided for the encrypting and decrypting the communication to the authentication server AS using the common key K_{AAS} of A and AS

- \<primitive\> object icons: A, B, AS, t_A, K_{AB}, Circle, R_ARROW, BOX
- action icon: K_{AAS}(composite icon)
- send icon with parameters sender, message from sender to receiver

The syntactic category \<primitive\> stands for different primitive patterns, and there is a simple Chomsky-2 grammar with "," (horizontal concatenation), & (spatial overlay), $\vee$, $\wedge$ (vertical concatenation) and "(" , ")" grouping

Concept Graph for K_{AAS}

key-lock_AAS,"encryption with common key of A and TTP", EVENT,,
[EVENT = ENCRYPTION] –
  (THEME) $\rightarrow$ [OBJECT=STRING]
  (event.OWNER) $\rightarrow$ [KEYHOLDER.1 = A]
  (event.OWNER) $\rightarrow$ [KEYHOLDER.2 = AS]
  (event.ALGORITHM) $\rightarrow$ [XXXX.1 = YYY].

This description should be combined with a string replacement at the same place.

Concept Graph for MOVE_STRING

MOVE_STRING, (fpp(CIRCLE)&fpp(A) $\vee$
        (fpp(BOXED_STRING), fpp(R_ARROW) $\wedge$ fpp(CIRCLE)& fpp(AS))
        "move a string to from an old place to a new place", EVENT,,
[EVENT = MOVE_STRING] –
        (THEME) $\rightarrow$ [OBJECT = STRING]
(event.GO) $\rightarrow$ [PATH = P.EAST] –
        (path.FROM) $\rightarrow$ [PLACE = BOX_A]
        (path.TO) $\rightarrow$ [PLACE = BOX_B].

Remark: A, B, AS, K_{AB}, K_{AAS}(.) can be replaced by images.

Action sendMessage1ToAS

- First action (createMessage1ForAS), which creates a message for the authenticity server
- Alternatively, the transition "!s*sonst" handles the error case.
- Second action (sendMessage1ToAS)
- The information content in the places must be available.

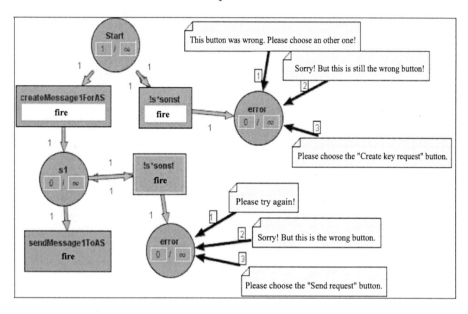

Fig. 3. Part of the Petri net–based representation of the AL of NSP

20 New Aspects in the Construction of Cryptographic Protocols

- AL implemented as Petri net using
  - self-executable and text-executable transitions
  - a scenario description with different actors and roles
  - situation-adapted error messages
  - method mapping: Methods are assigned to a key
- SwixML used for describing graphical user interfaces directly in XML for Java
- This approach allows one to check the user action against AL and verify the formal correctness of the generated CK.

21 Adaptation to Our Scenario

VL- to PN-based representation
- Implement XML-based parser
- VL2PN converter
  - Situation conversion
    - Inscribe places with type
  - Operation conversion : Operation to transition
    - Inscribe edges with type
  - Context conversion : Involved objects and operations
    - Inscribe edges and places in the basic topology of the subnet
    - Initial and final marking derived from context
- Simulation using model tracer

22 Interface Reconfiguration in a Distributed Simulation Environment

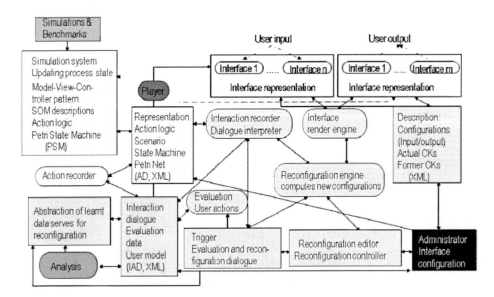

Fig. 4. System architecture of a reconfiguration system [10]

Formal Reconfiguration and Redesign of Human-Computer Interfaces

Benjamin Weyers[1] and Wolfram Luther[1]

[1] University of Duisburg-Essen
Department of Computational and Cognitive Sciences, Lotharstr. 65
47057 Duisburg, Germany
{weyers, luther}@inf.uni-due.de

Abstract. Adaptation of interfaces is mainly motivated by one aspect: the fitting of the user's plan to solve a specific task (formally described by a task model) to the (cognitive) computational process model that represents the possible task-solving strategies offered by a given machine. The physical interface has a great impact on the understanding of how to solve a task using the computational process model. The problem addressed in this paper is the inflexibility of the user interface provided by the machine, which does not allow reconfiguration and redesign operations to make the user's computational process model fit the task model. This paper describes a new approach to adaptive interfaces from the cognitive model point of view. We will present a formal description of Interaction Logic and formal reconfiguration and redesign techniques for human-computer interfaces.

Keywords: Formal Reconfiguration, Formal Redesign, Human-Computer Interfaces, Human-Computer Interaction, Adaptive Interface

1 Introduction

Human-Computer interaction and especially the adaptation of user interfaces is an important research area nowadays. Well-known approaches to problems in Human-Computer interaction often concentrate on analyzing users [12], describing interaction patterns [13] and evaluating users and interaction [14]. Cognitive architectures, like GOMS [15] or the SOAR model [16], are used to describe the user before the interface is designed. Adaptive interfaces use approaches like logging interaction and thus create user profiles and models as is done in ITS systems [17]. In this way, the interface can be modified to be less error-prone than the previous version. Often usability issues [18] are the center of interest for the interface designer; these issues are also closely related to the occurrence of errors in interaction [19]. But there are other ways to address these problems. In this paper we present an alternative approach to the question of how interface redesign and reconfiguration can be described, modeled and implemented in interactive systems.

Three central aspects are important in this context:

1. the formal description of interaction logic

2. the formal description of reconfiguration and redesign
3. the combination of both approaches from adaptive user interfaces to formal modeling of user interfaces.

To address these aspects and to describe an alternative approach to adaptive interface creation, we will define formal interaction logic and describe how to use it in the context of interface reconfiguration and redesign.

The concepts and formalisms presented are based on past research [9, 20] and software implementation [21] as well as evaluations [22]. In June 2009 we evaluated a system for interface design in the context of learning cryptographic protocols. Positive results from the evaluation, like the highly rated usability of the user interface for modeling, motivated us to continue bringing these approaches and ideas to a more general and formal level (described in Sections 3 and 4).

The validation of the created interfaces through testing was conducted by students based on a manual, computer-aided simulation. Future work and implementation will target the automatic validation and verification of formally described user interfaces as well as computer-aided reconfiguration and redesign of error-prone user interfaces (described in Section 5).

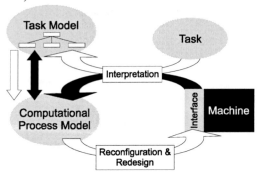

Fig. 1. Motivation of adaptive interfaces and formal interaction logic

2 Motivation

The main motivation for this new approach to adaptive interfaces is to fill the gap between the (cognitive) computational process model of a given machine and the task model defined by a given task (Figure 1). If the computational process model is error-prone, the user will be unable to fit it to his or her task model and will not succeed. It is also possible to view this issue from another perspective—that of the creation of the task model, which is directly influenced by the computational process model. When the user thinks about how to solve a task, he or she will analyze the computational process model and make decisions such as which steps are necessary to solve the task.

The problem we are addressing here is the inflexibility of the user interface implemented as part of the machine that does not allow reconfiguration and redesign operations to make the computational process model fit the task model. The user interface and the machine should not constitute the computational process model; it is the task model that should constitute the computational process model. This is the reason why reconfiguration and redesign techniques for user interfaces are necessary.

To let the user constitute the computational process model, the user interface should be described formally. Therefore, two perspectives on a user interface have been identified: (a) the physical interface composed by physical interaction elements called widgets and (b) its logic, which describes the frame of interaction and which is often reflexively implied by the physical interaction elements. These two correlated perspectives have to be described formally. There are diverse reasons why a formal description is necessary. Identification of problems in interaction can be analyzed using formal approaches. Reconfiguration and redesign can be described as formal rules using various formal or semi-formal languages. Automatic changes to the interface can be implemented, and so on. Without a formal description of the user interface such approaches cannot be implemented in a computer-based way.

From this point of view, a less error-prone interaction will result. If it is possible to identify problems in the formal description of the interface design and configuration, it can be fixed in an automatic or semi-automatic way. Without the possibility of a formalization of design and logic, such results cannot be applied to interfaces in the redesign and reconfiguration process. Without formal description there is no chance to apply redesign or reconfiguration during runtime. Long and cost-intensive reengineering processes have to be applied to acquire better designed interfaces. Nevertheless, the problem remains that these reengineering processes only match the interface to a special group of people, and so there will still be a lot of people making errors when interacting with an interface that has not been adapted to them.

3   Definitions

3.1 Interface Redesign

Definition 1 (Interface Redesign) Interface Redesign is the modification process of the physical representation (design) of a user interface.

Interface redesign means modification of the position and appearance of physical interaction elements, extending the interface by new elements or deleting old ones. Also, changing the style aspects of an interface is part of interface redesign.

It is important to note that the process of designing an interface from scratch should be separated from the term of interface redesign. Interface creation is not the modification but the generation of a physical representation. The motivation, the initial data and the point in time separate the two processes. Nonetheless, both approaches are not entirely different in their construction methods. For instance, adding or deleting (etc.) of widgets can be found in both approaches. Based on this observation, the use of a common formalism (for creation and for redesign) is adequate.

3.2 What Can Interface Creation and Redesign Do?

In [9] we presented a new approach to the cooperative creation of concept keyboards [23] for learning cryptographic algorithms using a distributed learning environment and an interface designing tool. The result is an iterative workflow, shown in Figure 2. The workflow starts with a thematic introduction of a group of students followed by an explanation of the task to be solved. In the context of learning cryptographic protocols, the students have to create a concept keyboard offering one button per step in the cryptographic protocol. After creating the keyboard, they have to evaluate their result through a distributed simulation of the protocol using their keyboard. If they have forgotten to add operations to the keyboard or if they have selected the wrong role for a given operation, they have to go back to the creation phase and fix the error in an iterative manner. The distributed simulation system therefore gives hints to help the students identify errors so that they can fix the problems.

In an evaluation of this workflow conducted at the University of Duisburg-Essen in June 2009, this concept was validated under various hypotheses with 66 students. In this evaluation, two groups were established. The first group created the keyboard cooperatively, while the students in the second group created their role-specific keyboards independently. Figure 3 shows these two settings—the cooperative one on the left, the non-cooperative on the right. The results of this study are still to be evaluated, but initial conclusions from interviews have shown that the cooperative group was more motivated and more effective than the non-cooperative group. Still, the devel-

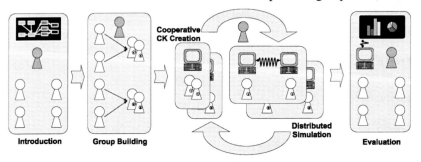

Fig. 2. Workflow for iterative creation of concept keyboards

Fig. 3. Cooperative (left) and non-cooperative (right) groups creating concept keyboards for the Needham-Schroeder protocol.

oped software for creating and redesigning the keyboards was well accepted and highly rated in both groups.

3.3 Formal Interaction Logic

Definition 2 (Interaction Logic) Interaction logic (IL) of a user interface formally describes the possible interaction (frame of interaction or interaction frame) supported by the interface.

IL describes a logical layer between the system interface and the physical representation of the user interface. Figure 4 shows the layered structure of a system with its system interface, the physical representation of the user interface and the intermediate IL layer. The system interface represents a subset of all possible operations and observable values of the underlying system. The user interface is the entity of physical representation and IL.

Definition 3 (Interface Reconfiguration) Interface reconfiguration is the modification process of the interaction logic of a user interface.

Thus, interface reconfiguration is to IL as interface redesign is to the design of a user interface. Nevertheless, they are not the same thing. A redesign of the physical representation of an interface need not change its IL, and the reconfiguration of an interface need not necessarily change its design. Changing the style of a button, like its color or its position, does not change the IL of the button. Conversely, changing the operation that is triggered by pressing a specific button has no influence on the button's color or position. Nonetheless, the design and the IL are closely related. The text on a button expresses its functionality, and a specific functionality corresponds to a specific interaction widget. The relationship and the differences between them motivate the differentiation and offer a close and formal look at both design and IL.

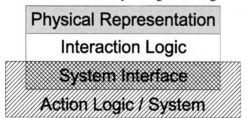

Fig. 4. Layered structure of an interactive system extended by a formal description of interaction logic.

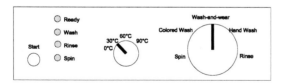

Fig. 5. Simple user interface of a washing machine

3.4 An Example of Formal Interaction Logic

The following example explains the term IL and the difference between the physical layer and the logic layer in greater detail. The example is a simple washing machine, which implements the interface shown in Figure 5. Three input widgets are shown for selecting the washing temperature, the washing program and a start button to begin the washing process. Four LEDs show the status of the washing process. Under the assumption that these operations are directly offered by the system interface, the IL is

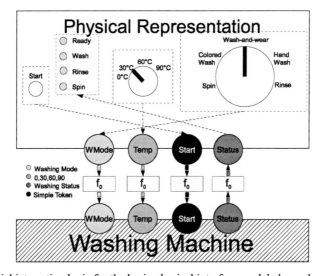

Fig. 6. Trivial interaction logic for the basic physical interface modeled as colored Petri net.

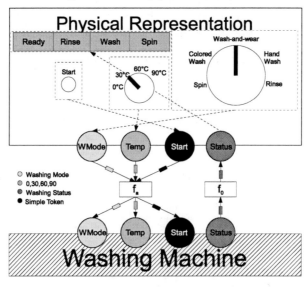

Fig. 7. Example of a non-correlated reconfiguration and redesign of a user interface.

trivial, as shown in Figure 6. It is a one-to-one mapping of physical widgets and their values to the system interface.

In this example, formal IL will be modeled using a colored Petri net (CPN). CPNs are an extension of Petri's formal modeling language [24] for dynamic, non-deterministic and parallel processes as defined in [25]. The main extension is the coloring of the marks in the net. Depending on the coloring of the places, the inscription of the edges and the function of the transitions, these nets become more compact and are closer to the object-oriented programming paradigm than original Petri nets are. Colors are often described as simple or complex data types.

In the washing machine example, an input operation made by the user generates a specific token of the given type and value selected. Suppose that the user selects 30°C for the next wash. This generates a token in the "Temp'" place of the type temperature and the value 30°C. The connected transition is now enabled and fires directly. The transition consumes the token and creates a new one in the place representing a part of the system interface called "Temp". This trivial consuming and creating without changing the type or the value of the consumed token is designated as function f_0.

Figure 7 shows an example of a redesign and a reconfiguration; neither influences the design or the IL. The redesign shown is a change in the output widget for the process status. This redesign does not influence the IL. It still shows the status that is transmitted from the system interface to the physical representation. The reconfiguration in Figure 7 deals with the problem that it is necessary to have all values (input parameters) for a wash defined before pressing the start button. The transition with function f_a can only fire if values for the washing mode and the temperature are de-

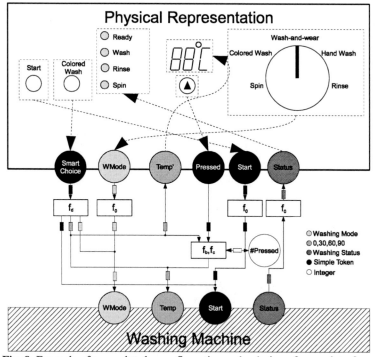

Fig. 8. Example of a correlated reconfiguration and redesign of a user interface.

fined and the start button has been pressed. The function f_a works like the function f_0 but with three input edges and three output edges.

Another possible reconfiguration and redesign of the washing machine interface is shown in Figure 8. This example of reconfiguration and redesign shows a close dependency between design and IL. In the first redesign, the temperature switch is changed to a button combined with a two number (seven-segment) output device. For this redesign, a modification of the IL takes place. The IL has to be changed such that with every button press event the temperature increases. The new temperature has to be shown in the output widget and communicated to the machine interface. The function f_b implements the counting functionality, which uses the value from the "#Pressed" place, which holds a token with the counting value. The value of this token is incremented with every press event. f_b is defined as follows:

$$f_b: \#Pressed := \#Pressed + 1$$

$$f_c: Temp = Temp' := (30*\#Pressed) \bmod 120$$

In these equations the name of a place implies the value of the token that is placed on it. A place on the right of the equal sign implies the consumption of a token; a place on the right of the equal sign implies the creation of the described token.

The second example of correlated reconfiguration and redesign is the implementation of a smart choice button. The user does not have to select all the parameters for a colored wash at 30°C but only has to put the laundry into the machine and press the smart choice button. The IL now has to describe the more complex operation using an extension of the Petri net. The result is a new transition with the function f_d. If the button is pressed, the new transition is enabled and can fire, executing the function f_d, which is defined as follows:

$$f_d: WMode = \text{"Colored Wash"}; Temp = Temp' = 30; Start = SimpleToken$$

The smart choice token is simply consumed without being used in further calculations.

3.5 What Can Formal Interaction Logic and Reconfiguration Do?

As mentioned above, IL defines the framework of the possible interaction of the user with the system. By combining this with a formal description of the physical representation of the user interface, the whole interface can be described formally. This method of describing user interfaces has several intended benefits:

1. Automatic reconfiguration/redesign is possible. Formal specifications and patterns like those expressed in [26], etc., can be used directly to modify the interface.

2. The user interface can be formally verified and validated with respect to different issues. Analyzing tools can be used to analyze the interface, the possible interaction and other elements, like requirements or specifications resulting from requirement analysis.

3. Automatic interface generation is possible, e.g., using interaction patterns. If the IL is once described, applying different interaction patterns to it can generate different physical representations of the user interface, which facilitates the interaction frame described by the IL and vice versa.

3.6 Visual Languages

The problem with formal languages, like Petri nets, is unreadability. In the case of CPNs, of course, there is a visual representation, but this visual representation is still formal and context-independent. Yet the modeling process for a user interface is highly context dependent. The creation of an interface for a nuclear power plant will result in a totally different interface description than will the creation of an interface for a car. Nonetheless, the Petri nets in both cases will have places and transitions. The language itself (especially the syntax) would not have any meaning to the modeler. Visual languages, on the other hand, are context-specific. A visual language, according to Chang [8], comprises a set of icons, which are defined as pairings of a physical representation and a meaning, as well as a set of icon operations describing the functionality for generating more complex icons from a set of atomic icons. Based on this approach, it is possible to generate visual languages to describe the interaction between the user and the machine in a context-specific manner. The explicit implementation is one of our current research topics.

In [20] we presented a conversation algorithm which generates CPN-based descriptions from visual languages. Based on this approach, it will be possible to offer context-dependent visual languages to the non-expert user for describing complex IL.

3.7 Operation-Centered Modeling of Formal Interaction Logic

Another approach to modeling complex IL is a graph-based description based on the term of operations. It can be viewed as a compromise between a formal description by CPNs and a context-dependent description using visual languages. This approach is based on the following definition of operations.

Definition 4 (Operation) An Operation O is a tuple of three elements $O=(P_i,P_o,f)$, where P_i is a set of Input-Parameters, P_o is a set of Output-Parameters and f describes its function. f can have pre- and post-conditions.

f is normally implemented as black box or part of the system the functionality of which is not known from the point of view of the user interface. Apart from these system operations, other types of operations can be used to model more complex operations based on an elementary system. Combining system operations, an IL can be described by a set of operations and can thus be reconfigured in different ways. This modeling approach can be facilitated by using software based on graphical data structures, as presented in the next section.

Figure 9 shows an algorithm for the conversion of an operation- and graph-based description to a CPN-based description of IL. According to the findings of Ehrig et al. [4], net transformation techniques can be applied to generate a subnet that results from this conversion, leading to more complex IL. Based on graph transformation as a high-level rule and pattern-based manipulation language for graph models, it is possible to integrate additional information into the CPN using meta-model approaches like those described in [27]. In this way, the semantics of context-specific pre- and post-conditions can be included in a formal graph-based description of IL.

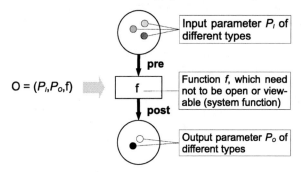

Fig. 9. Conversion rule to convert operation-based descriptions to CPN-based ones.

5 Implementation and Architecture

A possible implementation of a visual modeling tool for a formal modeling, redesign and reconfiguration of user interfaces is shown in Figure 10. This tool is an extension of the existing one used in the study described in Section 3. This extension is separated into two perspectives corresponding to the two aspects of a user interface: (a) the IL and (b) the physical interface representation, or design. Figure 10, therefore, is split into two parts. The upper part shows the perspective for modeling formal IL using the operation-based approach described in Section 4. The lower part shows the perspective for modeling the physical representation of the user interface.

A user who wants to create or reconfigure/redesign a user interface using this tool must complete the following steps: After loading the interface to the tool, the physical representation perspective will pop up, presenting the physical representation to the user. Now, there are several possibilities. One is to change the existing widgets by giving them new positions or styles (color, etc.). Another is to add new widgets from the widget palette on the left by dragging and dropping or to remove widgets from the interface canvas. After carrying out the redesign, the user may want to change the IL of selected widgets. To do so, it is necessary to select one or more widgets and then change to the IL perspective. The tool has to offer the selection of more than one widget at the same time because a part of the IL is sometimes connected to more than one widget. Figure 10 provides an example of this. The value selected with the slider should be shown in the seven-segment output widget. Thus, the IL of the slider is closely related to the IL of the output widget. By grouping these two, the user can now define the formal IL for these two widgets.

The IL perspective is separated into three different areas. From left to right: the operation palette, the operation canvas and the pre- and post-condition canvases. The operation palette offers different types of operations visualized by little boxes. Every box representing an operation offers input and output ports that represent the various input and output parameters of any specific operation. The user can select between system operations, which are part of the system interface, and special operations, which are used to combine these elementary system operations to more complex operations. These "design" operations can be any mathematical function changing the value of one parameter and passing this new value as input to another operation, and so on.

Nevertheless, it is important to define the context of an operation as pre- and post-conditions. In this context, visual languages are again of great interest. Pre- and post-conditions describe the context in which the modeled complex operation can be executed. Using the conversion algorithm from [20], the subnets resulting from the graph-based modeling approach for complex operations can be modified such that pre- and post- conditions are integrated.

After the user has defined the IL for every widget on the user interface, the resulting operation graphs are converted to CPNs automatically involving the pre- and post-

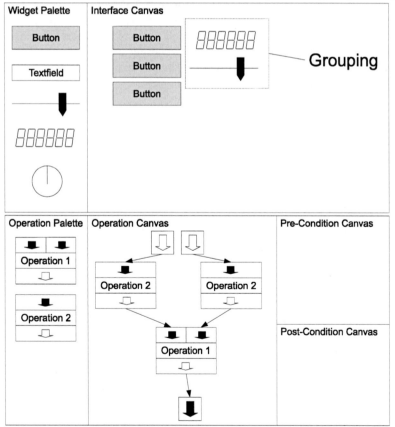

Fig. 10. Mock-up of a visual editor to create a user interface by modeling the formal interaction logic (above) and the physical representation of the interface (below).

conditions. The collectivity of all these subnets builds the IL of the modeled user interface. The formal descriptions of the physical and logic layers will be stored as XML data files for further use. Different XML dialects are of major interest in this context. For CPNs, the Petri Net Markup Language PNML is one suitable option. For the description of the physical representation of user interfaces, different languages have been developed. SwiXML is one of those that are closely related to a specific programming language, in this case JAVA with its SWING library.

In addition to the visual interface for modeling and the conversion algorithms, the software should offer a set of further analyzing tools. Based on the XML data, techniques like style sheets (XSL-T) or search engines like XQuery offer many different technologies for using such formal description for further analysis. Reconfiguration and redesign can be formalized in rule-based systems and descriptions. Automatic Reconfiguration and redesign can be applied to such formalizations influenced by monitoring user's behavior and identifying errors in interaction. Combining results from monitoring and rules, such as those generated by interaction patterns [13], automatic reconfiguration and redesign can be applied to formal user interfaces.

On the level of CPNs, many tools and research results exist concerning state space analysis and net transformation techniques [4]. For example, state-space analysis applied to a formal IL description could show the whole reachable interaction frame that the interface offers for interaction with a system. Based on this, it can be decided whether an interface offers too low or too high a degree of freedom for the application. Another example is an interface that has to change according to the classification of the user. A normal worker, for example, should have a lower degree of freedom than the boss.

6 Conclusion and Future Work

This paper introduces a new approach to adaptive interface modeling. Based on formal languages and description of the physical and the logic aspects of a user interface, it becomes possible to identify problems and to address issues concerning adaptive user interface creation and reconfiguration. In addition to defining terms and describing a formal approach, we have used the simple example of a washing machine to describe the possibilities of a formal approach to user interface creation and design. Furthermore, we have described basic ideas for implementing a visual modeling tool for formal IL and context design.

These concepts were tested in a learning scenario for cryptographic protocols. The study described demonstrated the many benefits of this approach as well as the usability of this kind of separation between the physical and logic layers of a user interface. However, the integration of visual languages and the tool described in the last section have yet to be implemented. The formalization concept also has to be finished, and further research and evaluation is planned for the middle of next year.

References

1. Palanque, P., Bastide, R.: Design, specification and verification of interactive systems. Springer, Wien (1995)
2. De Carolis, B., Rosis, F. de, Errore, S.: A user-adapted iconic language for the medical domain, In: International Journal of Human-Computer Studies, 561–577 (1995)
3. Rosis, F. de, Pizzutilo, S.: Formal description and evaluation of user-adapted interfaces, In: International Journal of Human-Computer Studies, 95–120 (1998)
4. Ehrig, H., Hoffmann, K., Padberg, J., Ermel, C., Prange, U., Biermann, E., Modica, T.: Petri Net Transformations. Petri Net: Theory and Applications, 534–550 (2008)
5. Ritter, H. T.: Sound and meaning in auditory data display. Proc. IEEE 92 4, 730–741 (2004)
6. Baloian, N., Luther, W.: Modeling Educational Software for People with Disabilities: Theory and Practice. Proceedings ASSETS 2002 conference, 111–118 (2002)
7. Andersen, P. B.: A theory of computer semiotics. Cambridge University Press, Cambridge (1990)
8. Chang, S. K., Tauber, M. J., Yu, B., Yu, J.-S.: A visual language compiler. IEEE Transactions on Software Engineering 15 (5), 506–525 (1989)
9. Weyers, B., Baloian, N., Luther, W.: Cooperative Creation of Concept Keyboards in Distributed Learning Environments. Proceedings of 13th International Conference on CSCW in Design, IEEE Press, 534–539 (2009)
10. Schubert, C.: Dynamical Interface Reconfiguration (dSrS) in a Distributed Simulation Environment, Diploma thesis, Duisburg (2007)
11. Baloian, Nelson; Luther, Wolfram; Söffker, D.; Urano, Y.: Multimodal Human-Machine Interaction in Different Application Scenarios. Logos, Berlin (2008)
12. Card, S. K., Moran, T. P., Newell, A.: The psychology of human-computer interaction. CRC Press, Boca Raton, Fla. (2008)
13. Tidwell, J.: Designing interfaces. O'Reilly, Beijing (2006)
14. Dix, A. J.: Human-computer interaction. Pearson Prentice-Hall, Harlow (2006)
15. Card, S. K., Moran, T. P., Newell, A.: The psychology of human-computer interaction. CRC Press, Boca Raton, Fla. (2008)
16. Rosenbloom, P. S., Laird, J. E., Newell, A.: The Soar papers. MIT Press, Cambridge, Mass. (1993)
17. Heraud, J.-M., France, L., Mille, A.: Pixed: An ITS that guides students with the help of learners' interaction log. ITS2004: 7th International Conference on Intelligent, 57–64 (2004)
18. Nielsen, J.: Usability engineering. Academic Press, Boston (1993)
19. Dörner, D.: Die Logik des Mißlingens. Rowohlt, Reinbek bei Hamburg (2002)
20. Weyers, B., Luther, W., Baloian, N.: Cooperative Model Reconstruction for Cryptographic Protocols Using Visual Languages. Groupware: Design, Implementation, and Use. CRIWG 2009, LNCS 5784 Springer, Berlin 311–318 (2009)
21. Kotthäuser, T., Kovacova, A., Liu, W., Luther, W., Selvanadurajan, L., Wander, M., Wang, S., Weyers, B., Yapo, A., Zhu, K.: Concept Keyboards zur Steuerung und Visualisierung interaktiver krypthographischer Algorithmen, Duisburg (2006)
22. Selvanadurajan, J.: Interaktive Visualisierung kryptographischer Protokolle mit Concept Keyboards—Testszenarien und Evaluation, Diploma thesis, Duisburg (2007)
23. Baloian, N., Breuer, H., Luther, W.: Concept keyboards in the animation of standard algorithms. Journal of Visual Languages and Computing 6, 652–674 (2008)
24. Petri, C. A.: Software Visualization—Programming as a Multimedia Experience, Bonn
25. Jensen, K.: Coloured petri nets. Springer, Berlin, New York (1997)
26. Jacky, J.: The way of Z. Cambridge Univ. Press, Cambridge (1997)
27. Ráth, I., Vágó, D., Varró, D.: Design-time Simulation of Domain-Specific Models by Incremental Pattern Matching in Proceedings of VL/HCC'08, 219 – 222 (2008)

Adaptive User Interfaces

Interactive Systems and Interaction Design

Prof. Dr. –Ing. Jürgen Ziegler

E-Mail: juergen.ziegler@uni-due.de
Web: http://interactivesystems.info

SADUEWA PhD Academy, Duisburg, July 30, 2009

INTERACTIVE SYSTEMS   Prof. Dr.-Ing. Jürgen Ziegler   -1-

Overview Research Areas
Interactive Systems Group

- Human-Computer Interaction
- Information Visualisation / Visual Retrieval and Exploration of Semantic Web data
- Model-based generation of user interfaces
- Cooperative development of ontologies
- Adaptive user interfaces
- Game Design & Entertainment computing
- Usability Engineering

INTERACTIVE SYSTEMS   Prof. Dr.-Ing. Jürgen Ziegler   -2-

Adaptive User Interfaces: Outline of Talk

1. definitions and characteristics of adaptive UI
2. adaptation paradigms and examples
3. user modeling and prediction approaches
4. adaptation strategies
5. usability of adaptive UI

INTERACTIVE SYSTEMS   Prof. Dr.-Ing. Jürgen Ziegler   -3-

A new problem?

"The term "adaptive systems/interfaces" designates one of the trendy areas of current research in HCI."

(H. U. Hoppe in a 1988 paper)

INTERACTIVE SYSTEMS   Prof. Dr.-Ing. Jürgen Ziegler   -4-

Adaptive User Interfaces - Definition

"An adaptive user interface is an interactive software system that improves its ability to interact with a user based on partial experience with that user."

Pat Langley, Stanford University (1997) in „Machine Learning"

- Adaptive user interfaces: „intelligent" user interfaces:
  - try to predict goals or preferences of the user
  - apply methods such as learning, inferencing or decision making (artificial intelligence methods)
  - can modify different aspects of an interactive system at runtime

INTERACTIVE SYSTEMS   Prof. Dr.-Ing. Jürgen Ziegler   -5-

General Schema for Adaptive Interaction

User model

User model acquisition

User model application

Information about the user

Predictions or decisions about the user

(Jameson / Faulring)

INTERACTIVE SYSTEMS   Prof. Dr.-Ing. Jürgen Ziegler   -6-

Basic Architecture of Adaptive UIs

User Interface

Capture User Behavior

User Model Acquisition

User or Group Model

Prediction/ Decision

Adaptation Mechanism

INTERACTIVE SYSTEMS   Prof. Dr.-Ing. Jürgen Ziegler   -7-

Adaptive, adapted, adaptable,…

- **Adaptive systems**
  - adapt to the user automatically during system use
  - → (auto)-adaption

- **Adapted systems**
  - Adaptation done prior to system use
  - → tayloring, customization

- **Adaptable (configurable) systems**
  - are taylored by users manually with respect to their requirements
  - → individualization, personalization

INTERACTIVE SYSTEMS   Prof. Dr.-Ing. Jürgen Ziegler   -8-

Approaches to User Modeling

	Individual Profiles	Stereotypical Profiles
Manual Construction	Hand-crafted Profiles	Hand-crafted Stereotypes
Automated Construction	Adaptive User Interfaces	Data-Mining Methods

(Source: P. Langley)

INTERACTIVE SYSTEMS   Prof. Dr.-Ing. Jürgen Ziegler   -4-

Goals of Adaptation

- increase efficiency of interaction by decreasing to number of task steps
- adjust to different physical or technical context
- provide assistance in performing tasks
- make user aware of relevant resources
- guide user learning
- …

INTERACTIVE SYSTEMS   Prof. Dr.-Ing. Jürgen Ziegler   -10-

Adaptation – a controversial issue

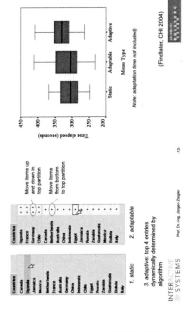

They optimize the UI for the individual!

They disorient the user!

(Gajos et al. 2006)

INTERACTIVE SYSTEMS   Prof. Dr.-Ing. Jürgen Ziegler   -11-

Comparison of static, adaptable and adaptive menus

1. static   2. adaptable

Move items up and down in top partition

Move items from bottom to top partition

3. adaptive: top 4 entries dynamically determined by algorithm

Note: adaptation time not included

(Findlater, CHI 2004)

INTERACTIVE SYSTEMS   Prof. Dr.-Ing. Jürgen Ziegler   -12-

Typical Examples / Paradigms for Adaptive UIs

- UIs that adapt to current task
- Learning personal assistants
- Virtual agents/assistants
- Intelligent Tutors
- Recommenders
- Critics, critique-based recommendation
- Personalized search
- Context-adaptive UIs
- Adaptation for Accessibility
- ...

(some of the following paradigm slides courtesy A. Jameson, DFKI, and K. Gajos, Harvard, CHI 2009 course notes)

INTERACTIVE SYSTEMS Prof. Dr.-Ing. Jürgen Ziegler -14-

About This Paradigm

- Features:
  - change the presentation and organization of user interface *functionality* in anticipation of the user's next most likely task
- Adaptation mechanisms:
  - Modeling and predicting user's actions
  - Computing and executing most helpful UI modifications

(mod. after A. Jameson & K. Gajos)

INTERACTIVE SYSTEMS Prof. Dr.-Ing. Jürgen Ziegler -16-

Adaptation Effects: Different Levels

- content/functionality level
  - filtering of content
  - generating recommendations (items, parameters…)
  - creating macros on the fly
- navigational level
  - filter/rearrange navigation entries
  - promote frequently accessed objects to higher level
- interaction level
  - changing/shortening menus
  - creating shortcuts
  - interaction mode, e.g. direct input vs. menu selection
- presentation level
  - change layout and presentation parameters (font, color…)
  - change input/output mode (e.g. screen vs. voice)

INTERACTIVE SYSTEMS Prof. Dr.-Ing. Jürgen Ziegler -15-

p. 59

Paradigm: User Interfaces that Adapt to the Current Task

(mod. after A. Jameson & K. Gajos)

INTERACTIVE SYSTEMS Prof. Dr.-Ing. Jürgen Ziegler -15-

Paradigm: Learning Personal Assistants

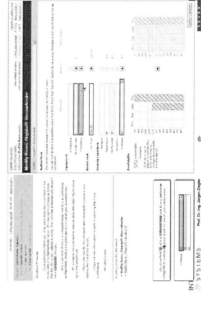

Example: RADAR system

(cf. Faulring, A., Mohnkern, K., Steinfeld, A., & Myers, B. (2008)

(mod. after A. Jameson & K. Gajos)

INTERACTIVE SYSTEMS · Prof. Dr.-Ing. Jürgen Ziegler · -19-

Agent-Assisted Form Filling

INTERACTIVE SYSTEMS · Prof. Dr.-Ing. Jürgen Ziegler · -20-

Paradigm in Practice: Examples from Mainstream Software

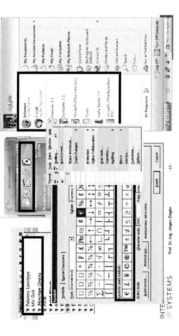

INTERACTIVE SYSTEMS · Prof. Dr.-Ing. Jürgen Ziegler · -17-

About This Paradigm

- *Features*
  - system observes users performing tasks and learns how to (help them to) perform the tasks
  - The system assists users by taking over parts of tasks
- *Adaptation mechanisms*
  - learning how to support particular tasks in a particular context
  - there may also be adaptation to the idiosyncrasies of individual users (person-specific tasks; preferred ways of performing a task)

(mod. after A. Jameson & K. Gajos)

INTERACTIVE SYSTEMS · Prof. Dr.-Ing. Jürgen Ziegler · -18-

Proposal of Values for a Form

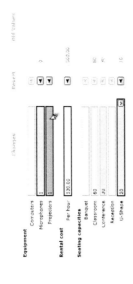

Fields for which RADAR has proposed a value are shown with an orange background. Moving the cursor over such a field causes the corresponding *anchor* in the email message to be highlighted

INTERACTIVE SYSTEMS   Prof. Dr.-Ing. Jürgen Ziegler   -21-

Showing Sources of Proposals

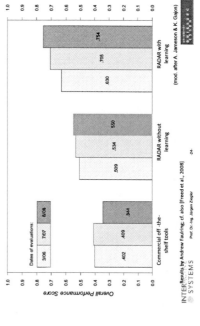

Moving the cursor over an anchor in the message opens a menu of proposed values.

INTERACTIVE SYSTEMS   Prof. Dr.-Ing. Jürgen Ziegler   -22-

Task-Centric Email Interface

SYSTEMS   Prof. Dr.-Ing. Jürgen Ziegler   -23-

Results of Large-Scale Evaluations

Results by Andrew Faulring; cf. also [Freed et al., 2008]
(mod. after A. Jameson & K. Gajos)

INTERACTIVE SYSTEMS   Prof. Dr.-Ing. Jürgen Ziegler   -24-

27

Paradigm: Embodied Virtual Agents

(J. Cassell et al.)

INTERACTIVE SYSTEMS Prof. Dr.-Ing. Jürgen Ziegler -26-

Paradigm: Recommender Systems
Example: Movielens (Konstan & Riedl)

INTERACTIVE SYSTEMS Prof. Dr.-Ing. Jürgen Ziegler -26-

Paradigm:
Critique-Based Recommendation

INTERACTIVE SYSTEMS Prof. Dr.-Ing. Jürgen Ziegler -27-

About This Paradigm

- *Features*
  - A user interacts with a system with the goal of finding an item (e.g., a product) that fulfills some current need of the user
  - basic mode of interaction is:
  - user provides an initial partial specification of their needs and preferences; or the system starts with an existing initial specification
  - Until the user has found an acceptable item,
    1. The system presents one or more items for consideration
    2. The user either
       - ... accepts an item
       - ... specifies one or more ways in which the desired item ought to differ from those presented, or
       - ... adds other new information about their preferences

(mod. after A. Jameson & K. Gajos)

INTERACTIVE SYSTEMS Prof. Dr.-Ing. Jürgen Ziegler -28-

CritiqueShop, Textual Interface

The selection of proposed compound critiques is based on the current model of the customer's preferences

Compound critiques

Unit critiques

INTERACTIVE SYSTEMS   Prof. Dr.-Ing. Jürgen Ziegler   -29-

Paradigm:
Personalized Web Search

INTERACTIVE SYSTEMS   Prof. Dr.-Ing. Jürgen Ziegler   -30-

Paradigm: Adaptation to Situational Impairments

"Sitting UI"   "Walking UI"

[Kane, 2008]

INTERACTIVE SYSTEMS   Prof. Dr.-Ing. Jürgen Ziegler   -31-

Methods can be structured with respect to phase of adaptation process

Model Acquisition → Prediction → Adaptation

INTERACTIVE SYSTEMS   Prof. Dr.-Ing. Jürgen Ziegler   -32-

Space of Prediction Approaches (I)

Sources for prediction

- single user characteristics or behavior
- group behavior
- data/content the user is dealing with
- context
  - external context factors such as location, time, device

Type of prediction

- action prediction
  - e.g. given a sequence of previous user actions predict the likely next action(s)
- resource prediction
  - determine relevance of information resources for the user's current task or context

INTERACTIVE SYSTEMS   Prof. Dr.-Ing. Jürgen Ziegler   -33-

Space of Prediction Approaches (II)

Prediction Principle

- history-based: only sequence of previous interactions considered
- model-based: explicit representation of user constructs, e.g. task model
- deterministic vs. probabilistic

Prediction methods

- large variety of AI and other methods:
  - machine learning,
  - rule-based inference, Bayesian techniques, neural networks
  - text mining, NLP
  - …

INTERACTIVE SYSTEMS   Prof. Dr.-Ing. Jürgen Ziegler   -34-

History-based action prediction: Example

- goal: identify patterns in command sequences

```
a) vi cw.tex
b) latex cw.tex
c) dvips cw.dvi
d) gv cw.ps
e) vi cw.tex
f) latex cw.tex
g) dvips cw.dvi
h) gv cw.ps
i) vi cw.tex
j) latex cw.tex
k) dvips cw.dvi
dvips: bad DUT file - text here not possible
l) dvips cw.dvi
m) gv cw.ps
n) Mail
Can anyone help me with latex???
?
```

Command i	Command i+1	Prob
vi cw.tex	latex cw.tex	1.0
latex cw.tex	dvips cw.dvi	0.8
	dvips cw.tex	0.2
dvips cw.dvi	gv cw.ps	1.0
dvips cw.dvi	vi cw.tex	0.8
gv cw.ps	mail	0.2

Quelle: Kirsten Kirsten: Space of Human Factors for Interactive Systems (Davison, Hirsh 2002)

INTERACTIVE SYSTEMS   Prof. Dr.-Ing. Jürgen Ziegler   -35-

Action Prediction

- **Goal:**
  - find patterns in interaction behavior
  - generate model to predict next action
  - offer the user a set of input options
- **sample accuracy levels achieved (UNIX commands, Davison & Hirsh):**
  - ~ 45% correct command predicted
  - ~ 75% for simple command without parameters

INTERACTIVE SYSTEMS   Prof. Dr.-Ing. Jürgen Ziegler   -36-

Algorithms for action prediction

- general problem: determine probability distribution of

$$P(x_{i+1}|x_{j..i})\ mit\ 1 \le j \le i$$

- Sample methods/algorithms
  - Markov models, Bayesian Networks
  - IPAM: Incremental Probabilistic Action Modeling
  - PPM: Prediction by Partial Matching
    based on longest matches of current tail of input sequence with longest subsequencies in earlier input
    derived methods: PPM*, PPMC+
  - Levenshtein distance

Prof. Dr.-Ing. Jürgen Ziegler   -37-

Sample Algorithm: IPAM (Davison & Hirsh 1998)

- Characteristics:
  - incremental, all previous events considered
  - does not store complete history, only matrix n x n for n commands)
  - no domain knowledge needed, realtime performance
- Method: update table of transition probabilities after each input

1. input

current Action \ next	a_1	a_2	...	a_{n-2}	a_{n-1}	a_n
a_1	p	p	p	p	p	p

Sum = 1

2. input

current Action \ next	a_1	a_2	...	a_{n-2}	a_{n-1}	a_n
a_1	p'·α	p'·α+ 1-α	p'·α	p'·α	p'·α	p
a_2	p	p	p	p	p	p

0 ≤ α ≤ 1, probability of current action increased

selecting α is decisive for quality

→repeat for each input, sort columns by highest probability

Prof. Dr.-Ing. Jürgen Ziegler   -38-

Prediction Accuracy for IPAM

Figure 6: Average per user accuracies of the top-n predictions. The likelihood of including the correct command goes up as the number of suggested commands increases.

Prof. Dr.-Ing. Jürgen Ziegler   -39-

Action Prediction in Smart Environments

- Context: Fraunhofer InHaus Duisburg
- Project: develop adaptive mobile control for smart home functions (Ressel, Ziegler, Naroska 2006)
- several adaption goals:
  - use different strategies: e.g. by room, by function
  - use familiar control functions in unknown environment (ontology-based approach)
  - adapt control interface for quick access to most likely actions

Prof. Dr.-Ing. Jürgen Ziegler   -40-

Using weighted hit lists for prediction

- probability of next action determined on basis of
  - occurences of sequences corresponding to current tail of input sequence (hits)
  - weighting hits by their length (longer sequences weighted higher)

INTERACTIVE SYSTEMS   Prof. Dr.-Ing. Jürgen Ziegler   -42-

Other history-based techniques

- n-grams
- t-pattern analysis (interesting for usabiliy research, not yet used in realtime interaction)
- ...

INTERACTIVE SYSTEMS   Prof. Dr.-Ing. Jürgen Ziegler   -44-

Prediction on the basis of similar patterns
(Ressel, Naroska, Ziegler 2007)

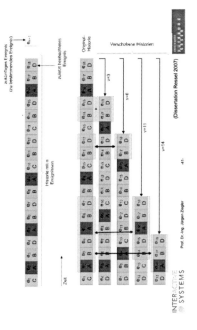

(Dissertation Ressel 2007)

INTERACTIVE SYSTEMS   Prof. Dr.-Ing. Jürgen Ziegler   -41-

Evaluation

- ex post analysis of 2 instrumented flats (inhabited)
- prediction only, no mobile control used
- high prediction rate, spatially constrained behavior of inhabitants leads to recurring patterns

INTERACTIVE SYSTEMS   Prof. Dr.-Ing. Jürgen Ziegler   -43-

Model-based Approaches for Action Prediction

Task & process models

- hierarchical task structures
  - e.g. Concur Task Trees (Paternò 1999), used for device adaptation
- grammatical models:
  - e.g. Task-oriented parsing (Hoppe 1988): Attribute grammar used to parse input sequences into higher-level task units
- process models
  - e.g. petri net models
- non-deterministic task models
  - Markov models
  - dynamic Bayesian networks
    e.g. LUMIERE project (Horvitz et al. 1998)

INTERACTIVE SYSTEMS   Prof. Dr.-Ing. Jürgen Ziegler   -45-

Lumiere Project: Influence diagram for providing intelligent assistance (Horvitz et al. 1998)

INTERACTIVE SYSTEMS   Prof. Dr.-Ing. Jürgen Ziegler   -46-

Portion of Bayesian User Model in Lumiere

- dependency between a pause after activity and the likelihood that a user would welcome assistance.
- a user being in the state of welcoming assistance would shift the probability distribution of observing pauses in activity.
- dto. probability of observing increased searching of menus is influenced

INTERACTIVE SYSTEMS   Prof. Dr.-Ing. Jürgen Ziegler   -47-

(One of the) commercial outcomes ....

INTERACTIVE SYSTEMS   Prof. Dr.-Ing. Jürgen Ziegler   -48-

Model-based Approaches for Resource Prediction

- Goal: Determine resources relevant for the user's current task and context
  - documents or document fragments
  - multimedia objects
  - semantic data (→e.g. for semantic desktops such as Haystack)
  - other resources such as communication channels
- Basis: handcrafted or (semi)automatically generated models:
  - thesauri
  - concept networks, topic maps
  - ontologies

Prof. Dr.-Ing. Jürgen Ziegler -49-

INTERACTIVE SYSTEMS

WISE Project: Ontology-based generation and adaption of Web applications
(Kaltz, Ziegler & Lohmann 2005)

Fragment of model for an e-commerce site:

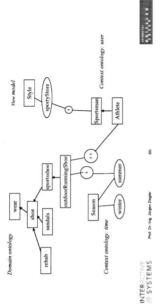

Prof. Dr.-Ing. Jürgen Ziegler -50-

INTERACTIVE SYSTEMS

CATWALK Framework

- Component-oriented framework (based on Apache Cocoon)
- Generates a context-adaptive Web application by interpreting models at runtime:
  - domain model, context model & navigation model + view model

white arrows: process flow - dotted-lined arrows: component calls

Prof. Dr.-Ing. Jürgen Ziegler -51-

INTERACTIVE SYSTEMS

Context Reasoning

- different context reasoning mechanisms can be plugged into the architecture

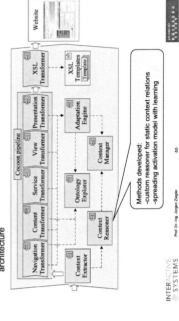

Methods developed:
-custom reasoner for static context relations
-spreading activation model with learning

Prof. Dr.-Ing. Jürgen Ziegler -52-

INTERACTIVE SYSTEMS

Context Reasoning

- different context reasoning mechanisms can be plugged into the architecture

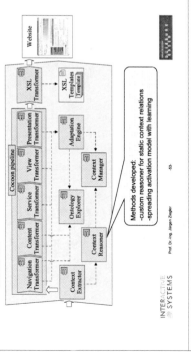

Methods developed:
- custom reasoner for static context relations
- spreading activation model with learning

Prof. Dr.-Ing. Jürgen Ziegler   -93-

Different Resulting Adaptations

Navigation structure

Content selection

Presentation features

Prof. Dr.-Ing. Jürgen Ziegler   -94-

Adapting parameters for service invocation

According to the contextual conditions …

Context Relations Model

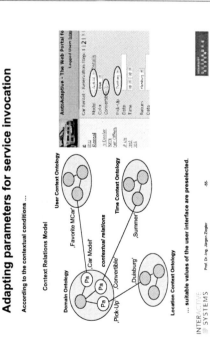

… suitable values of the user interface are preselected.

Prof. Dr.-Ing. Jürgen Ziegler   -95-

Contici (Adaptive Interaction for Collaborative Work) - Uniting Domain and Context Ontologies

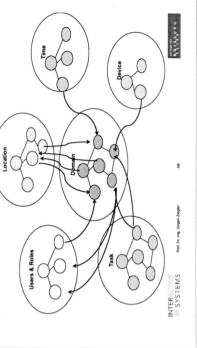

Prof. Dr.-Ing. Jürgen Ziegler   -96-

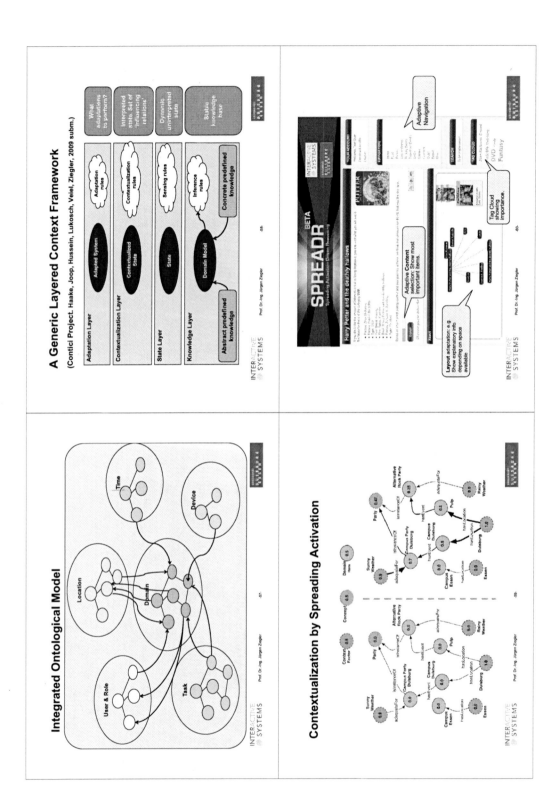

Adaptation Design Issues

- skill level of the user
  - adaptation may be less effective or even counterproductive for proceduralized behavior
- elective vs. mandatory use of adaptation
- spatial stability
- locality
- persistent vs. ephemeral
- embeddedness vs. embodiment

INTERACTIVE SYSTEMS   Prof. Dr.-Ing. Jürgen Ziegler   -42-

Performance Vs. Adaptation Type

Completion time (seconds)

Participants were significantly faster using Split Interface than Non-adaptive baseline ($p<0.003$)

(chart with bars: None, Split, Moving; axis values 70, 75, 80, 85, 90, 95)

(Gajos, Czerwinski et al. 2006)

INTERACTIVE SYSTEMS   Prof. Dr.-Ing. Jürgen Ziegler   -44-

Methods can be structured with respect to phase of adaptation process

Model Acquisition → Prediction → Adaptation

INTERACTIVE SYSTEMS   Prof. Dr.-Ing. Jürgen Ziegler   -41-

Study of adaptive toolbars

(Gajos, Czerwinski et al. 2006)

	Potential Benefit	Potential Disorientation
The Split Interface	Medium	Low
The Moving Interface	High	Medium
The Visual Popout Interface	Low	Low

INTERACTIVE SYSTEMS

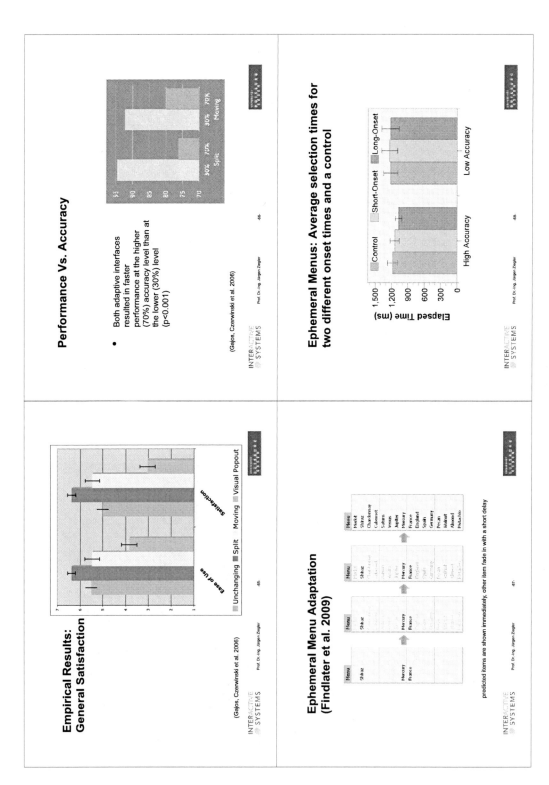

Conclusions

- Adaptive UIs have improved over time and some of them have gone mainstream
- Potential growing eg due to advances in areas like text mining and language processing, but...
- Features that are seamlessly integrated in applications seem more promising (but may depend on interaction style and application)
- Content or parameter-oriented adaptation seems to be more effective than adapting the interaction itself (in many cases
- Building adaptive interfaces is hard, but evaluating them in a valid fashion may even be harder

INTERACTIVE
SYSTEMS

Prof. Dr.-Ing. Jürgen Ziegler   -49-

Context-aware Recommendations

Tim Hussein

University of Duisburg-Essen, Germany
http://interactivesystems.info/hussein
tim.hussein@uni-due.de

Abstract. This article illustrates the vivid research field of hybrid and context-aware recommender systems. Moreover, two own approaches to deal with context-awareness in recommender systems, are described in detail.

1 Introduction

With the help of recommendations, large collections of products, or services are made accessible. Recommender systems support users by recommending content considered as being particularly interesting for them. They play an important role in handling large amounts of information. Often, the content and artifacts a person might be interested in, depend on the specific situation: The current location, season, user role, temperature, etc. Context-aware recommender systems try to exploit the usage context to improve the recommendation generation process.

Unfortunately, to this day, no commonly accepted technical definition of context does exist. Just for the term "context", there are more than 150 definitions from various disciplines. One of the most frequently cited definitions was proposed by Abowd, Dey, and others [1]:

> *"Context is any information that can be used to characterize the situation of an entity. An entity is a person, place, or object that is considered relevant to the interaction between a user and an application, including the user, and applications themselves."*

This rather broad definition lets the designer decide what he or she considers as relevant contextual information. This paper illustrates the state of the art regarding context-aware recommendations and introduces two techniques that incorporate both context information derived from system interaction (clickstream, history) as well as information about the external circumstances (location, time, season, etc.).

2 State of the Art

This section introduces into the research field of Recommender Systems. Beginning with basic techniques, it explains state-of-the-art approaches of combining them and, finally, integrating contextual information into a recommendation process.

2.1 Basic Recommendation Algorithms

Recommender systems have been established as an independent research area during the 1990s, having their roots in various disciplines like cognitive science and information retrieval. Most techniques can be roughly divided into content-based ([2]), collaboration-based ([3]), and hybrid approaches ([4, 5]).

Content-based systems incorporate features associated to the objects of interest. User ratings or transactions can be analysed in order to find out his or her interests, to recommend items similar to those bought in the past or rated as positive. For instance, neural nets, decision trees and vector-based representations can be used for that purpose. Collaborative filtering (CF) methods are supposed to be the most widely implemented recommendation techniques. They can be partitioned into classical User-based-CF and Item-based CF methods. User-based techniques identify so-called mentors for a user by generating vectors from the user's ratings and comparing those vectors, for instance, by correlation measurement or cosine. They assume that similar users are interested in similar items. So the mentors ratings for items are multiplied by the mentors similarity in order to predict the recommendations.

These computations may be time consuming and are often inappropriate for real-time recommendations with massive data sets and tens of millions of customers. Companies like Amazon.com therefore often use so-called Item-based collaborative filtering, that is based on the ideas of Sarwar et al. [6]. For each product a recommendation list of similar items is being pre-computed regularly based on what users tend to purchase together.

2.2 Hybrid Approaches

Different recommendation approaches are often combined into so called hybrid recommender systems (which may also incorporate information like social or demographic data for instance). The majority of hybrid recommender systems use collaborative filtering as the core method while content-based filtering offers solutions to the shortcomings of CF.

Balabanovic & Shoham [7] force items to be, at the same time, close to the user thematic profile, and highly rated by his neighbors as well. Pazzani [8] compares users according to their content profiles and thereupon uses collaborative filtering to generate recommendations. Other commonly cited approaches that combine content-based and collaborative filtering have been introduced by Melville et al. [9], Han & Karypis [10], and Wang et al. [11].

2.3 Context-aware Recommender Systems

Combining different techniques has been one of the main research interests within the field of recommender systems as well as incorporating contextual information [12, 13, 5, 14]. Context can be used in several ways to enhance recommender systems. Shepitsen et al. for instance introduce an agglomerative hierarchical clustering algorithm for social tagging systems [15]: A user-selected tag is used for a context-dependent limitation of the selected set of clusters considered for the recommendation process.

A content-based model for adaptive recommendations with the help of a use context is described by Kim and Kwon [16] using a set of four ontologies from which the "use context" for a user is derived: Product, location, shopping record and consumer. Most valued products are taken from the product ontology with help of the consumer preferences and shopping record. The most valued recommendations are taken and displayed in more detail. Products are ordered in a concept hierarchy from broad to most specific. If the user chooses a concept, the context switches and more specific information is shown. In this way, context is used to control the information detail of recommendations.

Adomavicius et al. add contextual information as additional dimensions to the given user and item dimension in an collaborative filtering approach [14]. The recommendations are derived from the item ratings under the given context.

Contextual information for both the involved items and recommendation process itself is proposed by Loizou et al. [17], who use an ontology containing information about items and the recommendation process. The ontology is build with the help of web services and expanded over time with new data to match the current recommendation context at runtime. Suchlike information could for instance contain metrics for usefulness for specific users. To extract recommendations, this ontology is mapped into a vector space from which only relevant parts are sliced out.

All theses systems work well in their specific environments, but there is still a research gap regarding systematic, generic and extensible integration of context information into the recommendation process. This paper introduces two frameworks that address these questions and, beyond that, can be very useful for hybrid recommender system prototyping as different recommender techniques and context sources can smoothly be combined.

3 Experiences with SPREADR

In 1975, Collins & Loftus introduced a technique called "Spreading Activation" [18]. This model was originally applied in the fields of psycho linguistics and semantic priming [19]. Later, the idea was adopted by computer scientists: Spreading activation techniques have successfully been used in several research areas in computer science, most notably in information retrieval ([20–22]). The principles of spreading activation have also been used by Pirolli & Card [23] in their information foraging theory.

The basic concept behind Spreading Activation is that all relevant information is mapped on a graph as nodes with a certain "activation level". Relations between two concepts are represented by a link between the corresponding nodes. If for any reason one or more nodes are activated their activation level arises and the activation is spread to the adjacent nodes (and the ones related to them and so on) like water running through a river bed. Thereby the flow of activation is attenuated the more it strides away from the initially activated node(s). At the end several nodes are activated to a certain degree that are semantically related to the concepts originally selected.

At the beginning, each node has an initial activation value of 0. We use the current context as the starting point for the Spreading Activation: When a new session starts all necessary context information is sensed and the nodes representing the recognized context factors are used as initial nodes to trigger the activation flow. As a result concepts and items that are related to the current context have a high activation value. A little example should illustrate this: The setting may be an information portal for leisure activities. Imagine the user starts a new session from Duisburg and the current time is evening. The system recognizes the time and the current location. This may result in raising the activation levels of all venues located in her city and events that take place on that particular evening are highly activated, too. Perhaps the system is configured to take local weather information into account as a context factor. So perhaps open air events may get a higher activation than indoor events. The flexible architecture allows a combination of arbitrary context information. Finally all nodes have a certain activation value that represents their degree of relevance in the current situation.

After that run the activation values are not reset but refined with every user action. If he clicks on a certain domain item - for instance a concert - this interaction is taken into account, too. The node representing that particular concert now is the initial node to another Spreading Activation run and transmit activation energy to all related concepts and items. That may include the concept of a concert in general (and thereby activating other concerts), the artist, the music genre, the venue of the concert and so on. Each interaction adopts the weights more and more to the current context and the user's interests.

At this point no adaptation is performed yet. Only the underlying models are adjusted to the current context and usage behavior. We believe that it is a good idea to separate these model adjustment mechanisms from the process of web page generation. Any changes in the page generation and presentation framework won't affect the reasoning part of the system and vice versa.

Several algorithms have been developed to implement the concept of spreading activation. Details and a comparison can be found in Huang et al. [24]. We chose the so called *Branch-and-bound* approach.

3.1 The branch-and-bound algorithm

The following steps describe a single Spreading Activation run. As mentioned earlier the activation values are not reset after each cycle so that the networks can develop into a kind of user and context profile. During a Spreading Activation run two phases can be distinguished: Initialization and execution.

Initialization: Before the actual execution of spreading activation begins, the network must be initialized:

1. The weights for the links are set based on the user's individual context model. Moreover, in our approach, the network is not necessarily in a blank state

when a spreading activation run starts. Therefore, initial activation levels for each node in the network are set. These are based on the resulting activation levels of the previous run.

2. The initial nodes are activated with a certain value. The activation received by the start nodes is added to their previous state. Optionally the new activation level is calculated by applying an activation function to this sum.

3. The initial nodes are inserted into a priority queue ordered by descending activation.

Execution: After initialization, the following steps are repeated until a defined termination condition is fulfilled or the priority queue is empty. The termination condition can be configured freely, but two pre-defined termination conditions are provided: (1) A maximum of *activated* nodes is reached, (2) a maximum of *processed* nodes is reached. A processed node is a node that has itself propagated activation to adjacent nodes.

1. The node with the highest weight is removed from the queue.

2. The activation of that node is passed on to all adjacent nodes, if this is not prevented by some restriction imposed on the spreading of activation. If a node j receives activation from an adjacent node i, a new activation level is computed for j.

$$A_j(t+1) = A_j(t) + O_i(t) \times w_{ij} \times a$$

where $A_j(t)$ is the previous activation of j, $O_i(t)$ is the output activation of i at the time t, w_{ij} is the weight of the relation between i and j and a is an attenuation factor. The output activation of a node is the activation it has received. An arbitrary function can be used to keep the values in a predefined range. In most cases a linear or parabolic function will be meaningful.

3. The adjacent nodes that have received activation are inserted into the priority queue unless they have already been marked as processed.

4. The node that passed on its activation to the neighboring nodes is marked as processed.

When a new spreading activation run is triggered the values are not reset, so that the network is refined every time the process is executed. We implemented an aging mechanism by attenuating each activation value by 5% before each new spreading activation run.

3.2 Configuration

Certain constraints and termination conditions can be defined to to prevent activation from spreading through the whole network and eventually activating every single node. Additionally this allows for refining the Spreading Activation process regarding performance. The process can be influenced for instance depending on the concept type, the outgoing edges or the path-distance between nodes. Details about those constraints can be found in [20] and [25].

In addition, the sub-functions described above can be configured - for instance the attenuation factor - or reverberation can either be allowed or prevented. This means that a node j must not propagate activation to a node i if node j has itself been activated by node i before in the same run. Finally, our spreading activation mechanism allows the adjustment of relation type weights. A relation type weight is used for each relation for which no individual weight has been set in the initialization phase of the algorithm.

Details about SPREADR can be found in [26].

4   Experiences with DISCOVR

Like many other context-aware approaches (including some of the systems presented in Section 2), DISCOVR utilizes semantic background information represented as ontologies. All item- and context-related information to be incorporated by the system has to be modeled in an ontology[1], for instance *[CD Garth Brooks - Beyond the Season]* → *[suitable for holiday]* → *[Christmas]*. Surely, this is a laborious task, but DISCOVR is mainly a framework for prototypical development and the scenarios will more likely be several hundred items and concepts rather than millions.

The components introduced in the upcoming section exploit this information and build context-aware recommendations upon.

4.1   A service architecture for recommendations

One important idea that was present throughout all our concepts was to realize the different components in the form of separate *services*. Each service has some kind of input and some kind of output, so that they can be connected to each other. While each service can present its data as a semantic model, for instance for visualization and explanation purposes, most of the communication between services takes place "on rails" in the way that the output type of one service matches the input type of another. We divided the input types (which we call *triggers* because they trigger the receiving component) and the output types into five distinct categories (Figure 1):

- *Semantic models*,
- *Sorted lists of resources* from our domain model, with the sorting order based upon the importance of the given resource,
- Lists of *weighted resources* with assigned weights between 0 (unimportant) and 1 (very important),
- *Numeric values*,
- *Textual data*.

---

[1] It may be useful to split the information into several ontologies for later reuse of parts in other scenarios

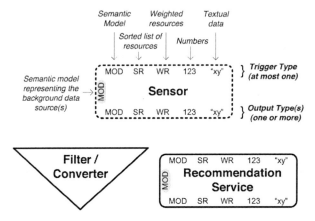

Fig. 1. Types of components of our service architecture, together with possible input and output data types.

Each service accepts triggering input of one specific type at most, which may be provided by one or more triggering services. The output of a service, on the other hand, can be manifold, depending on the particular implementation.[2] Additionally, each service can possess one or more background data source(s) in the form of semantic models (RDF triples) if needed.

In DISCOVR, we distinguish three different categories of services (Figure 1): *Sensor, recommendation* and *utility services*, all of them now explained in more detail.

Sensor Services A sensor is a service that acquires information about the user's context: Information derived from system interaction or information about external circumstances like the current temperature, which might be determined by contacting a web service. For a sensor to operate, it might first be necessary to retrieve already known information from another sensor: A weather sensor might need to know the user's current location, for example.

Most sensors' output has the form of a list of weighted resources (for instance closest cities along with their degree of adjacency). Some sensors, on the other hand, simply return literal values like strings or numbers (IP address, geographic coordinates).

Recommendation Services Recommendation services use their input in order to generate recommendations (context-aware ones, if the output of sensors is being incorporated). Typically, recommendation services require a background

---

[2] Item-based recommendations for instance could be delivered both as ordered or weighted resources.

data source containing items to recommended and their relations to each other in order to work properly.

The output of recommendation services is usually twofold: First, a recommendation service produces a list of ordered or weighted resources that can (after a possible filtering step) be presented to the user. Second, a recommendation service also returns a semantic model that is a sub-model of the background data source input and can be utilized as the background data source of yet another recommendation service, such that these services can be chained.

Utility Services The last kind of services are utility services. Such a service might *filter* its input according to specific criteria, like selecting only resources that have a specific type, or limit the amount of results. Another example of a utility service is a weighting service that assigns weights to a given, sorted list of resources according to a specific formula (virtually acting as a *converter* between sorted and weighted resources).

4.2   Experiences

We developed a virtual shopping and leisure portal including about 500 items like DVDs, CDs, sport events, concerts, etc. to demonstrate DISCOVR's potential (Figure 2) and implemented a set of components as reusable building blocks for hybrid, context-aware recommender systems.

4.3   Portal architecture

We implemented DISCOVR on top of the Spring Framework[3] as a Java web application including interfaces and abstract classes reflecting the components introduced in Section 4. In addition, we realized several concrete sensor, recommender and filter modules for testing purposes: 8 Sensors for location, click-stream, weather, season, etc.; 3 recommenders (Item-based Collaborative Filtering, Spreading Activation and Rule-based) as well as 5 filters like a Sorted Resource Weighter or a Weighted Resource Filter.

We assume that the general principles of item-based CF and rule-based recommendations are commonly known among the readership. Spreading Activation is a concept proposed in the 1970s by Collins and Loftus [18] and was originally applied in the fields of psycholinguistics and semantic priming. Later, computer scientists adopted the idea: The principles have successfully been used in several research areas in computer science, most notably in information retrieval [21] or for predicting user behavior [27]. The basic idea is that within a semantic network, certain elements are initially activated and spread this activation to adjacent elements. This activation flow runs through the network until a certain stop condition is met. In our case, the semantic model supplied by the background data source is converted into a directed graph, and those elements

---

[3] http://www.springsource.org

Fig. 2. Screenshot of a web-portal powered by DISCOVR including different areas for recommendations. In this case: (1) is a 'traditional' recommendation block for product recommendations based on a Spreading Activation algorithm and the latest user clicks. (2) shows local events suitable to current weather conditions. In (3) recommendations for a chosen category (e. g. CDs) are presented with certain items (with special relevance to upcoming holidays) presented as highlights (4).

reflecting the input values are initially activated and spread this energy in a highly customizable fashion within the network. The service's output is then a list of resources together with their activation weights corresponding to the activation values obtained during the activation process.

The portal makes strong use of the *MVC* design pattern, so that the information contained in the model can be displayed in various ways with the components only being loosely coupled.

Recommendations are generated using DISCOVR's service framework. A *service processor* builds a dependency graph of all registered services and then executes them in order. These services are realized as Java beans that are set up using an XML configuration file. Possible configuration parameters of a given service include the services that trigger this service, the background data source (which is, in most cases, the domain model), or service-specific items like certain filter criteria for a filtering service. A virtual service editor is planned as a future extension to make the whole setup of the service chain configurable at run-time.

4.4 Context-aware recommendations

Now we want to give an example of a service processes that produce context-aware recommendations of products associated with upcoming holidays (for instance 'Christmas', see Figure 3). For example, when the user's last click was on a romantic movie, we would recommend (romantic) movies that are, in some way, related to Christmas.

To achieve this, the output of a Holiday Sensor triggers a rule applying service restricting the domain model to only those elements related to just this holiday. This sub-model then serves as the background data source for an item-based collaborative filtering triggered by the user's last visited item. For the sake of brevity, the additional background data required for the item-based collaborative filtering approach (clicked items of other users) is not modeled here.

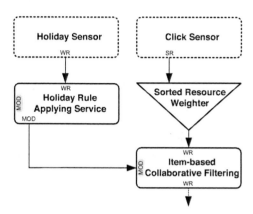

Fig. 3. Another example of a service process. In this case, a combination of a rule-applying selection service and an item-based collaborative filtering approach has been chosen.

[28] contains details on the DISCOVR Framework.

5   Summary

This article introduced the field of context-aware (and hybrid) recommendation generation. Furthermore, two approaches have been explained in detail.

6   Acknowledgements

The research presented in this paper is part of the CONTICI project, in which the Universities of Duisburg-Essen, Siegen, Hagen, and Aachen take part. CONTICI is funded by the German Research Foundation (Deutsche Forschungsgemeinschaft).

References

1. Gregory D. Abowd, Anind K. Dey, Peter J. Brown, Nigel Davies, Mark Smith, and Pete Steggles. Towards a better understanding of context and context-awareness.

In *HUC '99: Proceedings of the 1st international symposium on Handheld and Ubiquitous Computing*, pages 304–307, London, UK, 1999. Springer.

2. Raymond J. Mooney and Loriene Roy. Content-based book recommending using learning for text categorization. In *Proceedings of the fifth ACM conference on Digital libraries*, pages 195–204, New York, NY, USA, 2000. ACM.

3. Paul Resnick, Neophytos Iacovou, Mitesh Suchak, Peter Bergstrom, and John Riedl. Grouplens: An open architecture for collaborative filtering of netnews. In *CSCW '94: Proceedings of the 1994 ACM conference on Computer supported cooperative work*, pages 175–186, New York, NY, USA, 1994. ACM.

4. Mark Claypool, Anuja Gokhale, Tim Miranda, Pavel Murnikov, Dmitry Netes, and Matthew Sartin. Combining content-based and collaborative filters in an online newspaper. In *Proceedings of ACM SIGIR Workshop on Recommender Systems*. ACM, 1999.

5. Robin Burke. Hybrid recommender systems: Survey and experiments. *User Modeling and User-Adapted Interaction*, 12(4):331–370, 2002.

6. Badrul Sarwar, George Karypis, Joseph A. Konstan, and John T. Riedl. Item-based collaborative filtering recommendation algorithms. In Vincent Y. Shen, Nobuo Saito, Michael R. Lyu, and Mary Ellen Zurko, editors, *Proceedings of the 10th international conference on World Wide Web*, pages 285–295, Hong Kong, 2001. ACM.

7. Marko Balabanovic and Yoav Shoham. Combining content-based and collaborative recommendation. *Communications of the ACM*, 40:66–72, 1997.

8. Michael J. Pazzani. A framework for collaborative, content-based and demographic filtering. *Artificial Intelligence Review*, 13(5-6):393–408, 1999.

9. Prem Melville, Raymod J. Mooney, and Ramadass Nagarajan. Content-boosted collaborative filtering for improved recommendations. In *Eighteenth national conference on Artificial intelligence*, pages 187–192, Menlo Park, CA, USA, 2002. American Association for Artificial Intelligence.

10. Eui-Hong Han and George Karypis. Feature-based recommendation system. In *CIKM '05: Proceedings of the 14th ACM international conference on Information and knowledge management*, pages 446–452, New York, NY, USA, 2005. ACM.

11. Jun Wang, Arjen P. de Vries, and Marcel J. T. Reinders. Unifying user-based and item-based collaborative filtering approaches by similarity fusion. In *SIGIR '06: Proceedings of the 29th annual international ACM SIGIR conference on Research and development in information retrieval*, pages 501–508, New York, NY, USA, 2006. ACM.

12. Jonathan L. Herlocker and Joseph A. Konstan. Content-independent task-focused recommendation. *IEEE Internet Computing*, 5(6):40–47, 2001.

13. Gediminas Adomavicius and Alexander Tuzhilin. Multidimensional recommender systems: A data warehousing approach. In *WELCOM '01: Proceedings of the Second International Workshop on Electronic Commerce*, pages 180–192, London, UK, 2001. Springer.

14. Gediminas Adomavicius, Ramesh Sankaranarayanan, Shahana Sen, and Alexander Tuzhilin. Incorporating contextual information in recommender systems using a multidimensional approach. *ACM Transactions on Information Systems*, 23(1):103–145, 2005.

15. Andriy Shepitsen, Jonathan Gemmell, Bamshad Mobasher, and Robin Burke. Personalized recommendation in social tagging systems using hierarchical clustering. In *Proceedings of the 2008 ACM conference on Recommender Systems (RecSys)*, pages 259–266, New York, NY, USA, 2008. ACM.

16. Sungrim Kim and Joonhee Kwon. Effective context-aware recommendation on the semantic web. *International Journal of Computer Science and Network Security*, 7(8):154–159, 2007.

17. Antonis Loizou and Srinandan Dasmahapatra. Recommender systems for the semantic web. In *ECAI 2006 Recommender Systems Workshop*, 2006.

18. Allan M. Collins and Elizabeth F. Loftus. A spreading activation theory of semantic processing. *Psychological Review*, 82(6):407–428, 1975.

19. John R. Anderson. A spreading activation theory of memory. *Journal of Verbal Learning and Verbal Behavior*, 22:261–295, 1983.

20. Paul R. Cohen and Rick Kjeldsen. Information retrieval by constrained spreading activation in semantic networks. *Information Processing and Management*, 23(4):255–268, 1987.

21. Fabio Crestani. Application of spreading activation techniques in information retrieval. *Artificial Intelligence Review*, 11(6):453–482, 1997.

22. Helmut Berger, Michael Dittenbach, and Dieter Merkl. An adaptive information retrieval system based on associative networks. In *APCCM '04: Proceedings of the first Asian-Pacific conference on Conceptual modelling*, pages 27–36, Darlinghurst, Australia, Australia, 2004. Australian Computer Society, Inc.

23. Peter Pirolli and Stuart Card. Information foraging in information access environments. In Irvin R. Katz, Robert Mack, Linn Marks, Mary Beth Rosson, and Jakob Nielsen, editors, *Proceedings of the SIGCHI conference on Human factors in computing systems*, pages 51–58, Denver, Colorado, USA, 1995. ACM Press.

24. Zan Huang, Hsinchun Chen, and Daniel Zeng. Applying associative retrieval techniques to alleviate the sparsity problem in collaborative filtering. *ACM Transactions on Information Systems*, 22(1):116–142, 2004.

25. Cristiano Rocha, Daniel Schwabe, and Marcus Poggi Aragao. A hybrid approach for searching in the semantic web. In *WWW '04: Proceedings of the 13th international conference on World Wide Web*, pages 374–383, New York, NY, USA, 2004. ACM.

26. Tim Hussein and Jürgen Ziegler. Adapting web sites by spreading activation in ontologies. In Lawrence Bergman, Kim, Jihie, Bamshad Mobasher, Stefan Rueger, Stefan Siersdorfer, Sergej Sizov, and Markus Stolze, editors, *Proceedings of International Workshop on Recommendation and Collaboration*, New York, USA, 2008. ACM.

27. Wai-Tat Fu and Peter Pirolli. Snif-act: a cognitive model of user navigation on the world wide web. *Human-Computer Interaction*, 22(4):355–412, 2007.

28. Tim Hussein, Timm Linder, Werner Gaulke, and Jürgen Ziegler. Context-aware recommendations on rails. In *Workshop on Context-Aware Recommender Systems (CARS-2009) in conjunction with the 3rd ACM Conference on Recommender Systems (ACM RecSys 2009)*, New York, NY, USA, 2009.

A framework for context-based adaptation (for collaboration)

Bjoern Joop, Juergen Ziegler
Department for Computer Science and Applied Cognition Science,
University of Duisburg-Essen
bjoern.joop@uni-due.de, juergen.ziegler@uni-due.de

Abstract. The topic of our talk focuses on definitions of context and approaches in computer science to model context in adaptive or context-aware systems. We present briefly an own context-understanding, a multi-layered framework for context-based adaptation. We present some current examples for context-based adaptation and conclude with some further thoughts about adding unstructured information such as tags to our context understanding to be able to mediate knowledge between different contexts and users.

Keywords: context, adaptation, context-awareness, collaboration, context modeling; co-location; co-recommendation

1 Introduction

Modern organizations work to a large extent collaborative. This is particularly true for knowledge work which is often performed by distributed teams cooperating over global distances. This poses a number of challenges that need to be addressed effectively for supporting the cooperative work.

Collaboration support requires a wide range of communication facilities, tools and information resources. These must be used in dynamically changing collaboration situations in an effective and efficient manner. This often leads to a high complexity of the collaboration environment, to cognitive overload on the users' side, inefficient interaction and thus suboptimal use or even outright rejection of sophisticated collaboration support systems [1]. To solve these problems, the functionality and interaction offered by the collaboration environment should be adjusted to the current collaboration situation. To date, users and teams wishing to adjust their working environment have to negotiate and perform such changes manually. This leads to a high cognitive overhead, ignoring the potential for improvement and thus lowers the team's performance.

The solution for these problems is to make the collaboration environment adaptive. Self-adaptation of systems to changing user needs and situations has been investigated in various application domains (e.g. intelligent tutoring systems, product recommendations, location-based services, etc.). In these approaches the focus has mainly been on the individual and not on collaboration situations.

The notion of context is paramount for any kind of adaptive system. Context-aware and context-adaptive systems have been a major research topic in fields such as mobile applications and ubiquitous computing. Even more, a generalized view of context and methods for its' systematic use in adaptive interactive systems are still missing.

We present an attempt to formulate a notion of context applicable for both single-user and collaborative work and introduce a method for managing dynamic context in an adaptive system.

2 Definitions of context

The word "context" shows its meaning inherently: *con* (meaning: with) *text*. This definition has its origin in linguistics expressing a communicative goal [2] or describes the surrounding situation for an easier interpretation [3, 4]. In philosophy context is used as a correlation between sentences or defines aspects of a situation with the goal to help understanding the semantic meaning of an expression [5]. Psychologists research context regarding how changes of the situation affect cognitive processes [6, 7].

In computer science the notion of context has played an increasingly important role especially in the area of ubiquitous computing with the aim of developing context-aware systems [8]. Context-aware systems usually use time, location, users and available resources as contextual information representing aspects of the physical world [9].

Fig. 1. Context-aware computing application scenarios, Schilit '94 [9]

Later on, these context dimensions were extended using sensors and object properties [10]. An general definition was provided by Dey et al [11, 12] defining context: *"context is any information characterizing the situation of an entity"*. Another popular definition was given by Winograd [13] defining context as an operational term for characterizing its role in communication. This means something is context because it is used in communication for interpretation and not due to its inherent properties. Winograd further distinguishes between context and setting. In his opinion, the setting includes all fixes information about users nearby, the place an action takes place, etc. On the other hand, context represents all information helping understanding a communication.

Approaches modeling context range from simple key-value models over graphical or hierarchical models up to sophisticated ontology-based context models which support validation and reasoning (cf. [14]).

3 Our understanding of context

We agree with Winograd, that we need a distinction between context and setting. But in our understanding, we need contextual (meaning: surrounding) information in regard to a center of attention (focus). The context depends on the current person's perspective, known facts and the state of the "real" world and applications. This includes information about the setting of the current situation.

But this also means, that context is ever-changing and dynamic. These changes can easily be captured and interpreted by humans; context-aware applications on the other hand have to use sensors to recognize these changes and have to interpret it due to predefined rules.

We see the contextualization as a selection process: In a complex situation, contextualization mechanisms are used to extract the most relevant elements. Therefore we need the following components for a conceptual context mode:

- Information about the current situation (state) provided by sensing components mapping internal or external information sources into state objects
- Background information about the application domain
- Contextualization rules to constitute a contextualized state
- Adaptation rules defining a set of meaningful adaptations in regard to the contextualized state.

4 A framework for context-based adaptation

In [15] we present a framework for context-based adaptation which has to meet a set of formal requirements:

- it must be a formal representation of context
- must be able to capture a wide range of adaptation purposes
- must be able to capture aspects of collaborative work
- must be able to support both single user and multi user scenarios

We proposed a multi-layered framework for such a framework. We distinguish between four layers: a knowledge layer, a state layer, a contextualization and an adaptation layer (see figure 2).

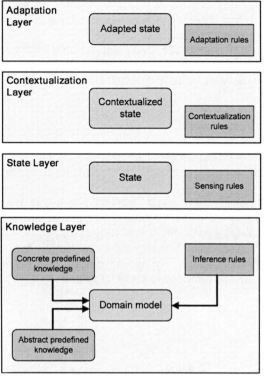

Fig. 2 A four-layered framework for context-based adaptation [15].

For more details see [15].

4.1 Knowledge Layer

The knowledge layer uses predefined information to represent aspects of the physical world, users, the computing environment and resources. The information can be represented using different techniques (e.g. Web Ontology Language using relations, classes and individuals). It is possible to distinguish between abstract and concrete knowledge.

Examples:
> *"Berlin is a city."* represents stable, predefined knowledge because this fact will not be easily changed.
> *"Every city has a name."* represents using classes and relations predefined abstract knowledge.

4.2 State Layer

The state layer represents the current situation including domain knowledge from the knowledge layer. Using sensors and rules we are able to filter and map external or internal (system) information into the state model.

For representing the current state, a directed graph $Gs = \{V,E,\sigma\}$ with vertices and V, edges E and an relation strength function σ: E x T $\rightarrow$ [0,1] is used (see [15]). This can be precisely represented by an RDF graph.

4.3 Contextualization Layer

The contextualization layer provides techniques that define which subset of the state is relevant for a given focus. We call those techniques contextualization techniques (e.g. rule-based).

A focus is a non-empty set of objects from the state representing the current center of attention. The focus can be set by the user or by an application and is used as the starting point for applying contextualization techniques.

Incorporating relation strength values inside the state is optional and depends on the contextualization technique. For example Spreading Activation [16, 17] has particularly been used in information retrieval systems [18, 19, 20] and would use relation strength.

4.4 Adaptation Layer

The contextualized state contains information about individuals relevant for the current focus. The adaptation layer contains adaptation rules, which describe which adaptation actions should be performed in which case. Adaptation rules include operations for changing properties, artifacts or in general any state variable ("show", "start", etc.). Effects of these adaptations have to be propagated to the user interface.

We propose to represent adaptation rules as IF-THEN rules such as:

IF ?document is_important THEN open ?document.

5 Context-based adaptations for collaboration scenarios

In [15] we discussed the applicability of this approach for four typical collaboration scenarios or episodes:

- Co-location denotes the situation where several people meet at a physical or virtual location
- Co-access denotes the situation where several people access the same artifact

- Co-recommendation denotes the situation where explicit or implicit actions of the users are used to suggest information resources potentially useful
- Co-dependency denotes the situation where several tasks, objects or users are dependent

We introduce co-location and co-recommendation as exemplary scenarios.

5.1 Co-location

Co-location occurs when two or more people, artifacts or devices are physically near to each other. Co-location affords a range of adaptations, for example, facilitating the use of nearby devices or automatically setting up the collaboration system for joint tasks or information access.

Scenario: Alice and Bob, jointly working on a report, gather in a meeting room equipped with a large shareable display. Sensors recognize and identify the two persons. The system infers that they will likely work on the current report. It activates the display and shows the report in the workspace. Alice and Bob can now immediately start discussing the latest version of the report.

For this scenario, we use the domain model shown in figure 3. An actor works with a device, such as a computer or a display, so the device must be able to display artifacts. Additionally, each actor and each device can be at some location. Actors who are at the same location are linked by an additional relation *isLocatedWith*.

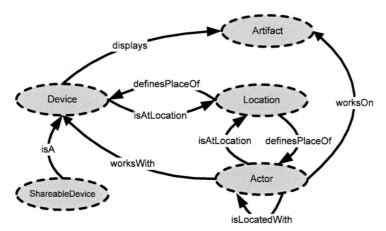

Fig. 3 An exemplary domain model including *"Actors"*, *"Location"* and *"Device"*

The state is contextualized by rules expressing which concepts are important for a given focus in this model. In the example, a rule could, for instance, state: *"IF at least two persons are in the same room AND work on the same artifact AND the room has a shareable device (e.g. a large display) THEN this particular artifact and device are important."* In this case, persons, shared artifacts and locations are the focus points, for which potentially important shared artifacts and matching shareable displays are computed as context. We define the context by examining the state using three conditions: Is the artifact simultaneously being worked on? Are the persons working on it in the same room? Does the room have a shareable display?

The contextualized state is shown in figure 4. In our scenario, it includes the location *Location:l_meetingRoom* where both *Actor:a_alice* and *Actor:a_bob* are and the devices at that location (here: *Device:d_shareableDisplay*). Furthermore, all artifacts (Artifact:a_report) on which both actors currently work on collaboratively are included.

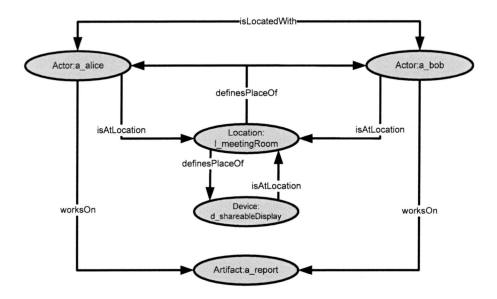

Fig. 4 Contextualized state after creating a co-located situation

An adaptation rule, which adapts all devices in the room based on the contextualized state, could be formulated as follows:

```
// Obtain artifacts and device from the contextualized
// state
artifacts := getArtifactsFromContextualizedState;
device := getDeviceFromContexutalizedState;
// If there are shared artifacts and a shareable device,
// then display the artifacts on the display
IF (notEmpty(artifacts) AND notEmpty(device)) THEN {
  display(artifacts,device);
}
```

The adaptation rule is triggered when all parts of the condition are fulfilled: The adaptation rule is triggered, because *Actor:a_bob* enters *Location:l_meetingRoom* which *Actor:a_alice* has entered before. Both work on several artifacts simultaneously and *Location:l_meetingRoom* provides a shareable display. Consequently, the adaptation rule obtains an artifact and a shareable display from the contextualized state (neither of the sets is empty) and *Device:d_sharableDisplay* will be activated and it will display *Artifact:a_report*.

5.2 Co-Recommendation

Co-recommendation is a technique in which the system suggests potentially relevant information resources based on prior action of other group members and one' own interest profile.

In this exemplary scenario, an actor Bob works for a building company specialized in refurbishments. He is an expert in the area of energy efficiency and frequently tags documents or web pages with keywords from this domain. On this basis, the system classifies documents into a predefined semantic model. Alice is a new colleague and enters the system to search for information regarding thermal insulation. The system recommends a number of documents concerning this topic.

Later on, Bob adds a new document to the system which he rates highly relevant to the topic of roof insulations. Based on Bob's rating, the system recommends this document to Alice through an appropriate awareness function or when Alice logs in the next time.

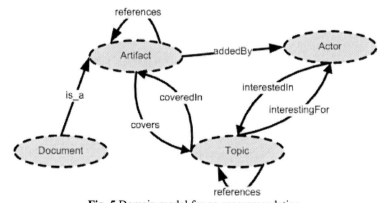

Fig. 5 Domain model for co-recommendation.

In order to allow the system to recommend Alice documents, we need a domain model (cf. figure 5) including classes for *"Topic"* and *"Document"* and create additional relations connecting them. In this example, we use a spreading activation algorithm for contextualization.

Each artifact has one or more topics assigned to it and may reference other artifacts. The relation strength represents the degree of 'relatedness' of two instances. In the example shown in figure 6, *Actor:a_alice* is very interested in the topic *Topic:t_energyInsulations* which is represented by a value of 0.9. On the other Hand, the topic *Topic:t_energyInsulations* is only peripherally covered in the document *Artifact:a_manualProofing* – maybe a manual for do-it-yourself house proofing – which is represented in the relation strength of 0.4.

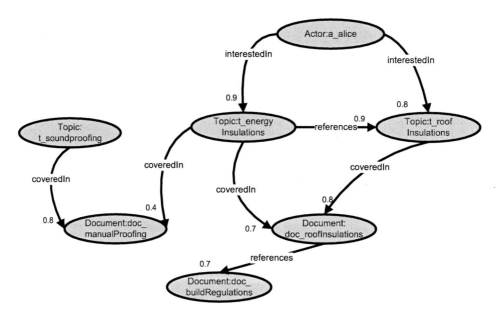

Fig. 6 A possible state for a co-recommendation scenario. Relations strengths are assigned to each relation. Note that not all relations from the domain model in figure 5 are included.

In this example, we use spreading activation (cf 4.3) as a contextualization technique. This could work as follows:
1. Select the node *Actor:a_alice* as initial nodes (the focus)
2. Activate all vertices connecting *Actor:a_alice* to adjacent ones
3. Propagate the activations until either:
   - the distance from the initial node to the current one is greater than α
   - the relation strength is greater than β
   - the propagating vertices' activation is smaller than γ
   using α, β and γ as predefined (terminating) parameters.

The result of the spreading activation algorithm applied on the graph is being shown in figure 7.

The interpreted state shown in figure 8 is the result of applying the spreading activation techniques and choosing only those objects with an activation greater than 0.5.

Based on the contextualized state, we can define an adaptation rule for recommending artifacts of interest to *Actor:a_alice*:

```
//select all documents from the contextualized state
//with an activation > 0
Documents := getDocumentsWithActivationLagergerThan(0.5);
//displaying all documents
IF (notEmtpy(documents))  display(Documents);
```

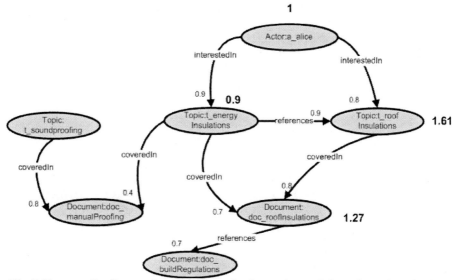

Fig. 7 (Contextualized) state after spreading activation on the graph from figure 6. Activations are shown bold highlighted.

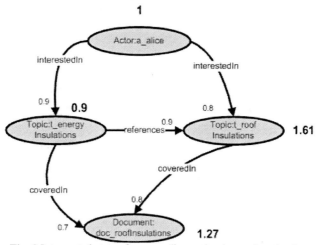

Fig. 8 Interpreted state after spreading activation and projection.

The function *getDocumentsWithActivationValueLargerThan* returns from the contextualized state a set of all documents with an activation greater than 0.5. Accordingly, *Actor:a_alice* will get a recommendation to read the document *Document:doc_roofInsulations* which covers some of the topics she is interested in.

After Bob adds a new document to the database (*Document:doc_newRoofInsulations*) – which leads to a new state (cf. figure 9) – the system has two alternatives for setting the focus: Firstly, it can use the newly added document as the new focus and thus as initial node for the contextualization by spreading activation for selecting all actors who are highly interested in the topics covered in the document. Secondly, the actor can be used as a new focus after login to recommend the most relevant documents.

Using the first alternative, awareness functions are able to directly inform actors interested in the topic *Topic:t_roofInsulations* about the new document *Document:doc_newRoofInsulations* added by *Actor:a_bob*.

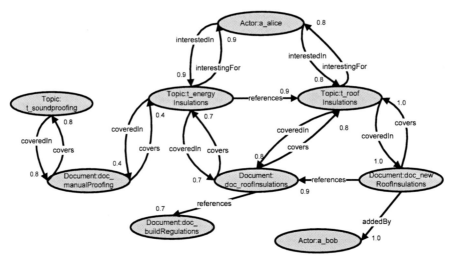

Fig. 9 Excerpt of the state after *Actor:a_bob* adds a new document *Document:doc_newRoofInsulations*. Note, that in this figure all relations from the domain model (cf. figure 5) are included.

The contextualized state after applying the spreading activation with the focus on *Document:doc_newRoofInsulations* is illustrated in figure 10.

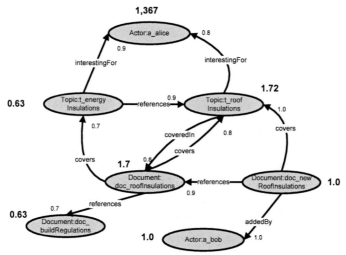

Fig. 10 Contextualized state after spreading activation with focus on new document. Note that not all nodes from figure 9 are included.

Further user-based adaptations can be made using a feedback mechanism. If a user is not satisfied with the recommendations for a specific topic, he can provide feedback which directly decreases the relation strength connecting the artifact with the given topics or to decrease the relation strength between references from artifact to artifact or topic to topic.

7 Future work

Currently we are easily able to use the context of an individual or a global, predefined shared context for all users working collaboratively. We are still missing a formal definition of a group context and a solution about how to create such a group context from individual contexts.

Additionally, we want to include unstructured information in form of individual and collaborative tagged information in our understanding of context. This approach focuses on further individualizing of user contexts using their own language and taxonomy for annotation of important information. To be able to share information in a more global context, we need to mediate between individual contexts using a shared group context from this information. This may lead to be able to switch between user contexts to "look at a situation from a totally different view".

Further work will be implementing and testing a collaborative context server to enable information transfer from one person to another. Therefore new collaboration tools with context-aware components have to be developed. Also, we will investigate new contextualization techniques and adaptation rules.

Acknowledgments. This work is supported by the German Research Foundation (DFG) within the cluster project "Context Adaptive Interaction in Cooperative Knowledge Processes" (CONTici).

References

1. V. Wulf and B. Golombek, Exploration Environments – Concepts and Empirical Evaluation, in Proceedings of the 2001 International ACM SIGGROUP Conference on Supporting Group Work (GROUP'01), 2001, pp. 107-116
2. H. Bunt, Context and Dialogue Control, *THINK Quarterly*, Vol. 3, 1994.
3. B. Malinowski, The Problem of Meaning in primitive Languages, *The Meaning of Meaning* (1923), pp. 146-152.
4. J. L. Austin, *How to Do Things with Words* (Oxford: O.U.P., 1962).
5. R. Carnap, *Meaning and Necessity: A Study in Semantics and Modal Logic,* 2nd Ed., 1988.
6. G. M. Davies and D. M. Thomson, Memory in Context; Context in Memory (John Wiley & Sons Inc., 1988), pp. 1-10.
7. T. Ziemke, Embodiment of Context, in *Proceedings of ECCS*, 1997.
8. H. Bunt, Context and Dialogue Control, *THINK Quarterly*, Vol. 3, 1994.
9. B. Schilit, N. Adams and R. Want, Context-Aware Computing Applications, (IEEE) Workshop on Mobile Computing Systems and Applications, 1994.
10. J. Roth, *Mobile Computing* (dpunkt.verlag, 2nd. Edition, 2005).
11. A. K. Dey, G. D. Abowd, P. J. Brown, N. D. Davies, M. Smith and Pete Steggles, Towards a Better Understanding of Context and Context-Awareness, in Proceedings of the 1st international symposium on Handheld and Ubiquitous Computing, 1999, pp. 304-307.
12. A. K. Dey, Understanding and using Context, Personal Ubiquitous Computing Nr. 1 Vol. 5 (2001), pp. 4-7.
13. T. Winograd, Architectures for Context, Human-Computer Interaction, Vol. 16 (1991), pp. 401-419.
14. T. Strang and C. Linnhoff-Popien, A Context Modeling Survey, Workshop on Advanced Context Modelling, Reasoning and Management, The Sixth International Conference on Ubiquitous Computing, 2004.
15. J. Haake, T. Hussein, B. Joop, S. Lukosch, D. Veiel, J. Ziegler (2009) Technische Berichte der Abteilung für Informatik und Angewandte Kognitionswissenschaft, Nr. 2009-02
16. A. M. Collins and E. F. Loftus, A Spreading Activation Theory of Semantic Processing. Psychological Review, 82(6) (1975), pp. 407–428.
17. J. R. Anderson, A spreading activation theory of memory. Journal of Verbal Learning and Verbal Behavior, 22 (1983), pp. 261–295.
18. G. Chen and D. Kotz, A survey of context-aware mobile computing research, Dartmouth College Technical Report, 2000.
19. F. Crestani, Application of spreading activation techniques in information retrieval. Artificial Intelligence Review, 11(6) (1997), pp. 453–482.
20. G. Salton and C. Buckley, On the use of spreading activation methods in automatic information. In Yves Chiaramella (Ed.), Proceedings of the 11th annual international ACM SIGIR conference on Research and development in information retrieval (pp. 147–160) 1988. Grenoble, France: ACM.

Integration and Activity Structuring in Ubiquitous and Mobile Learning Environments

H. Ulrich Hoppe

Department of Computer Science and Cognitive Science,
University of Duisburg-Essen, Germany

hoppe@collide.info

The Integration Challenge

Recently, we have begun to see integration as a theme and purpose of educational media usage of its own right, beyond issues of efficiency and acceleration. The value of integration is primarily characterised by improving the richness and directness of educational interactions. We can distinguish several aspects of integration: (1) the integration of media and processes to support a smooth and seamless information flow in both virtual and face-to-face classroom scenarios, (2) the use of ICT to bridge between different conditions of learning, such as individual, small group or large community activities as well as between synchronous and asynchronous settings, and recently (3) model-based integration based on learning process modelling languages. In this presentation, I will focus on issue (1), first relating back to experience in the European NIMIS project, then talking up current issues of mobile learning scenarios. A broader treatment of all these integration issues can be found in Hoppe (2007).

Media Integration in Computer-Integrated Classrooms

Traditional classroom scenarios suffer from discontinuities caused by incompatibilities of media and representations ("media breaks"). Often, e.g., results developed in small groups using paper and pencil are copied to the chalkboard in a redundant activity. The chalkboard, on the other hand, allows for flexible and spontaneous note taking and visualisation, but it is a leak in terms of persistence and re-use. Technology can help to bridge media breaks without introducing serious additional constraints. This is exemplified by the European project NIMIS (1998-2000) in primary school classrooms (Lingnau, Hoppe & Mannhaupt, 2003).

Computer *integrated* classrooms

The NIMIS CiC
(1999)

Application area:
"Early Reading/
Writing"

Classroom information flow

*... from small to
large group*

NIMIS has adopted ubiquitous computing technologies, particularly supporting pen and finger based interaction, for an early learning classroom and combined it with speech technology to support reading and writing. The NIMIS environment has been specially designed for the needs of learners who do not (yet) have full reading and writing skills by introducing a new visual desktop. It has several groupware functions for synchronous and asynchronous cooperation.

The NIMIS desktop

- General procedures and tools (incl. synchronous collab.)
- Non-standard login policy:
  max. two students logged in in one place, only one login per student at a time

Activity Monitor:
Visualisation of action logs

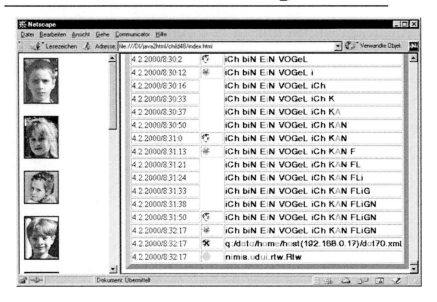

NIMIS integration features

- Media integration
  - uniform representation of learning materials and student products
  - archiving support
  - integration of digital representation with pen-based input
- Process integration / support
  - supervision support for teachers (action logs, spatial trajectories)
  - remote intervention

10

NIMIS success factors

- "Ecological validity" (part of a real school environment)
- Curricular relevance
- Responsibility of teachers for methods and content
- Evolutionary design
- Reduction of routine work created new possibilities

11

CiC in Taiwan

Media integration: "digital mimicry"

the
"ruler episode"
(project SEED)

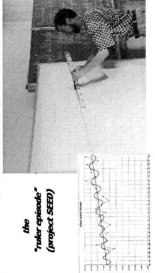

"Interactive Lecture" scenario

... integrates lecture (pen based presentation) with archive, forum and exercise distribution/ correction (since 1998)

Classroom Quiz (Miguel Nussbaum)

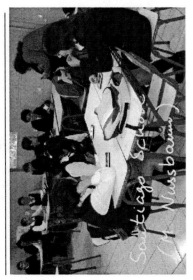

Tools for Classroom and Lecturing Environments

Integrative types of technology potentially provide an added value to grown learning scenarios such as the classroom or a lecture hall. In a *computer-integrated classroom*, a mixture of traditional (or natural) forms of communication and media may co-exist with digital media serving different functions which may be partly identical to traditional media use and in other parts actually qualitatively new. We have used the term "digital mimicry" to characterise interactive digital media functions which mimic traditional forms such as the use of a pen based big electronic display instead of a chalkboard (cf. Hoppe, 2007). Interactive simulations are a typical example of a genuine new media function which is bound to the digital modality. However, there is a general added value that we expect already experience from combining digitised traditional media (e.g. scanned-in paper notes) with digital mimicry applications and real new media into a new form of digital information flow with specific forms of recording, re-use, re-enactment and extension/modification.

In our teaching practice, we are using NIMIS-like approaches in so-called „interactive lecturing" scenarios (Hoppe et al., 1999). Similar approaches have been suggested by Bacher et al. (1996) with more emphasis on the use of streaming media. Instead, we have focused our work on multi-representational software tools that support various types of modeling and sketching, both for presentation in a lecture as well for cooperation in small groups with communicating "shared workspaces". As a result of these efforts, our *FreeStyler* environment (Hoppe & Gassner, 2002) supports a variety of visual languages such as Petri Nets, system dynamics modelling, Toulmin-like argumentation structures, several mathematics tools and several types of UML diagrams. These applications have been used and are being used both in high school and academic settings.

FreeStyler: stochastics palette

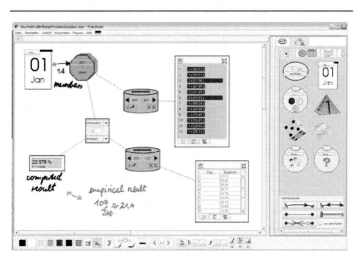

CiC Technologies

Basic technologies

- *Groupware construction tools (MatchMaker, ...)*
- *Pen based tools*
- *Recognition of action patterns*

New issues /challenges

- *Mobile devices*   <- **Software Patterns**
- *Wireless communication*

16

Mobile Devices in Integrated Classroom Scenarios

Recently, we have explored face-to-face learning scenarios integrating mobile devices. Taking into account the different profiles of different mobile and other devices (including embedded, fixed location devices such as big interactive displays or sensitive surfaces), it is important to define adequate distributions of functionality over these devices and to design and implement interoperability mechanisms. "Interoperability", in this context, includes technical interoperability, i.e. data exchange and continuous information flow, but also "educational interoperability" in terms of the enabling of teaching/learning workflows and the support of re-usability of emerging learning objects. Here, mobile devices are a relevant facet of a much larger picture.

Our "Mobile Notes" system supports discussions by integrating PDAs with a big interactive screen (Bollen et al., 2006). Following Liu and Kao (2005), public interactive displays complement the lack of shared visual focus with smaller personal devices. In Mobile Notes", the PDA is essentially only used as an input device to initially prepare and enter discussion contributions. When a contribution (either text based or a hand written sketch) is completed, it is sent to a database from which it can be retrieved and transferred to the public display application. All public discussions would only refer to the public display area. This has turned out to be a very generally usable scenario.

Small mobile devices are unlikely to be a primary interface for visual information processing (such as visual/graphical modelling environments). Here, we should explore such devices with auxiliary functions, e.g. as input devices and note taking instruments. However, there is a central role for smart phones and the like in language learning, or any other type of voice or audio based interaction. Mobile devices have a great potential for educational games, but the educational value of interactive games has to be specified in a global picture of TEL.

On the pedagogical level, the idea of mobile learning is often associated with informal learning settings in which could be triggered by situational affordances or could just take place whenever and wherever the learners want to. It is an issue if this kind of learning yields the necessary degree of systematisation and coherence (or maybe these factors are over-estimated based existing justifications of institutionalised learning?). Again, (second) language learning appears to be a good candidate for learning in informal settings, but how about mathematics or geography? From the integration point of view, research on mobile learning needs to be connected to other areas of learning and learning support methodologies such as CSCL. It would also benefit from using intelligent technologies to develop improved contextualisation and awareness mechanisms.

M. Nussbaum's project in Chile (see above) exemplifies process integration using one type of device (a PDA) with different functions for the teacher and for learning groups. Of particular interest are functions that support supervision and reflection as part of the teacher's interface.

Knowledge integration was seen as a challenge for learning settings orchestrated with mobile devices, both for formal and for informal types of scenarios. There are a couple of questions which may guide further work: Do we have a problem with fragmented experience and fragmented learning activities in technology enhanced learning? If yes, is the fragmentation problem a particular challenge for mobile learning scenarios? Do we have pedagogical strategies for de-fragmentation which could be supported by adequate technologies?

An adequate integrative design for mobile learning needs also a deep understanding of the affordances and inherent functional constraints of the technological components, and that this would not come as a consequence of the theoretical underpinning. So, an elaborate model of the educational situation and requirements, theory based structuring principles and technical expertise about the available and adequate technologies are all needed in a synergetic approach.

Pen-based Technologies

Pen based computing interfaces have been developed and propagated for a variety of applications related to learning. The applications range from note taking and annotation over brainstorming seminars to lecturing in big lecture theatres. Often, pen based technologies are combined with synchronous collaboration mechanisms to support group work. Due to their smaller form factor, many mobile devices rely on pen based input. For this reason, the use of mobile devices in educational scenarios may introduce pen based technologies as a side effect.

Based on our own practice and on the above mentioned references, typical advantages of pen based input can be identified in

-   the minimization of space requirements (as opposed to keyboard and mouse),
-   the exploitation of two dimensions in note taking (sketching) and graphical annotation,
-   the potential of free form expression for supporting spontaneity and reactivity (as, e.g., in lecturing),
-   the possibility of inventing new representations on the fly as an aspect of creativity.

We would see the last three points in the list all related to what could be called "representational flexibility".

Conventional computer interfaces usually pre-define the concrete representations that can be used. Also, usually, one specific tool only supports a small range of such predefined representations. The study reported here was motivated by exploring the potential benefits of representational flexibility provided by pen based devices in a problem solving task. Many problem solving strategies involve the use of external representations of both symbolic and graphical or iconic nature. The external representation can serve as an external memory, it can be the concrete material to work with (as in some diagrammatic and geometrical problems) or it can serve as a concrete visual proxy of a more abstract problem state. Also, Gibson's concept of "affordance" relates to this issue in that it explains the influence of representations on choices of action. As Norman points out, it is important that the affordances of an environment be not only logically given in inherent form but also perceived.

Representational flexibility afforded by P(L)Ts

-   The exploitation of two dimensions in note taking (sketching) and graphical annotation

-   The potential of free form expression for supporting spontaneity and reactivity (as, e.g., in lecturing)

-   The possibility of inventing new representations on the fly as an aspect of creativity

Sudoku study

Initial idea : Compare
   Sudoku solving with a pen based tool (*NoteIt!* on tablet)
   Sudoku solving with a standard tool (*Simple Sudoku*)

Expectation (hypothesis)

Subjects (students) would use (develop?)
richer and more differentiated strategies
in their Sudoku solving;

"richness" would be substantiated
also in the use of external representations,
potentially of original/idiosyncratic nature.

Design of Experiment I

	Group A (6)	Group B (6)
	Pre-test – Prior Knowledge Assessment	
Session 1	Pen based (using *NoteIt!*)	Keyboard-based
	Questionnaires	
Session 2	Keyboard-based	*NoteIt!*
	Questionnaires, Interviews	

38

Findings I

- Performance advantage for *Simple Sudoku*
- No difference in reported standard strategies
- Keyboard-based tool more "fun"
- Almost no annotations with *NoteIt!*
- Annotations seen as useful by 80%

39

Sudoku strategies

Sample->	Pen based *NoteIt!* (6)	Keyboard-based (6)	Total
naked single	5	6	11
hidden single	2	2	4
combined	4	2	6
Total	11	10	21

40

Findings II

- Less difference in performance between tools (overall higher performance)

- Again no difference in reported standard strategies

- Massive difference in annotation behaviour between *NoteIt!* and *Paper&Pencil*

42

Annotations

Task related annotations

		Much	Little	Sample
Pen based	A1&B2	0	1	8
Pencil & Paper	C1&D2	5	2	8

Non-task related annotations

		Much	Little	Sample
Pen based	A1&B2	1	4	8
Pencil & Paper	C1&D2	0	0	8

43

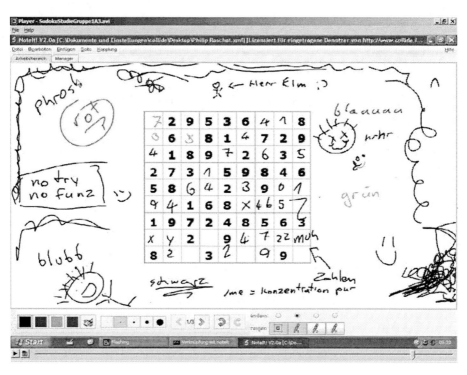

Sudoku study – interpretation

Prior experience of computer use created specific expectations or "mental constraints", which prevented the students from making use of a computerised tool in an unexpected way: "You do not use dirty handwriting in serious computer tasks!"

This would correspond to a general *dilemma*: Here, technology seems to create expectations which limit its own usage in that they prevent users from perceiving non standard affordances.

45

"Take Home Messages"

- Define mobile/ubiquitous learning in terms of the specific affordances of the enabling technologies (not in terms of general learning characteristics)

- Design rich integrated learning scenarios, exploiting the different affordances of devices

- Assure that affordances are perceived/realised

- Develop specific and adequate architectures, support re-use and transfer of these solutions

- Add intelligent monitoring and support

65

References

1. Bacher, C., Müller, R., Ottmann, T., Will, M. (1997). Authoring on the Fly: a new way of integrating telepresentation and courseware production. *Proceedings of ICCE '97*, Kuching (Malysia), Dec. 1997.
2. Bollen, L., Juarez, G., Westermann, M., Hoppe, H.U. (2006). PDAs as input devices in brainstorming and creative discussions. In Proceedings of *4th International Workshop on Wireless, Mobile and Ubiquitous Technologies in Education* (WMUTE 2006). Los Alamitos, CA (IEEE Computer Society), pp. 137-141.
3. Chan, T.W., Roschelle, J., Hsi, S., Kinshuk, Sharples, M., Brown, T., Patton, C., Cherniavsky, J., Pea, R., Norris, C., Soloway, E., Balacheff, N., Scardamalia, M., Dillenbourg, P., Looi, C.-K., Milrad, M., and Hoppe, H.U. (2006). One-to-one technology-enhanced learning: An opportunity for global research collaboration. *Research and Practice in Technology Enhanced Learning,* 1(1), 3-29.
4. Hoppe, H.U., Luther, W.; Mühlenbrock, M.; Otten, W.; Tewissen, F. (1999). Interactive presentation support for an electronic lecture hall - a practice report. *Proceedings of ICCE '99.* Chiba (Japan), November 1999.
5. Hoppe, H.U., Pinkwart, N., Oelinger, M., Zeini, S., Verdejo, F., Barros, B., Mayorga, J.I. (2005). Building bridges within Learning communities through ontologies and "thematic objects". In *Proceedings of CSCL 2005*, Taipei (Taiwan), June 2005.
6. Hoppe, H.U. & Gaßner, K. (2002). Integrating collaborative concept mapping tools with group memory and retrieval functions. In Proceedings of *CSCL 2002*, Boulder (USA), January 2002, pp. 716-725.
7. Hoppe, H.U. (2007). Integrating learning processes across boundaries of media, time and group scale. *Research and Practice in Technology Enhanced Learning* (RPTEL) 2 (1), 2007, 31-49.
8. Lingnau, A., Hoppe, H.U., Mannhaupt, G. (2003). Computer supported collaborative writing in an early learning classroom. *JCAL* 19, 186-194.
9. Liu, C. & Kao, L. (2005). Handheld devices with large shared display groupware: tools to facilitate group communication in one-to-one collaborative learning activities. In *Proceedings. of the 3rd IEEE Workshop on Wireless and Mobile Technologies in Education (WMTE 2005)*. Tokushima (Japan), November 2005. pp. 128-135.
10. Norman, D.A. (1999). Affordances, Conventions and Design. *Interactions* 6(3):38-43, May 1999, ACM Press.

Flexible Architectures for Learning Environments

Adam Giemza

Department of Computer Science and Cognitive Science,
University of Duisburg-Essen, Germany

giemza@collide.info

Abstract. Regarding existing frameworks and architectures for distributed collaborative learning environments, it can be observed that most do not support flexible approaches with heterogeneous language support and loosely coupling. In this talk a flexible approach for architectures in distributed and collaborative learning environments using the TupleSpaces will be introduced. The TupleSpaces approach will be presented for collaborative desktop applications as well as for mobile scenarios.

Keywords: architectures, collaboration, tuplespace, mobiles

1. Introduction

In CSCL collaboration is one of the main aspects. Learners collaborate to increase learning and to gain social interaction behavior. When talking about collaboration of learners and mapping collaboration to the application level, the technical realization will always be based on data synchronization. The synchronized data can be arbitrary data, beginning from simple text data (e.g., chats) to complex data (e.g., multi-media data or graph structures).

FreeStyler Collaboration

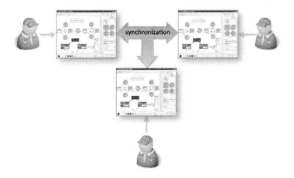

In the FreeStyler collaborative modeling environment [1,2], the synchronized data consists of user actions and graph structures containing nodes and edges. All synchronized objects are described by attributes that are shared among the multiple FreeStyler instances in a collaborative session. The MatchMaker framework provides this data synchronization. It allows for synchronizing arbitrary Java objects in a tree-based manner. MatchMaker is implemented using Java RMI, which led to difficulties with firewalls and furthermore is limited to the Java world. This makes it quite difficult to embed intelligent components (e.g., agents) written in different languages.

MatchMaker Synchronization

- Implemented in Java
- Based on Java RMI
- Flexible Synchronization using *SyncTree* and *SyncLabels*

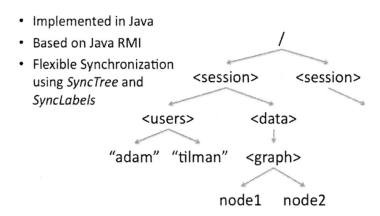

Problems with MatchMaker

- Firewall problems with RMI and bi-directional communication

- Limited to Java World

2. New Approach

With limitations in the existing MatchMaker framework, a new approach was required. The most promising and flexible approach was based on a tuple space (cf. Gelernter [3]) implementation called TSpaces.

What is a TupleSpace?

- Concept dates back to coordination language Linda (Gelernter, 1985)
- Model for several parallel processes to operate on objects stored in a shared memory cf. *blackboard concept*
- Objects stored as several primitives on ordered sequence of typed data objects -> tuples
- Primitive operations (in, out, rd, eval)

David Gelernter. *Generative Communication in Linda. ACM Trans. Program. Lang. Syst., 7 (1): 80–112, 1985.*

Why TupleSpaces / (IBM) TSpaces?

- Simple Programming Interface
- Loosely coupled Architecture
- Client-Server-Architecture
- Indirect communication paradigm
- Multi-purpose protocol
- Data represented by tuples with fields
- E.g., <"Adam", "Giemza", 26, true>
- Simple operations (read, write, take, update)
- Extended Features
  - Notifications, Transactions, Persistency

The IBM TSpaces have been used as the basis for the collaborative application Group Scribbles by Roschelle, et al. [4].

Related Work: Group Scribbles

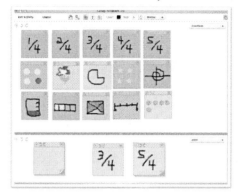

Roschelle, et al., SRI International's Center for Technology in Learning

Giemza [5] implemented a first data synchronization platform based on TSpaces called Colmid – the COLlaborative MIDdleware. Colmid provides a flexible interface for synchronizing arbitrary data.

Colmid – Collaborative Middleware

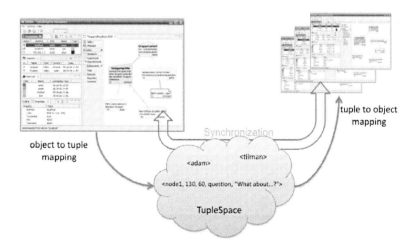

The objects are mapped to tuples and written into the tuple space. Other clients register for events on the tuple space and get notified on changes like new tuples, modifications or deletions. The mapping of objects (cf. Object Mapping Component) has to be configured for all objects as the mapping is application dependent.

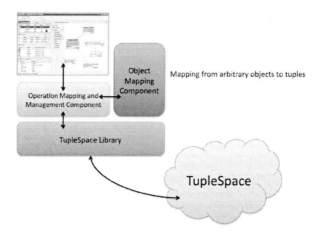

Coldisc [5,6] is a collaborative discussion environment using Colmid for synchronizing a graph-based discussion. The discussion elements (nodes and edges) are mapped to a tuple structure. Furthermore, the user management and the user awareness are represented in the tuple spaces as tuple.

Coldisc – Collaborative Discussion

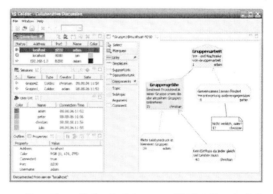

Weinbrenner, Giemza, Hoppe, "Engineering Heterogeneous Distributed Learning Environments
Using Tuple Spaces as an Architectural Platform", ICALT 2007

As mentioned in the introduction, the lack of support for flexibly embedding heterogeneous intelligent components like agents into the architecture was one of the reasons to investigate new approaches. Weinbrenner [7] has achieved this requirement by providing an interface for prolog to the TSpaces. This interface allows writing or reusing intelligent algorithms written in Prolog in combination with the data synchronization framework Colmid [6]. A first usage of this approach was the analysis and evaluation of the data stored in the tuple space in Coldisc sessions.

Action analysis agents have been adapted to process the tuple formats of Coldisc and have generated statistics of user actions and user interaction patterns.

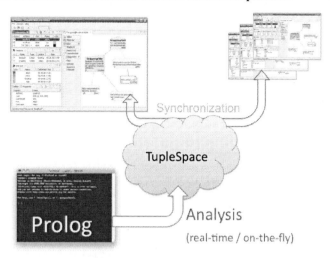

Example Analysis

?- analyze('Group1').

* * * General Statistics for Session Gruppe1
Users: [adam, jan, peter]
* Nodes created: 7
* Nodes updated: 3
* Nodes deleted: 1
* Edges created: 5
* Edges created: 1
* Edges deleted: 5
* Actions overall: 22

* * * Linking of topics of others
* [adam, jan]: 0
* [adam, peter]: 2
* [jan, adam]: 0
* [jan, peter]: 0
* [peter, adam]: 1
* [peter, jan]: 0

3. Implementation of SQLSpaces

The first results from the Colmid, Coldisc and the analyzing agents were very promising. However, the usage of TSpaces was very problematic. The licensing of the TSpaces was very strict and did not allow any distribution of the framework and had a limited runtime for testing for six months. Furthermore, the development was not very vivid and the support was very limited. Overall the future of this project was quite uncertain, which led to a new implementation of the tuple space concept called SQLSpaces [8].

Solution: Our own TupleSpaces!

SQLSpaces

- Implemented in Java
- Reuse of XML bridge
- Interface close to TSpaces
- Using SQL database as storage
- Meanwhile much more functionality and...

... Open Source!

- SQLSpaces Server distributed under AGPL 3.0
  – Any changes needs to go back to the community
- SQLSpaces Client distributed under LGPL 3.0
  – Can also be used in closed source projects

http://sqlspaces.collide.info

4. Flexible Architectures

Whereas the Colmid framework, the Coldisc environment and the analyzing agents can be seen as first trials or proof of concepts of the framework, the SQLSpaces quickly became the architectural foundation for multiple projects.

The common aspects of the projects are the flexible and the loosely coupled nature supported by heterogeneous devices and programming languages. An interface for mobiles has been developed to support mobile learning applications in combination with agents and FreeStyler. This chapter will present some of these projects and summarize aspects of the flexible architecture.

4.1 MobileQOC

MobileQOC [9] was the first application that has taken full benefit from the flexible and heterogeneous approach using the SQLSpaces. MobileQOC is an application that uses the mobile devices as input devices for collaborative, moderated design rationale sessions with *Questions, Options, Criteria (QOC)*. Agents analyze the session content and the user actions to support the moderator by providing feedback on detected user interaction patterns.

Mobile QOC Scenario

Bollen, Kebe, Giemza, Hoppe, "Analysing Cooperation in a
Language andDevice Heterogeneous Architecture", MULE 2007

Mobile QOC Architecture

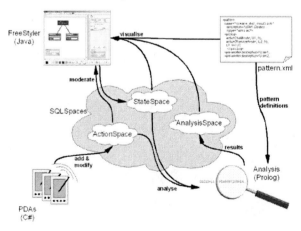

The architecture of MobileQOC is based on the SQLSpaces as a central data repository and allows for communication between heterogeneous programming languages (here: Java, C# and Prolog). Thus it can also be seen as a "language switch board" [10].

The MobileQOC approach also provides a flexible way to author the agent framework. A knowledge engineer can develop and evaluate agents using direct interaction with the tuple space and data. The resulting Prolog pattern predicates can be compiled into an exchangeable XML format that agents use for dynamic configuration.

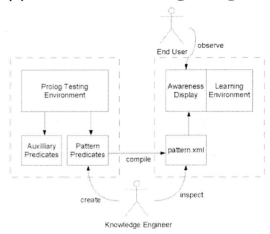

4.2 Argunaut

The main emphasis of the Argunaut project (http://www.argunaut.org) is moderation of e-discussions. The typical scenario is a co-located classroom discussion using e-discussion tools (Digalo and FreeStyler), which is moderated by a teacher using a special application called *Moderator's Interface*.

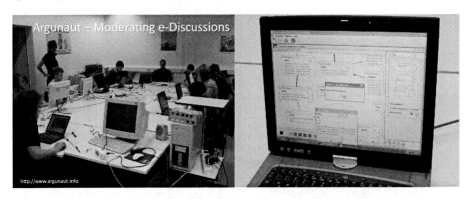

The Argunaut architecture has been based on the tuple space approach to support loosely coupling of different components and agents. However, the initial mapping of actions and tuple has not been adequate and flexible enough, thus the architecture and the communication have been revised and extended. Further more the scenario of Argunaut has been extended to support more visual languages (Petri Nets, QOC), intelligent support has been added with flexibly configurable agents (cf. MobileQOC) and finally new feedback agents to provide automatic feedback to learners.

Argunaut (Reloaded) Architecture

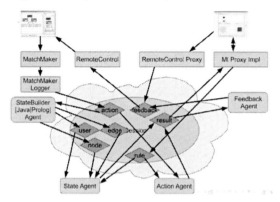

Benefits Using TupleSpace Platform

- Flexible approach for agent architecture
  - Flexibility in programming language – agents written in Prolog as well as in Java
  - Loosely coupled architecture – easy to add (plug-in) new agents providing new functionality
  - Indirect communication paradigm – new agents can pick up existing analysis results and generate new results without changing existing architecture (communication, formats)

4.3 Lemonade

Most existing learning environments focusing on field trips with mobile devices either only support specific activity structures, or do not support authoring or are limited to specific domains or contents. LEMONADE is a fully integrated framework with a full cycle support for authoring and conducting field trips with mobile devices as well as for post-trip reporting and reflection analysis.

LEMONADE

- *"Learning Environment for MObile Network-Attached DEvices"*
- Fully integrated, full cycle support for field trips with mobile devices

The full integration into FreeStyler allows for integrating field trips in regular FreeStyler school activities as well as for combining field trip results with other FreeStyler plug-ins (e.g. for concept mapping, modeling, etc.).

Fully Integrated

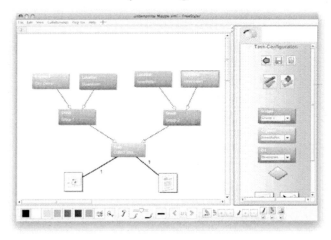

LEMONADE provides a full-cycle support, i.e., the teacher can set-up projects, create groups, configure tasks on the one hand and retrieve results, monitor students and create reports on the other hand. All this can be done using one environment. On the other side, students use mobile devices for conducting the field trip by downloading the configuration, collecting the data and finally storing the results in the repository. In the background agents process, organize and check the data.

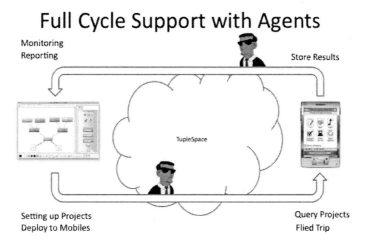

LEMONADE uses the SQLSpaces to allow for the heterogeneous setting as well as for a persistent repository to store field trip projects and the collected student data. The architecture contains a set of several agents and a configuration of distinct spaces for different purposes like storing project configurations, providing a project catalog and finally the group spaces to store the field trip data.

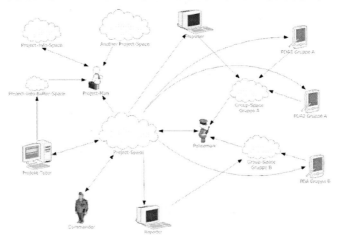

5. Conclusion

Overall, the tuple space approach allows for designing and building flexible architectures for various application scenarios. The flexibility of this approach stems from the loose coupling and the heterogeneous programming language support. The presented applications have shown the flexible adaptation of this approach and the flexibility in programming languages, devices and agent support.

6. References

[1] Hoppe, H. Ulrich, Gaßner, Katrin – "Integrating Collaborative Concept Mapping Tools with Group Memory and Retrieval Functions", Proceedings of the International Conference on Computer Supported Collaborative Learning (CSCL2002), New Jersey, USA, 2002, pp. 716-725.

[2] Gaßner, K.: "Diskussionen als Szenario zur Ko-Konstruktion von Wissen mit visuellen Sprachen", PhD thesis, Universität Duisburg-Essen, (2003)

[3] David Gelernter. *Generative Communication in Linda. ACM Trans. Program. Lang. Syst., 7 (1): 80–112, 1985*

[4] Roschelle, J., Tatar, D., Chaudhury, S. R., Dimitriadis, Y., Patton, C., & DiGiano, C. (2007). Ink, improvisation, and interactive engagement: Learning with tablets. Computer, 40(9), 38-44.

[5] Adam Giemza, "Using Java TSpaces (IBM) for Representing and Managing Visual Languages in Cooperative Applications", Diploma thesis, Universität Duisburg-Essen, 2006

[6] Weinbrenner, Giemza, Hoppe, "Engineering Heterogeneous Distributed Learning Environments Using Tuple Spaces as an Architectural Platform", ICALT 2007

[7] Stefan Weinbrenner, "Development and Testing of an architecture for Heterogeneous Distributed Systems with TupleSpaces and Prolog", Diploma thesis, Universität Duisburg-Essen, 2006

[8] SQLSpaces, COLLIDE Research Group, http://sqlspaces.collide.info

[9] Bollen, Kebe, Giemza, Hoppe, "Analysing Cooperation in a Language and Device Heterogeneous Architecture", MULE 2007

[10] Bollen, L. (2009, in press). "Activity Structuring and Activity Monitoring in Heterogeneous Learning Scenarios with Mobile Devices", Verlag Dr. Kovac, Hamburg.

Undo for Collaborative Modelling and Simulation Environments

Tilman Göhnert

Department of Computer Science and Cognitive Science,
University of Duisburg-Essen, Germany

goehnert@collide.info

Abstract. The following slides are from a talk at the PhD Summer Academy 2009 in Duisburg. They present a flexible multi-mode undo framework for a collaborative modeling environment supporting different types of graph representations (including Petri Nets and System Dynamics models) as well as free-hand annotations. The undo mechanism is first introduced on a formal basis. It is implemented as an extension of the underlying MatchMaker collaboration server and allows for selecting from and making use of several undo variants with minimal adaptation effort. This is a basis for future usability studies comparing different versions of undo and for better adapting the undo effects to the actual user goals.

Motivation I

Chen and Sun, 2001

"Undo can be used to recover from erronous operations, learn new system features by trial-and-failure, and explore alternative solutions by back tracking."

Motivation II

Prakash and Knister, 1992

"Undo is important in collaborative applications because it provides freedom to interact and experiment in a shared workspace."

Chen and Sun, 2001

- *"multi-user applications must have all the features in single user applications,*
- *the potential cost of an individual user's mistake is multiplied many times since it may adversely affect the work of a large number of collaborative users,*
- *the number of alternatives to be explored in a collaborative setting increases due to the presence of many users."*

Definitions

Undo

to reverse the effect of an action

Redo

to restore the effect of an undone action
(by undoing the undo)

Repeat

to execute an action again

Requirements for Undo

Action History
- executed actions
- order of execution
- further information depending on the context

Invertibility of Actions
- existence of an inverse action
- availability of information needed to construct an inverse action

Dependency Handling
- concept for dependency between actions and a mechanism to handle them

Mode and Mechanism

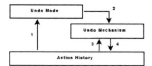

Mode
The undo mode defines the action to be undone.

Mechanismus
The undo mechanism is responsible for the execution of the undo.

Mode: Single-Step Undo

- The History alway contains only the currently latest action
$$... x\, y\, (z)$$
- By an undo the inverse action of the until-then latest actions becomes the new latest action
$$... x\, y\, z\, (\bar{z})$$
- A further undo then is a redo which in this case is a repeat of the original action
$$... x\, y\, z\, \bar{z}\, (z)$$
- This way multiple execution of undo leads to alternation of "last action is effective" and "last action is not effective"
$$(z) \to (\bar{z}) \to (z) \to (\bar{z}) \to (z) \to ...$$

Mode: Linear Undo

- The history may contain any number of actions

$$(\ldots x\,y\,z)$$

- Execution of undo reverses the effect of the latest action

$$(\ldots x\,y\,z) \xrightarrow{\overline{z}} (\ldots x\,y)$$

- A further undo reverses the effect of the new latest action

$$(\ldots x\,y) \xrightarrow{\overline{y}} (\ldots x)$$

- Undo may be repeated until the beginning of the history is reached

Mode: Linear Undo, selective variant

- The history may contain any number of actions

$$(\ldots u\,v\,w\,x\,y\,z)$$

- Any action contained in the history may be selected for undo

$$(\ldots u\,v\,w\,x\,y\,z) \xrightarrow{choice} x$$

- Linear undo is performed until the selected action has been undone

$$(\ldots u\,v\,w\,x\,y\,z) \xrightarrow{\overline{z}} \cdots \xrightarrow{\overline{x}} (\ldots u\,v\,w)$$

Selective Undo

- The history may contain any number of actions

$$(\ldots j\,k\,l\,\ldots)$$

- Any action contained in the history may be selected for undo

$$(\ldots j\,k\,l\,\ldots) \xrightarrow{choice} k$$

- Only the effect of the selected action will be reversed

$$(\ldots j\,k\,l\,\ldots) \xrightarrow{\overline{k}} (\ldots j\,l\,\ldots)$$

- Usually this mode requires recognition and handling of dependencies between the selected actions and those coming later in the history

New Dimension for Undo in Collaborative Systems

Local
Local undo considers only actions performed by the user requesting the undo.

Global
Global undo considers all actions performed by any user.

Mechanism

Function of the Mechanism
- Generation of an appropriate inverse action
- Dependency checking
- Execution of the inverse action if dependencies allow it

Example for a Mechanism: Limited Selective Undo
[Prakash, Knister, 1994]

Prerequisites
- Existence of a well-defined inverse for every action
  $a \longmapsto \overline{a}$
- Dependency recognition for every pair of actions
  $$(a, b) \longmapsto \begin{cases} true & \text{, dependent} \\ false & \text{, independent} \end{cases}$$
- Computability of transposed actions for every pair of actions
  $(a\,b) \longmapsto (b\,a)$, if not (a, b) dependent

Transposed Actions
Original order: $a\,b$

Reversed order, same result: $b\,a$

Limited Selective Undo: Example for Execution 1
Independent Actions

Independent Actions

given:
- history: $(a\,b\,c)$
- action selected for undo: b
- all actions independent

Limited Selective Undo: Example for Execution 1
Independent Actions

Execution

- Creation of a copy of the history beginning with the selected action: $[b\,c]$
- Check for dependencies between the selected and the following action in the copy of the history: (b, c) independent
- Transposition of the selected and the following action in the copy of the history: $[c\,b]$
- The selected action is the last one in the history: Computation of the inverse action: $b \mapsto \overline{b}$
- Execution of the inverse action and appending it to the original history: $(a\,b\,c\,\overline{b})$

Limited Selective Undo: Example for Execution 2
Dependent Actions

Dependent Actions

given:
- history: $(a\,b\,c)$
- action selected for undo: a
- action c depends on action a

Motivation   Undo and Redo   Developing an Undo Framework   Conclusion and Future Work

Limited Selective Undo: Example for Execution 2
Dependent Actions

Execution

- Creation of a copy of the history beginning with the selected action: [a b c]
- Check for dependencies between the selected and the following action in the copy of the history: (a, b) independent
- Transposition of the selected and the following action in the copy of the history: [b a c]
- Check for dependencies between the selected and the following action in the copy of the history: (a, c) dependent
- Cancelation of the undo, keeping the original history: (a b c)

Tilman Göhnert   University Duisburg-Essen, COLLIDE group

Motivation   Undo and Redo   Developing an Undo Framework   Conclusion and Future Work

Undo for the FreeStyler

Task
Enhance the existing collaborative modelling environment FreeStyler with an undo functionality.

Problem
The existing undo frameworks cannot be directly used in the FreeStyler.

Tilman Göhnert   University Duisburg-Essen, COLLIDE group

Motivation   Undo and Redo   Developing an Undo Framework   Conclusion and Future Work

FreeStyler

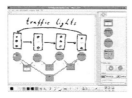

- collaborative sketching, modelling and simulation tool created in the COLLIDE research group
- uses MatchMaker as synchronization service

Tilman Göhnert   University Duisburg-Essen, COLLIDE group

MatchMaker

- collaboration server created in the COLLIDE research group
- used for FreeStyler
- organizes synchronized data in a tree structure
- offers creation, deletion, replacement of objects
- offers execution of methods of the synchronized (Java-)objects

Architecture: Data Structures in FreeStyler and MatchMaker

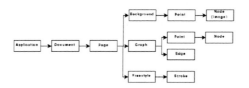

Architecture: Collaboration with FreeStyler

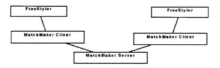

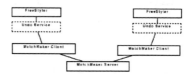

Approach: Enhancing the Synchronization

Advantages
- existing interface for
  - logging actions
  - requesting the performance of actions
- offers concurrency control

Challenges for Undo in Collaborative Environments

Concurrency
use of the CC offered by the underlying synchronization service

Cooperation with Changing Participants
use of a local history containing all local and global actions which can be undone, missing actions can not be undone by that user

Local vs Global Undo
both variations are offered as which one is to be used depends on the context

Special Challenges in the Context of FreeStyler and MatchMaker I

Challenge - MatchMaker
- MatchMaker offers *execution* of methods on the objects
- in contrast to *create*, *delete* and *replace* (which are also offered) this does not have a global inverse

Solution
- the formulation of an abstract generic inverse is possible
- has to be instantiated for every single method

Examples for Execution of Methods

Execution of Methods via MatchMaker

- Classic form of the action
  - `execAction{ID, Action, Argument}`
- Adaptations for Undo
  - Definition of an `InverseAction` for every single `Action`
  - Adaptation of the argument
  - Examples
    - `setText ← setText ; (Text) → (TextOld, TextNew)`
    - `increase ↔ decrease ; (Diff) → (Diff)`
  - Adapted form for the history
    `execAction{ID, Action, InverseAction, Argument, InverseArgument}`
- Mapping action ↔ inverse
  - `change{ID, Act, InvAct, Arg, InvArg} ↔ change{ID, InvAct, Act, InvArg, Arg}`

Tilman Göhnert — University Duisburg-Essen, COLLIDE group

Special Challenges in the Context of FreeStyler and MatchMaker II

Challenge - FreeStyler

- FreeStyler splits single user actions into multiple synchronization actions
- in case of undo this requires multiple execution of undo for undoing one user action

Solution

- grouping of actions is used to solve this problem

Tilman Göhnert — University Duisburg-Essen, COLLIDE group

An Example for Grouping: Petri-Nets

Before

User-Action
firing the transaction

Synchronised System-Actions
- fire transition
- place 1: -1
- place 2: -3
- place A: +1
- place B: +1
- place C: +3

After

Tilman Göhnert — University Duisburg-Essen, COLLIDE group

Undo Algorithm I

Input

- List L_1 of actions to be undone.
- Boolean variable B determining if dependent actions should also be undone.

Undo Algorithm II

Algorithm

- Check if all actions provide the necessary information to be undone. If not all information is available: abort undo.
- Generate a list L_2 with all actions depending on the initial set of actions to be undone.
- Remove all members of L_1 from L_2.
- Remove all do-undo pairs from L_2.
- Examine with the help of B if dependent actions shall be undone.
  - If they shall be undone, append L_2 to L_1.
  - If they shall not be undone and L_2 is not empty, abort undo.
- Sort the resulting list L_1 by the reverse execution order of the actions.
- Undo the actions in L_1 successively beginning with the first entry.

Architecture

Conclusion Undo Framework

The presented Undo Framework...

- enriches the collaboration service provided by the MatchMaker
- adds undo functionality to the FreeStyler
- offers flexibility in terms of undo mode
- can be used as basis for further research about undo

Tilman Göhnert   University Duisburg-Essen, COLLIDE group

Future Work I - Research on Undo

Undo Modes

- Which mode is best used in the given context?
- Cass, Fernandes und Polidore, 2006: Pen and Paper Study

Usefulnes of Undo

- How does Undo influence the users' collaborative behaviour?
- Does Undo increase the quality of the collaborative results?

Users' Intention

- Abowd and Dix, 1992: What does the undo button do? = What is the undo button for?
- In which situations the effect of undo is achieved by the use of other functions?

Tilman Göhnert   University Duisburg-Essen, COLLIDE group

Future Work II - Research on Action Logs

Action Logs can be used for...

- Manual analysis of user action (offline)
- Teacher and student support by awareness functionalities (online)
  - Argunaut project
- Building models for tutoring systems (offline)
- Giving input to tutoring systems (online)
  - Cognitive Tutors in cooperation with CMU (Harrer et. al., 2005)
  - Trace based tutors
- Building process models by process mining (offline)

Tilman Göhnert   University Duisburg-Essen, COLLIDE group

References

1. Chen, D., Sun, C.: Undoing any operation in collaborative graphics editing systems. In: GROUP '01: Proceedings of the 2001 International ACM SIGGROUP Conference on Supporting Group Work, New York, NY, USA, ACM (2001) 197-206
2. Prakash, A., Knister, M.J.: Undoing actions in collaborative work. In: CSCW '92: Proceedings of the 1992 ACM conference on Computer-supported cooperative work, New York, NY, USA, ACM (1992) 273-280
3. Prakash, A., Knister, M.J.: A framework for undoing actions in collaborative systems. ACM Transactions on Computer-Human Interaction 1(4) (1994) 295-330
4. Cass, A.G., Fernandes, C.S.T.: Using task models for cascading selective undo. In: TAMODIA. (2006) 186-201
5. Abowd, G.D., Dix, A.J.: Giving undo attention. Interacting with Computers 4(3) (1992) 317-342
6. Harrer, A., McLaren, B. M., Walker, E., Bollen, L., Sewell, J. Collaboration and cognitive tutoring: Integration, empirical results, and future directions. Artificial Intelligence in Education - Supporting Learning through Intelligent and Socially Informed Technology, Amsterdam (The Netherlands) (2005) 266-273

Development of Mobile and Ubiquitous Learning Environments

Hiroaki Ogata, Naka Gotoda, Masayuki Miyata, Yoneo Yano

[1]The University of Tokushima, 2-1 Minamijosanjima, Tokushima, Japan
{ogata, gotoda, miyata, yano}@is.tokushima-u.ac.jp

Abstract. CSUL (Computer Supported Ubiquitous Learning) is defined as a ubiquitous learning environment that is supported by embedded and invisible computers. CSUL has integrated high mobility with the pervasive learning environments. While the learner is moving with his/her mobile device, the system dynamically supports his/her learning by communicating with embedded computers in the environment. We describe the design and the use of such CSUL environments through systems developed in our projects. First, this paper mentions context-aware language-learning support systems for learning vocabularies, onomatopoeia and mimicry, polite expressions, and conversational expressions by leveraging PDA, GPS, RFID tags and sensor networks. Second, it describes the latest language-learning support systems with a new architecture of sensor networks. Third, it presents a web-based video repository for sharing and retrieving learning experiences. This system was used in the scenarios of computer hardware assembling and cooking. Forth, it describes the learning of physical (motor) skills developing in popular sports. This system organizes the online community based on learners' logs of physical activity through GPS, HRM (Heart Rate Monitor) and so on. Finally, the paper is ended with the discussions and future works.

Keywords: Technology Enhanced Learning, Ubiquitous Learning, Mobile Learning, SNS

1   What is Computer Supported Ubiquitous Learning?

Context-aware computing [1] will help in the organization and mediation of social interactions wherever and whenever these contexts might occur. Its evolution has recently been accelerated by improved wireless telecommunications capabilities, open networks, continuous increase in computing power, improved battery technology, and the emergence of flexible software architectures. With those technologies, an individual learning environment can be embedded in daily real life.

Computer Supported Ubiquitous Learning (CSUL) has integrated high mobility with embedded computing environments [14] according to [11]. While the learner is moving with his/her mobile device, the system dynamically supports his/her learning by communicating with embedded computers and sensors in the real world.

The main characteristics of CSUL are shown as follows [14]:

(1) Permanency: Learners never lose their work unless it is purposefully deleted. In addition, all the learning processes are recorded continuously every day.

(2) Accessibility: Learners have access to their documents, data, or videos from anywhere. That information is provided based on their requests. Therefore, the learning involved is self-directed.

(3) Immediacy: Wherever learners are, they can get any information immediately. Thus, learners can solve problems quickly. Otherwise, the learner can record the questions and look for the answer later.

(4) Interactivity: Learners can interact with experts, teachers, or peers in the form of synchronies or asynchronous communication. Hence, the experts are more reachable and the knowledge becomes more available.

(5) Situating of instructional activities: The learning could be embedded in our daily life. The problems encountered as well as the knowledge required are all presented in their natural and authentic forms. This helps learners notice the features of problem situations that make particular actions relevant.

(6) Authentic and learner-centered learning: CSUL is advocated by pedagogical theories such as on-demand learning, hands-on or minds-on learning, and authentic learning [3]. CSUL system provides learners on-demand information such as advices from teachers or experts at the spot at the precise moment they want to know something.

First, this paper focuses on CSCL for language learning because of the following reasons:

(1) Language learning is life-long activity, and it needs to be supported by computers permanently.

(2) Language learning takes place any time at any place. Therefore, learners need high accessibility to get information.

(3) If learners have problems in conversations, they will need immediate help.

(4) Learners can need interactive support from experts or peers, because they have to explain the current situation.

(5) Language learning is strongly influenced by situations.

We believe that language is mainly acquired through authentic learning. Miller and Gildea [12] worked on vocabulary teaching, and described how children are taught words from dictionary definitions and a few exemplary sentences. They learned lots of words outside school normally. Therefore, we believe that it is very important to support language learning in their everyday life with ubiquitous computing technologies.

Therefore, we have been investigating on computer supported ubiquitous language-learning environments. For example, we have developed

(1) TANGO (Tag Added Learning Objects) [14] system to support vocabulary learning with RFID tags,

(2) JAPELAS (Japanese Polite Expressions Learning Assisting System) [19]18 to support polite expressions.

(3) LOCH (Language-learning Outside the Classroom with Handhelds) [5] system in order that overseas students can notify teachers their location and teachers can give location specific advice leveraging GPS, PDA and data communication card.

(4) JAMIOLAS (Japanese Mimicry and Onomatopoeia Learning Assisting System) [15] to support to learn mimicry and onomatopoeia with sensor networks.

Second, in addition to these systems, this paper describes the latest language-learning support systems with a new architecture of sensor networks called "MOTE". Second, it presents a video sharing system called LORAMS [16], which support to capture, share and retrieve learning experiences that happen at anytime and anyplace. Also PERKAM (Personalized Knowledge Awareness Map) [2] system is to support the learner with the Knowledge Awareness Map, which recommends peer helpers. Third, it describes the learning of physical (motor) skills developing. This system organizes the online community based on learners' logs of physical activity through GPS, HRM (Heart Rate Monitor) and so on [20][21]. Finally, the paper is ended with the discussions and future works.

2   Classification of the learning environments

CSUL (Computer Supported Ubiquitous Learning) is defined as a ubiquitous learning environment that is enhanced by embedded and mobile computers in every-day life. Figure 1 shows the comparison of four learning environments [14]. The CAL (Computer Assisted Learning) systems and ITSs (Intelligent Tutoring System) leveraging desktop computers are not embedded in the real world and difficult to move. Therefore, those systems hardly support learning at anytime and anywhere.

high	CSPL (Computer Supported Pervasive Learning)	**CSUL (Computer Supported Ubiquitous Learning)**
low	DCBL (Desktop-Computer Based Learning)	CSML (Computer Supported Mobile Learning)

Level of embeddedness

low   *Level of mobility*   *high*

Fig. 1. Classification of the learning environments.

Compared with Desktop Computer Based Learning (DCBL), the concept of Computer Supported Mobile Learning (CSML) is to increase the learners' capability to physically move their own learning environment. CSML uses lightweight devices such as PDA (Personal Digital Assistant), cellular mobile phones, and so on. Those mobile devices can connect to the Internet through wireless communication technologies that enable to learn at anytime and anywhere. For example, Houser and Thornton [7] developed an English text message system leveraging mobile phone. Uther et al [18] developed a mobile learning application for speech/audio language training. Also PhotoStudy [9] was developed in order to support vocabulary study with mobile phones. In addition, there are a lot of commercial products and Podcast contents to support mobile language learning. In this case, computers are not embedded in the learner's surrounding environment, and they cannot seamlessly and automatically obtain information about the context of his learning. Therefore, they cannot provide suitable information for the learner's context.

In Computer Supported Pervasive Learning (CSPL), computers can obtain information about the context of the learning from the learning environment where small devices such as sensors, pads, badges, RFID tags and so on, are embedded and communicate mutually. CSPL environments can be built either by embedding models of a specific environment into dedicated computers, or by building generic capabilities with computers to inquire, detect, explore, and dynamically build models of the environments. NIMES (Networked Interactive Media in Schools) project [10] is one of the examples of CSPL environments. The aim of this project is to support classroom activities by leveraging embedded computers in the classroom, e.g., on students' desks and on black boards. However, the availability and the usefulness of CSPL are limited and highly localized.

Finally, CSUL has integrated high mobility with pervasive learning environments. While the learner is moving with his mobile device, the system dynamically supports his learning by communicating with embedded computers in the environment. TANGO is one of CSUL environments. This system allows learners to move with their PDAs and to communicate with the surrounding objects through RFID tags. Also RFID tags are used in museums [8]. As for the broad definition of CSUL, it includes both CSPL and CSML.

In terms of human computer interaction, the challenge in an information-rich world is not only to make information available to people at any time, at any place, and in any form, but specifically to say the right thing at the right time at the right place in the right way [4]. Therefore, CSUL environment should provide learners the right educational materials at the right time at the right place in the right way.

3 CSUL for language learning

3.1 LOCH

LOCH (Language-learning Outside the Classroom with Handhelds) system [5] has been developed in order that overseas students can notify teachers their location and teachers can give location specific advice using GPS, PDA and data communication card. This system is a specific application to support language learning and supports the following processes:

(1) Enhancing the applicability of the sentences that students learnt during the course;

(2) Learning on-site Japanese language in real life situations such as in a shopping market;

(3) Learning local Japanese language and culture though the conversation with local Japanese people;

(4) Sharing strategies and knowledge to solve problems when overseas students face.

Using the provided interfaces, the teacher assigns tasks to the students to go around the town, interact with native speakers and bring back their findings and/or questions.

Teachers give overseas students the following tasks in a meeting room at the beginning of the one day trip (figure 2 (1)):

(1) Interview with a person: Students go to an office and make an interview with a person in Japanese for ten minutes or so. The mission is recording the interview and taking a picture of the person with PDA. For example, a student goes to the dean's office and interview with him

(2) Gather information: The mission is going to the specific location and getting information. For example, student goes to the bicycle-parking space at the station, and asks the staff about the fee, business hours, the number of the parking lots, etc.

(3) Buy something local: For example, student goes to the super market, buy "fish sausage" and asks how to make it.

(4) Have an experience: For example, the mission was going to the University health center and take blood pressure.

By carrying out those tasks, we expect overseas students to enhancing the communication skill in Japanese, and to perceive the local culture such as foods, activities, etc. Students can make use of their PDAs for writing down annotations, recording questions, taking pictures and reporting back to the teacher (figure 2 (2)). At anytime, the teacher is monitoring the position of the students on the map and can establish communication with them, either through instant messaging or BBS (bulletin board system) (figure 2 (3)). Then, the teacher guides the students through the task activities, giving suggestions or hints (such as "Ask somebody how to get there" or "You have to find the post office first"). After finishing the task, the teacher gives the student another task according to the student's language skill, the location and the remaining time.

After all the students conclude their tasks, they meet together at the classroom. The classroom is equipped with a smart board. The teacher has being following their advances (figure 2 (4)). All the gathered information is displayed and discussed, and each student explains his/her strategies to the rest of the group. Similar situations are identified, and their solutions are shared under the guidance of the teacher. Also, the teachers link the problems and the knowledge that they taught during the course. This is a kind of "seamless learning", where students can seamlessly learn Japanese language not only inside the classroom but also outside the classroom.

Fig. 2. Learning process using LOCH.

Certainly, this approach contributes with a better insight of the foreign students during their daily life in Japan. There are a myriad of expressions that students are unfamiliar with, and the purpose of the teacher is to give them the tools to respond and behave according to the situation. Furthermore, students are encouraged to go around because the usage of mobile devices seems new and interesting, and they have the assurance that the teacher can be immediately reached in case something goes wrong.

3.2 JAMIOLAS

Japanese language is very rich in mimicry and onomatopoeia (MIO) words. Mimicry words are imitating situations and body movements. For example, "uro uro suru" means walking around aimlessly. Onomatopoeia shows sounds of something, e.g., animals, natural phenomena, etc. For example, "gaya gaya suru" means a very noisy situation. Japanese language has over 2,000 MIO words in total. If students can use these expressions correctly, their conversation will be more rich, natural, and emotional. For example, MIO words are often used in word balloons in Japanese cartoons, "Manga." In addition, those words are much related to Japanese culture itself. Therefore, learning MIO words are very useful not only to have rich communication with Japanese native speakers, but also to understand Japanese culture.

Generally, four skills (reading, writing, hearing, and speaking) are main objectives in language learning. Because time is limited in Japanese language learning course for overseas students, only a few onomatopoeia words could be taught. Therefore, students have to acquire more words in their daily life. However, it is very difficult to learn those words because the expressions vary according to the situation. If the expressions are not used properly, they might sound comical and strange. Moreover, it might lead to misunderstanding in conversation. Therefore, it is very important for foreigners to have the solid understanding of the situation.

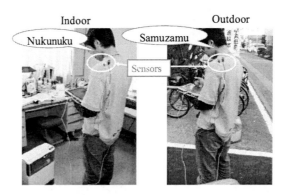

Fig. 3. Usage Scene of JAPELAS.

The usage of MIO words depends on the situation where the speaker is. Therefore, JAMIOLAS [15] has been developed to support learning MIO words using sensors, which detects the speaker's situation. Phidgets [9] sensors and ZigBee sensor network are used because it is easy to connect to PC and to control with program languages.

As shown in figure 4 (A), the system asks a question to the user according to the data of the rain sensor. In this case, the question is how it rains now. After the user selects one word from the list, the system tells whether the answer is correct or not. By double clicking a word in the list, the control window appears like (B). From this window, detailed information will be provided by pushing the buttons. For example, the usage situation is explained with the painting in the right upper window in figure 4. In addition, the user can change the sensor data using a slider in order to learn similar MIO words in different situations. For example, if it is high humidity in the user's situation, it can be described "mushi mushi." However, if the user changes to the sensor data for the low humidity, the user can learn "saratto suru."

Japanese language teachers and Japanese students can register MIO words into the database and setup the thresholds of sensors for each words. They wear sensors at that time and the system shows the current values from sensors. When an overseas student uses JAMIOLAS, the system shows the histogram of the entries for each MIO word corresponding to the current sensor data.

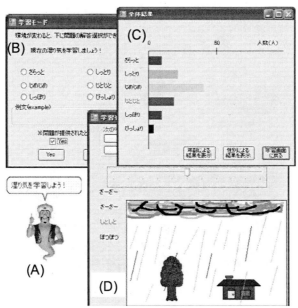

Fig. 4. User interface of JAMIOLAS.

3.3 TANGO

TANGO (Tag Added Learning Objects) system helps a learner to memorize for-eign language vocabularies, which detects the objects around the learner using RFID tags, and provides the learner with the right information in that context [14]. Figure 5 shows an example of an educational environment (room) where RFID tags are at-tached to almost all real objects. When the leaner enters a room with his PDA, the TANGO system detects the learner's location by reading the location RFID tag, and asks him some questions based on the available real objects and the learner's model. For example, the system asks him the following question "Where is the remote con-trol of the air conditioner?" If the learner cannot recognize the voice, the system shows the question as a text. If the learner scans the tag attached to the remote con-trol, the answer will be correct. Then the system will ask the learner to put it on the wooden desk. The interaction between the learner and the system goes on in this way.

3.4 JAPELAS

It is very difficult for overseas students to learn Japanese polite expressions be-cause the expressions change in complicated way according to the context, e.g. hypo-nymy, social distance, and the formality of conversation scenes. Moreover, the feeling of social distance in Japan often varies from that in a learner's country. This differ-ence may result in misunderstanding for the overseas students. Therefore, it is very important for the learners to learn the social situation in Japan, and to use polite expressions properly accordingly. We have implemented a PDA (Personal digital Assistant)-based language-learning support system for Japanese polite expressions learning, which is called JAPELAS (Japanese polite expressions learning assisting system) [19].

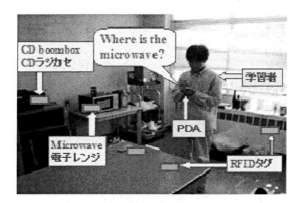

Fig. 5. Usage scene of TANGO.

Figure 6 shows a scene of learning polite expressions with JAPELAS. Every user has a PDA and inputs his in-formation into the database, e.g., name, grade, age etc. When Mr. X talks to Mr. Z, the system tells Mr. X a casual expression. That is because Mr. X is older than Mr. Z. On the other hand, when Mr. X turns to Mr. Y in order to talk, the system tells Mr. X a formal expression. That is because the year of Mr. X is lower than the year of Mr. Y. The system detects the location by scanning a RFID tag. If the room is not a lab room but a formal meeting room, the system recommends the learner to use formal expressions for everyone.

3.5   JAMIOLAS 2.0

3.5.1   Issues of JAMIOLAS 2.0

We developed JAMIOLAS system in our previous research. This system supports learning MIO using a sensor called Phidgets. The learner wears Phidgets connected to the system, and the system can receive information as digital data from environment around learner. The system presents the question about MIO, suitable for the situation by the received data, and the learner can learn MIO. However JAMIOLAS has following limitations:

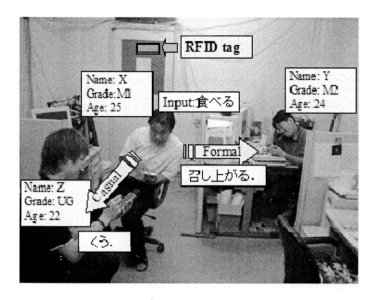

Fig. 6. Usage scene of JAPELAS.

4   Latest researches of CSUL environments

(1) The learner might not be able to know what kind of MIO can learn from other places by the system. Therefore the learner may miss out learning chance.
(2) There is a possibility that the learner becomes worried because s/he needs to carry the system.
(3) There is a possibility that the learner must go around in a blind way in order to look for places to be able to learn MIO.

We should install a sensor in the various places in order to solve these issues. Therefore this paper proposes JAMIOLAS 2.0 supported learning MIO with wireless sensor network "MOTE".

4.1.1   Wireless sensor network "MOTE"

Wireless sensor network is defined as "network of autonomously dispersion type which can collect information without wire using sensor nodes in real time". In this paper, we use "MOTE", as a wireless sensor network. The gateway of MOTE acquires data automatically just to put sensor nodes at every spot. Sensor nodes will response to temperature, illuminance, sound, and so on.

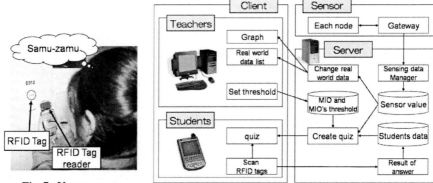

Fig. 7. Usage scene

Fig. 8. System architecture

4.1.2 Implementation

We have developed the prototype system of JAMIOLAS 2.0 on Pocket PC with Windows Mobile 5.0, Server with LAMP (Vine Linux 4.1 + Apache2 + PHP5 + MySQL5), RFID tags reader/writer, and MOTE. The program has been implementing using Visual C# 2005.

As shown in figure 8, JAMIOLAS 2.0 consists of a main client-server and sensor components. The client consists of the computers used by Japanese-language teacher's part and the PDA's used by the students outside the classroom. On the other hand, the server can be divided into two main parts, namely the interface and the data processing component. The database stores sensor value, MIO, MIO thresholds and students' data.

4.1.3 System interface and function

As shown in Figure 9, JAMIOLAS 2.0 for students has following interface:

(1) Select quiz format: The student can select either multiple-choice quiz or orienteering quiz from quiz format. When the student selects multiple-choice quiz, the screen page of PDA displays the page, the student has gone freely the spot placed RFID tag and node of MOTE. When the student selects orienteering quiz, the screen page of PDA display page of orienteering quiz.

(2) Multiple-choice quiz: When the student goes to the spot placed a node of MOTE and a RFID tag and scan it with RFID tags reader attached PDA, screen page of PDA display this page. The student selects and solves MIO suitable for the spot where s/he is now from multiple MIO presented by this system.

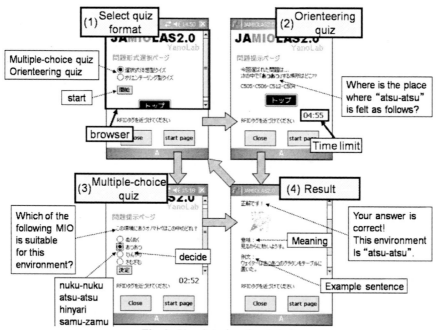

Fig. 9. User interface for student

(3) Orienteering quiz: When the student select orienteering quiz, screen page of PDA display this page. The system presents one MIO and multiple spots placed a node of MOTE and a RFID tag. The student looks for and goes to the spot where s/he can feel MIO suitable the situation from the multiple spots.

(4) Result: The screen page of PDA displays the result. When the student chooses the correct answer, the system presents meaning and example sentence of the MIO. As a result, the student can reach in depth of his/her understanding about the MIO. When the student chooses the wrong answer from multiple-choice quiz, the system recommends the spot, where s/he can learn the MIO that s/he selected.

Each quiz has set time limit and the screen page will display remaining time. In addition, MIO selected by this system appeared randomly. The system changes appearance ratio of the MIO with the level of understanding of the student.

As shown in figure 10, JAMIOLAS 2.0 for teacher has following functions:

(1) Function to support setting threshold of MIO: This system needs to set the threshold of MIO by Japanese feeling. However it is difficult to set the threshold, without referring to anything. The system can set the threshold by varied functions, For example, line graph as shown in figure 10 (a), list of real world data. The line graph can visualize real world data stored in the database on an hourly, a daily or monthly. Figure 10 (a) is line graph about temperature on a day

at each place put sensor node. The list of real world data can look at quantified real world data in the database, and has search function.

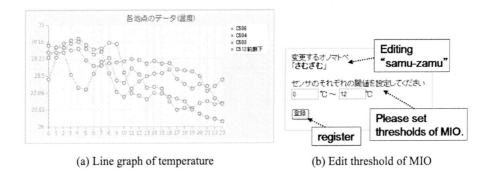

(a) Line graph of temperature   (b) Edit threshold of MIO

Fig. 10. User interface for teacher

(2) Set threshold of MIO: The teacher can look over all registered MIO and their kind and threshold. S/he can select MIO from list and set their threshold, for example, threshold of "Samu-zamu" is from 0 to 12 degrees centigrade as shown in **Fig. 10.** (b). In this case, it is highly possible that each teacher set piecemeal threshold. To solve this problem, the system selects MIO of majority in coincident MIO between thresholds.

4.1.4 Evaluation and Result

An experiment was done in order to evaluate the JAMIOLAS 2.0 usages. 2 groups were involved with the experiment. 16 Japanese undergraduates and postgraduates take part as Japanese-language teachers and 4 international students who have studied Japanese language take part as learners.

Firstly, as shown in figure 11, we prepared 6 rooms and the corridor where conditions varied, for example, we made a room hot with air conditioner (C506) and turned off a light in a room (C504 and C508). 10 words shown in Table 1. were registered in the database. Afterwards, Each Japanese student registered thresholds of these MIO with web browser of notebook PC, tablet PC, PDA and so on. Since, international students went out pretest. They studied MIO with dictionary for 10 minutes. They went out mid test. Afterwards, they felt free to learn using this system with PDA for 10 minutes. Lastly, they went out posttest.

Each test has 2 category, feeling type and example sentence type. The feeling type was with multiple choice questions from which they can select MIO suitable for each situation. The example sentence type was with fill-in-the-blank type questions that they select suitable MIO to complete a sentence. There were 5 questions in each category and 10 questions in total. After this experiment, Japanese and international students who used this system answered different questionnaires respectively. The questionnaire of 5 ranges from 1 to 5, of which 5 is the highest value.

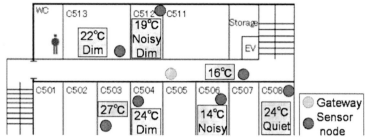

Fig. 11. Environment of Evaluation experiment

Table 1. Mimetic words and onomatopoeia used in the experimentation

Subject	Sensor	MIO words
Temperature	Temperature	samu-zamu, hinyari, nuku-nuku, atsu-atsu, poka-poka
Light	Illuminance	chira-chira, pika-pika, gira-gira
Sound	Sound	shiin, gaya-gaya

Table 2. Result of the questionnaire by Japanese students

No.	Question item	Average	SD
Q1	Were there mimetic words and onomatopoeia close to your sense?	3.5	1.16
Q2	Were you able to set the threshold easily?	3.1	0.92

Table 2. shows result of the questionnaire by Japanese students group. From the result of Q1, we can conclude that some students could not find the suitable MIO that is close to their sense. This is because we have registered MIO beforehand for the convenience of the experiment and we have made them not be able to register MIO. The result of Q2 shows that it was a bit difficult for Japanese students to set thresholds of MIO. This is due to not being able to set them while looking at functions to support setting them. In addition, this is partly because Japanese students cannot set thresholds of MIO while comparing other. This is because this system can set thresholds by only one MIO.

Table 3. shows result of the questionnaire by international students group. Results of Q3, Q5, Q6 and Q7 show that learning MIO with this system holds promise of learning effect than conventional learning and the learner can learn amusing and effectively. However MIO which are answer of quiz were often different in the similar situation from Q4. This is attributed to the fact that illuminance and sound sensor have likely a margin of error.

As shown in figure 12, question of the sense type raise international students' grades with this system. Therefore it is thought that international students understood what kind of MIO they used in varied situations. However example sentence type is little to choose between after learning with dictionary and after learning with this system. The sentences used in this system are also available in dictionary. In addition, international students did not understand meaning of words using example sentences which each test used and they understand situations of example sentence.

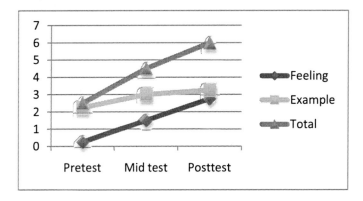

Fig. 12. Average score of test by international students

We received feedback from subjects, for example, the learning with this system is interesting and informative and MIO make impression. To give an actual example, a situation which is hot uses "atsu atsu". When a learner learned with this system in the situation, s/he made a mistake at first, but answered it correctly all the time afterwards. However, we received feedback that it is difficult for international students to understand with the interface of this system. This is because the interface is for Japanese. Therefore it was a little bit hard for them to understand MIO and to enjoy with this system. Accordingly, we will improve interface of this system for international students, thereby the system will hold promise of further learning effects.

Table 3. Result of the questionnaire by international students

No.	Question item	Average	SD
Q3	Were you able to learn mimetic words and onomatopoeia by this system?	4.4	0.55
Q4	Was the answer of presented quiz appropriate to the situation?	3.4	1.52
Q5	Were you able to learn mimetic words and onomatopoeia with them enjoying?	4.2	1.3
Q6	Which do you think enhance learning, conventional learning or this system?	3.8	1.3
Q7	Do you want to learn by this system in the future?	4.0	1.22

4.2 LORAMS

4.2.1 Introduction

The fundamental issues in ubiquitous learning are
(1) how to capture and share learning experiences that happen at anytime and any-place; and
(2) how to retrieve and reuse them for learning.

As for the first issue, video recording with handheld devices will allow us to capture learning experiences. Also consumer generated media (CGM) services helps to share those videos. The second issue will be solved, by identifying objects in a video with RFID so that the system can recommend the videos in similar situations to the situation where the learner has a problem.

We have developed LORAMS (Linking of RFID and Movie System) 15 to cope with those issues. There are two kinds of users in this system. One is a provider who records his/her experience into videos. The other is a user who has some problems and retrieves the videos. In this system, a user uses his/her own PDA with RFID tag reader and digital camera, and links real objects and the corresponding objects in a movie and shares it among other learners. Scanning RFID tags around the learner enables us to bridge the real objects and their information into the virtual world. LO-RAMS detects the objects around the user using RFID tags, and provides the user with the right information in that context.

Video recording process needs PDA as shown in figure 13 (1), RFID tag reader, video camera and wireless access to the Internet. First, a user has to start recording video at the beginning of the task. Before using objects, the user scans RFID tags and the system automatically sends the data and its time stamp to the server. After completing the task, the user uploads the video file to the server and the server automatically generate SMIL (Synchronized Multimedia Integration Language) file to link the video and the RFID tags.

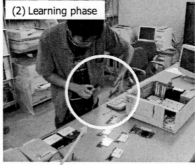

Reading RFID tag

Fig. 13. Usage scene of LORAMS.

4.2.2 Feature

The characteristics of LORAMS are as follows:

(1) Learner's experience is recorded into a video and linked to RFID tags of physical objects. The video can be shared with other learners.
(2) When the learner up-loads the video, it will be automatically encoded with the server.
(3) Learners can find suitable videos by scanning RFID tags and/or entering keywords of physical objects around them.
(4) The learner can compare the video of a similar situation with the learner's video.
(5) All learners can freely add the annotation to videos.

There are three phases for LORAMS as follows:
(1) Video recording phase.
(2) Video search phase.
(3) Video replay phase.
    A) Normal Replay (NR)
    B) Comparing Multi Replay (CMR)

Video recording process needs PDA, RFID tag reader, video camera and wireless access to the Internet. First, the user has to start recording video at the beginning of the task. Before using the objects, the user scans RFID tags and the system automatically sends the object data to the server. This data recorded in the database with time-stamp. The user scans RFID tags again when the user finishes using the object. The user repeats the previous procedure until finishing the task. After completing the task, the user uploads the video file to the server. Then, the server automatically starts encoding the video file. After encoding, the user inputs some personal information.

On the other hand, video search and replay processes need PDA, RFID tag reader, and Web browser. The learner scans RFID tags around him and/or enters some keywords, then the system sends them to the server and shows the list of the videos that match the objects and/or the keywords.

4.2.3 User Interface

In recording phase, the learner sets up the information for the RFID reader such as port number and code type. At the beginning of the task, the learner inputs the user name and pushes on "Send" button (1). Then, the learner pushes on "Start-Read" button at the same time that recording starts (2). When you read RFID tags, the data will be automatically stored in the server. As shown in the right side of figure 14, the RFIDs are linked to the video.

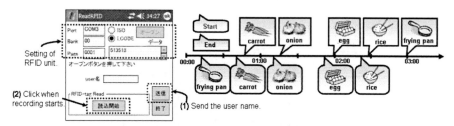

Fig. 14. The interface of the recording phase (left) and video timeline (right).

In the search phase, as shown in figure 15, the user scans RFIDs and/or enters keywords in (B), then the images of the scanned objects will be automatically displayed at the top of the page as shown in (A). Also, the system will display the retrieval results in the right side of figure 15. In (C), the system recommends the videos according to the evaluation from learners. It is easy to recognize the content of the video from its thumbnail. The video can be replayed using Flash 8 player as shown in figure 16. The list of the used objects in the video is displayed in (D). By drugging & dropping the icon shown in (E) on the screen, all learners can freely add the annotation to the video. And, the system automatically retrieves similar situations to learner's video in (F). In figure 17, two videos are replayed to make a comparison. In (G), a bar shows when and what objects the learner is using.

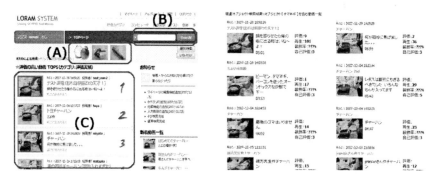

Fig. 15. The interface of index page (left) and retrieval results (right).

Fig. 16. The interface of Normal Replay

4.2.4 System Configuration

We have developed LORAMS, which works on a Fujitsu Pocket Loox v70 with Windows Mobile 2003 2nd Edition, RFID tag reader/writer (OMRON V720S-HMF01), and WiFi (IEEE 802.11b) access. RFID tag reader/writer is attached on a CF (Compact Flash) card slot of PDA. The tag unit can read and write data into and from RFID tags within 5 cm distance, and it works with a wireless LAN at the same time. The LORAMS program has been implemented using Embedded Visual C++ 4.0, PHP 5.2.0, Perl 5.8.8 and Flash 8. Figure 18 shows the system configuration.

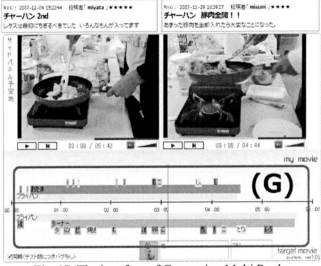

Fig. 17. The interface of Comparing Multi Replay.

The video is played according to following mechanism:

1) The player (A) sends a unique ID of the video to the server.
2) XML conversion module (B) receives the video ID and extracts video information from the database (C) and converts it into XML formats.
3) The XML file is passed to the player, then the file is analyzed using ActionScript.
4) When the player (A) receives the video information, the video file will be downloaded. Because the file is downloaded by the progressive download method, it is possible to replay while downloading it.

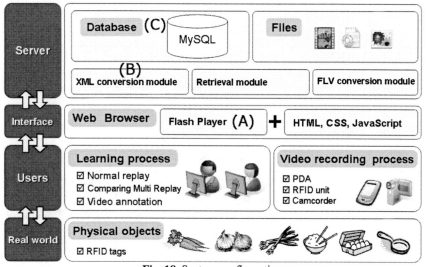

Fig. 18. System configuration

4.2.5 Recommend method of similar situation with the learner's video

The following algorithms are used in LORAMS to look for a video which contains a similar situation to the learner's video. There are two criteria. One is to consider the rate of the same objects, while the other is to calculate the similarity of the order of the objects, as follows:

1) The videos are listed according to the rates of the same objects in the different videos.
2) If the rates of 1) are the same, then the videos are listed according to the similarity of the order of the objects.

We use "Kendall's rank correlation coefficient" in the second algorithm. To apply this algorithm, we selected common objects of two videos. The common objects are re-numbered according to the order in which the objects were used. Then, the algorithm is applied to the set as shown in Table 4. And, the learner can visually confirm the similarity in the graph as shown in Figure 19.

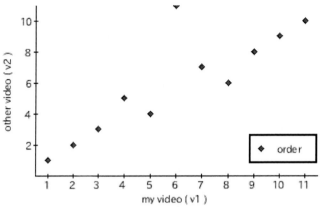

Fig. 19. Graph of similarity

Table 4. Object table

Object ID	Object name	Order (v1 , v2)
E1000005	flying-pan	(1 , 1)
EC000002	cooking oil	(2 , 2)
E0000012	onion	(3 , 3)
E0000013	carrot	(4 , 5)
E1000002	ladle	(5 , 4)
...	...	...
EC000005	salt	(9 , 8)
EC000006	pepper	(10 , 9)
EC000010	soy sauce	(11 , 10)

4.2.6 Experimentation

We investigated the effect of using the video comparison. The task was cooking a fried rice. The cooking method, utensil and ingredient vary from person to person, therefore we think that cooking is a suitable task for the evaluation process.

Twenty-one students from the department of computer science in the University of Tokushima were involved in the experiment. These 21 people were divided into groups A (11 people) who were experts in cooking and groups B (10 people) who were beginners.

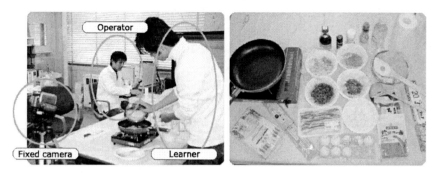

Fig. 20. Appearance of the experiment and a part of the ingredients and toolS

We assume that learner is cooking at home and shoots a video by himself. There-fore, the camera is fixed and captures at hand activity. It is difficult for learners to cook fried rice while scanning RFID tags. So, in this evaluation, an operator was scanning RFID tags for the learner. In the future, if the RFID reader becomes smaller, it will be easy for the learner to read the RFID tags by himself. The left side of figure 20 shows an actual appearance.

The learner can freely cook and select various utensil and ingredients. We prepared 8 kinds of seasonings, 17 kinds of ingredients and 5 kinds of utensil. The right side of figure 20 shows a part of the ingredients.

4.2.7 Result

After the experiment, all students filled in a questionnaire. They gave a rate from 1 (the worst) to 5 (the best) as an answer for each question. The result is shown in table 5. The average (Avg.) and standard deviation (SD) for the learners' answers are illu-strated.

Table 5. Results of the questionnaire

No.	Questionnaire	Avg	SD
Q1	Does the LORAMS serve as a reference in cooking?	4.3	0.59
Q2	Did you get the new knowledge by using LO-RAMS?	4.3	0.47
Q3	Are you able to recognize your mistake and the difference with others by watching the video that the system offered?	4.6	0.62
Q4	Is it easy to compare multi replay?	4.1	0.86
Q5	Which learning method is easy to learn, com-parison multi replay or normal replay?	4.1	0.93

Q6	Can you notice your mistake by using LO-RAMS?	4.6	0.51
Q7	Do you want to make some studies use of LO-RAMS in the future?	4.4	0.71
Q8	Do you want to share your learning experience with others?	4.0	1.00
Q9	How about the taste of the fried rice that you made?	3.1	0.94

The learner watched and compared other learners' videos by using the system after cooking. And some learners cooked again later. Consequently, the learner who had made the same kind of fried rice had a tendency to become skillful. Some learners were stimulated to other learners' video, and challenged a different kind of fried rice.

According to Q7 and Q8, almost everyone wants to use LORAMS as a learning assistance. By contrast, they are not enthusiastic about sharing videos. This result can be understood from the followings reasons.

— "I am ashamed to share clumsy videos."
— "I want to share videos after improving my cooking."

Table 6. Number of replay

Group	Replay	NR	Avg.	CMR	Avg.
A	205	157	11.3	48	4.4
B	367	316	31.6	51	5.1
Total	572	473	22.5	99	4.7

Table 7. Reflection points

(A) Timing in which egg in put
(B) Timing in which vegetable is put
(C) Stir-fried time
(D) How to handle frying-pan
(E) Smoothness of work
...

According to Table 6, the total replaying were 572 in two days. It shows that the learners have a deep interest in the experience videos. Table 7 is a part of the reflection points that the learner obtained by the comparison. It seems that there are three types of reflection point. The first is timing such as (A) and (B). The reflection point of this type can be get from the timeline. The second is time such as (C). This can be get from the timeline, too. The last is the actions such as (D) and (E). The reflection point of this type is obtained by comparing the video. Timing and actions are important in the cooking. This result shows that the learners are able to learn the important point by using LORAMS.

Figure 21 shows an example of the comparison. This is a timeline of an expert learner in cooking (upper) and the learner who has scorched the fried rice (bottom). We can notice two points that should be paid attention from the timeline. First, this learner takes longer time to finish up the cooking compared with the period (A) of the expert learner. Second, the learner spent longer time than the expert, without putting anything in the frying pan in (B). Expert is regularly putting the ingredients. The temperature of the frying-pan falls by putting the foodstuff. Therefore, the time that this learner spent without putting the foodstuff in frying-pan caused to scorch it. Figure 22 shows the timeline of the learner before using LORAMS (upper) and after using it (bottom). The learner becomes good cooker after using LORAMS.

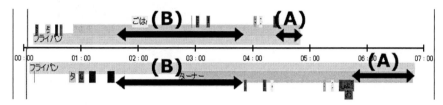

Fig. 21. Example of the comparison.

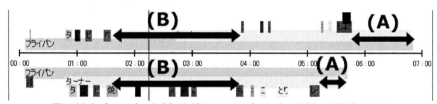

Fig. 22. before using LORAMS (upper), after using LORAMS (bottom)

4.3 PERKAM

The aim of PERKAM (Personalized Knowledge Awareness Map) system 1 is to support the learner with the Knowledge Awareness Map, which is personalized according to his current need and location. The system can recognize the environmental objects that surround the learner those he uses during his practice study. The system uses RFID tags to detect the surrounding physical space objects then it generates the learner's digital space where each object in the physical space has its corresponding one in the digital space. The system matches between the learner's current need and the other learners' interests and locations, recommends the best peer helpers and visualizes the relative distance between the learner's current need and the peer helpers' interests and locations. The learner can contact with one or more peer helpers, forward to him/them his Environmental Objects Map, interact and collaborate.

While the learner is interacting with another learner remotely, trying to explain him his current environment and situation, it may be difficult or at least need long time to describe exactly the available objects that he uses during his practice. The role of Environmental Objects Map is to map the physical space to a digital space, where each object in the physical space is detected, recognized and presented graphically by this system (figure 23). The learner can forward this digital space to the peer helper in order to facilitate easy understanding of his environment that augments the collaboration between the learners.

This map displays a two dimensions knowledge space of the recommended learners who are using the system and have enough knowledge about the learner's request (figure 24). This map represents the level of recommendation for each learner depending on his interests. The closer the recommended learner to the learner's request presents in the vertical (y) dimension, the nearer his physical location to the learner.

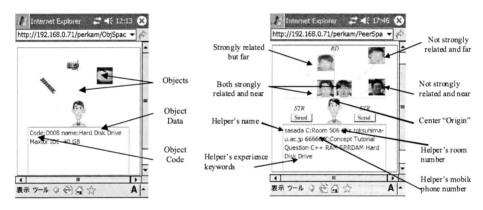

Fig. 23. Environmental objects map.   **Fig. 24.** Peer helper map.

4.4   e-Running SNS

4.4.1 Introduction

SNS has quickly become known by a diverse range of people. There are various web-based community sites such as Wiki-like application, XOOPS module, educational Blog [21] etc., which have educational support functionality. SNS is able to deal with virtual/real world human relationships. Human relationship is one of the key factors for CSCW/L (Computer Supported Collaborative Work/Learning). Therefore, it is reasonably conceivable that SNS is more appropriate for collaborative learning than other web applications.

However, learning in web based communities brings about common problems. In most cases, learning over long periods causes learners to decrease their motivation. Since this phenomenon is quite noticeable in physical training learning, our research group has already proposed its standpoint in a specific case study [21]. As to the essential factors for keeping motivation in physical training, a learner needs a proper partner for mutual encouragement and an indicator to show the corresponding steady progress.

When learners try to find a partner, they can easily get candidates through the keyword searching method on a community site. Nevertheless since physical learning with high variability is inexpressible, detailed descriptions of their states are not necessarily always consistent.

As to the indicator, a certain attainment in learning some specific skills; i.e. juggling the ball in soccer, is clearly identified by the number of bounces as well as the correct physical position for juggling the ball with the use of playback video technique etc. But, in the case of learning physical activities that does not require special skills; i.e. running, the ideal indicator can't just be defined. In many cases, although learners have a concrete image of their own future goals, the truth is that their training plans differ respectively from their individual abilities. For this reason, in the case of learning physical activities that does not require special skills, in order to achieve goals, it is vital to substitute appropriate knowledge of long-term training for skill, but it is also crucial the architecture to keep the reflected progress under constant observation. This research deals with this specific type of learning: no special skill is required, to be precise, the activity or sport of running, including beginners.

Hence, with respect to this particular viewpoint for keeping or increasing motivation, this research adopted the model of behavior modification (BM) based on the real world oriented style [22]. Furthermore, for the purpose of compensating shortcomings of this model, we have incorporated into the architecture the methodology for organizing communities based on real world log with GPS and HRM. This approach enables a variety of learners to get an opportunity to meet and interact with proper partners, and keep continuous goal-oriented activity through online learning-community.

4.4.2 Organizing online learning-community

The model of BM is composed of five stages (See Table 8) [23]. In this model, there are regular relationships between learner's motivation and learner's behavior that have effect on each other. The basic guideline to solve problems of how to promote learners' motivation and behavior is to encourage them to train themselves. In this research, the system supports the necessary activities from 2nd stage to 5th stage. The system is intended for learners who at least have some will to try physical activities.

The problems in introducing BM model into SNS are classified into two types. The first one is concerned with the organization of an online community, which is linked to the principle of 2nd stage. The second one is about the classification based on activities, which is related to the principle from 3rd stage to 5th stage.

About the former, learners in this model receive the instructions at the same time in one location. But in most existing online communities the information goes through asynchronous communication. For this reason, it is of the primary importance that the system supports an organization that promotes competition as well as cooperation on the web community.

As to the latter, how to understand each learner's BM is the special assignment. Additionally, during the design and implementation of this method, digitalization and visualization of learner's goal are required.

Table 8. Relationship between stage and task through BM

Stage number	Ability to take action	Example of teaching	Task for learners
1st	No interest at all	Explain advantage of physical activities	Open own mind
2nd	Feel like trying	Make learner put start.	Try activity
3rd	Participate in physical activities	Make learners increase their activity intensity.	Define clear goal
4th	Do active exercises	Keep learner's active interest	Redefine own goals
5th	Get accustomed to regular physical training	Suggest own training and leadership to other learners.	Independent training

There are many researchers who study the applications with sensor network from technical viewpoint. Most of these applications handle daily life activities in the real world. Our definition of the real world log is not the same as these researches. When we mention real world log, we particularly mean that it monitors and records the existing information such as the position from GPS and the physical condition from HRM.

By such real world log, our research can come up with an answer to the above mentioned problems about time restriction on 2nd stage and the understanding from 3rd stage to 5th stage (See Table. 9).

Generally, the methodology for organizing communities, tagged by specific characters, causes learners to pass up the opportunity to participate actively in the communities. But by automatic extraction the system brings the opportunities through the recommendation based on their log files. These log files contain information regarding the possible areas for learners' activities and their respective kinetic information, and the system can differentiate subtle differences in improvements using precise information such as pace of running and rate of heart beat during exercise. Since the communities consist of learners who have close correlation in their goals and in their common activities characteristics, the community is adapted in order to increase learners' awareness and to foster the learning process.

Moreover, from the objective viewpoint, to consider the classification between 3rd and 5th stage in Table.9 is of great significance for the learning. Therefore, the system has to detect the learner's current status automatically as well as controlling / navigating the learning process. For example, the system defines some fundamental indicators using the simple parameter method that would be used for processing the learners' profiles by simple parameter extraction method. Hence, learners can set their goals and confirm their activity progress through the suitable intensity for their re-spective level and indicators [24].

Table 9. Comparison of the General Community against the proposed method.

Stage number	Existing community	Proposal Community	Advantage of proposal
2nd	Consciously search or register in community by tags	Automatically extract and recommend a community	Not only by tags (key-words)
3rd previous term	Largely-subjective goal defined in the commu-nity	Set a goal through discussion with first training log activity	Visualization of improvements
3rd later term	Goal attainment level subjectively judged	Objective evaluation based on training results	
4th	Subjective goals not clearly defined.	Be promoted to 5th or return to 4th based on record of achievements	Clear goal identification

4.4.3 Development

We developed the online community site to implement the above-mentioned model. The system, which supports running beginners' learning, has a client-server architec-ture on the web (Fig.25). With regard to the client part, there are two situations: run-ning with a tiny client-device and using the web without running. The web application supports these client activities through HTTP.

Learners' viewpoint

When a learner is running, a tiny wearable device records the runner's position by GPS and heart rate by HRM. It also includes a simple navigation function, indicating the correct direction and the route that anyone has already run in the past. As a prere-quisite for the use of this function, a learner must download the track file from the server and load it to the portable device in advance. Learners can get comparative records of other learners' performances under the same training environment, since learners from different activity areas can use the same routes running at different time.

On the other hand, after running, the learner uploads log data to the server. The learner uses a data I/O tool made using C#.net, and the system automatically put the data file in the administrative sharing folder on the PC and uploads it to the server via the internet. In addition to objective data by logger, the learner sends some relevant comments as well as the respective answers to the items of a survey; i.e. (What is the purpose of this activity? Option: training, updating the record). This operation is done through the after-mentioned user interface.

System functionality

As to the server, in addition to general SNS functions, five unique modules were embedded in the system.

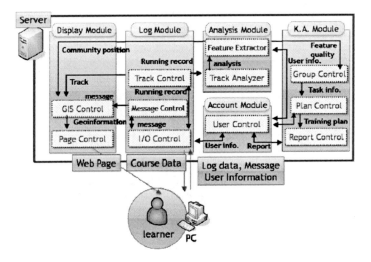

Fig. 25. Development of the online community on the real world log

First, a log module unifies the management of log data. The function of this module preserves all records that are linked to the physical logs. Also the system separates and stores them in each database in order to easily apply to other module. The position information of track log is converted into geographical weight points for the navigation.

Moreover, a displaying module plays an effective role in visualizing communities and traces of the learner's activities through Google Maps. Learners can find out more about information related to the areas of the activities, including their own associated information.

An analysis module pursues the correlation among running records and profiles of learners. At the beginning of this process, the system checks the positioning track data against a possibly existing activity area as a tentative community. If not existed, the system asks the learner whether to allow generate a new community or not. The system not only receive and process requests of participation from learners but also makes recommendations to them to take part in specific new communities as well.

When a community attracts many participants, more than about ten learners, the system move a community forward to the next stage. The system makes a comparison between learners' goal and tracks them also in relation to their physical pace and tracks in relation to the physical pace). Groups are created in a cooperative learning environment based on close correlation. These groups in a community are used to facilitate a clear understanding of learner's training knowledge through the aforementioned Knowledge Acquisition (K.A.) module. However, if a learner would not belong to any community, the system would not be able to support the learner's goal. For this reason, the system based on two principles may propose a participant from another community in order to attract some learners and to make an intended learning possible. For example, in case that a specific learner's goals have no correlation with the learners' goals of a given community, the system recommends another community which has strongly-correlated learners in the neighborhood of that specific learner's activity area.

Lastly, K.A. module follows the guidelines for BM. Learners are required to change from their present level to their suitable level. Figure.26 shows the process of K.A. to proceed to the upper stage. First, the system shows learners their training analysis results and proposes some candidates for the basic training plan. These are based on the systematized practice in sports science or on past successful experiences according to other learner's log. At this point, the system provides three assignments which are designed to lead learners to understand the training process through a discussion in a same community.

(1) To understand what their displayed results means.
(2) To understand why the candidates for the basic plan have been proposed.
(3) To modify the basic plan through an animated discussion.

Next step, learners continue their training under these modified plans. Finally the system sends a report to every learner comparing their own results with their respective plans. After a certain period of time, the system changes learners' level according to their respective scores based on their individual performance.

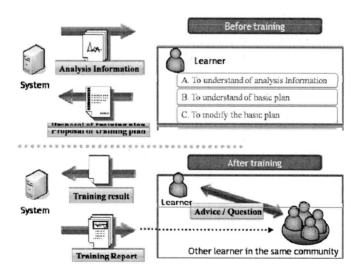

Fig. 26. The process of Knowledge Acquisition

4.5 User Interface

A learner uses this SNS environment after logging in to the system (Fig 2). Aside from general functions commonly used in SNS, the system provides learner with various services, i.e. distance recorder, personal weight control with a graph, and search function of the training place etc.

This screenshot illustrates learner's own training page. Part of the left side shows one learner's name and profile inputted by the learner. The top-bar shows the menu list. Furthermore, the organized information below menu is the training report. The upper part shows search condition owing to show community, if a learner works with multiple course or has much log, s/he can acquire at the information as to community one wants in no time at all. Next, the middle part shows on a Google Map the learner' recoded run track. The maker shows the position the learner began to run. Lastly, the lower part shows an analysis of the training. The graph shows the relationship between time and physical barometer. The barometer includes two types: speed pace at which a learner moves measured by GPS and heart rate by HRM.

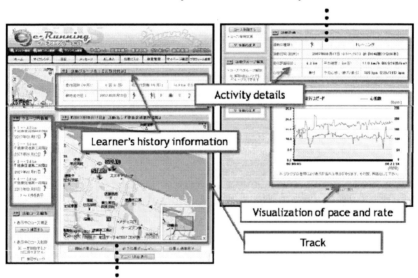

Fig. 27. Screenshot of the Interface

5 Conclusions

This paper overviewed our projects of CSUL. Authors developed such environments as follows:

(a) Context-aware language-learning support systems with PDA, GPS, RFID tags and sensor networks.
(b) Second-generation language-learning support systems with sophisticated sensor networks.

(c) Web-based video sharing system for sharing and retrieving learning experiences. with RFID tags.
(d) Social networking service supporting organization of online communities and joggers' motor-skill with HRM and GPS.

Those systems can augment learning experiences using ambient media. For further information, the web page is available at http://www-b4.is.tokushima-u.ac.jp/
The future works are shown below:

(1) Rich user interface: Everyone should be able to use CSUL easily. For example, voice input and output should be implemented in CSUL.
(2) Persistent learner model: The system should understand what the learner has learnt so far and what the learner has not learnt. Therefore, the learner's activities should be recorded permanently and they should be accessed by other educational systems.
(3) Personalization: CSUL should be personalized to provide the right information at the right place at the right time in the right way to the right person.
(4) Learning support: CSUL should provide the right scaffolding and fading tool in terms of short and long term perspectives. Also CSUL should be supported seamlessly across the learning contexts.
(5) Evaluation: CSUL should be evaluated for short and long term. We need to investigate how to evaluate. Also, we should take account of privacy issue.

References

1. Abowd, G.D., and Mynatt, E.D. "Charting Past, Present, and Future Research in Ubiquitous Computing", *ACM Transaction on Computer-Human Interaction*, Vol.7, No.1, 2000, pp.29-58.
2. Bishouty, M., Ogata, H., and Yano, Y., "Personalized Knowledge Awareness Map in Computer Supported Ubiquitous Learning", *Educational Technology and Society Journal*, vol.10, no.3, 2007, pp.122-134.
3. Brown, J. S., Collins, A., and Duguid, P., "Situated Cognition and the Culture of Learning", *Educational Researcher*, (Jan.-Feb.), 1989, pp.32-42.
4. Fischer, G. and Konomi, S., "Innovative Media in Support of Distributed Intelligence and Lifelong Learning", *Proc. of IEEE WMTE2005*, 2005, pp.3-10.
5. Gan, L.H., Wada, M., Ogata, H., Oishi, Y., Ueda, T., and Yano, Y. "Language Learning Outside the Classroom with Handhelds with Knowledge Management", *Proc. of ICCE 2007, Supporting Learning Flow through Integrative Technologies*, T. Hirashima et al.(Eds.), ISO Press, 2007, pp.361-368.
6. Greenberg, S. and Fitchett, C., "Phidgets: Easy development of physical interfaces through physical widgets", *Proceedings of the ACM UIST 2001, 14th Annual ACM Symposium on User Interface Software and Technology*, 2001, pp.209-218.
7. Houser, C. and Thornton, P. "Using mobile phones in English Education in Japan", *Journal of Computer Assisted Learning*, Vol.21, No.3, 2005, pp.217-228.

8. Hsi, S., "I-Guides in Progress: Two Prototype Applications for Museum Educators and Visitors Using Wireless Technologies to Support Informal Science Learning", *Proc. of IEEE WMTE 2004*, 2004, pp.187-192.

9. Joseph, S., Binsted K. and Suthers, D., "PhotoStudy: Vocabulary Learning and Collaboration on Fixed and Mobile Devices", *Proc. of WMTE 2005*, 2005,pp.206-210.

10. Lingnau, A., Hoppe, H.U., and Mannhaupt, G., "Computer Supported Collaborative Learning in an Early Learning Classroom", *Journal of Computer Assisted Learning*, vol.19, no.2, 2003, pp.186-194.

11. Lyytinen, K. and Yoo, Y. "Issues and Challenges in Ubiquitous Computing", *Communications of ACM*, vol.45, no.12, 2002, pp.63-65.

12. Miller, G. A., and Gildea, P.M., "How children learn words" *Scientific American*, no.257, 1987, pp.94–99.

13. Ogata, H., and Yano, Y., "Knowledge Awareness Map for Computer-Supported Ubiquitous Language-Learning", *Proc. of IEEE WMTE 2004*, 2004. pp.19-26.

14. Ogata, H., and Yano, Y., "Context-Aware Support for Computer Supported Ubiquitous Learning", *Proc. of IEEE WMTE 2004*, 2004, pp.27-34.

15. Ogata, H. and Yano, Y., "JAMIOLAS: Supporting Japanese Mimicry and Onomatopoeia Learning with Sensors", *Proc. of IEEE WMUTE 2006*, 2006, pp.111-115.

16. Ogata, H., Matsuka, Y., Bishouty, M. and Yano, Y., "LORAMS: Capturing sharing and reusing experiences by linking physical objects and videos", *International Workshop on Pervasive Learning 2007*, 2007, pp.34-42.

17. Ogata, H., Saito, N., Paredes, R., Ayala, G., Yano, Y., "Supporting Classroom Activities with the BSUL System", *Educational Technology and Society Journal*, 2008, in press.

18. Uther, M. Zipitria, I. Uther J. and Singh P., "Mobile Adaptive CALL: A case-study in developing a mobile learning application for speech/audio language training", *Proc. of IEEE WMTE 2005*, IEEE Computer Society Press. 2005, pp.187-191.

19. Yin, C., Ogata, H. and Yano, Y., "JAPELAS: Supporting Japanese-Polite-Expressions Learning Using PDA(s) Toward Ubiquitous Learning," *International Journal of Information and Systems in Education*, Vol.3, No.1, 2005, pp.33-39.

20. Gotoda, N., Matsuura, K., Kanenishi, K. and Yano, Y., "Organizing Online Learning-Community Based on the Real World Log," *Knowledge-Based Intelligent Information and Engineering Systems*, Vol. LNAI 4694, 2007, pp.608-615.

21. Matsuura, K., Kanenishi, K., Miyoshi, Y,, Terao, S., Gotoda, N. and Yano, Y., "DEVELOPMENT OF THE VLOG-BASED SCENARIO WITH CYBERCOMMUNITIES OF INTEREST FOR EXPERIENCED LEARNING," *Proceedings of IADIS International Conference on Web Based Communities 2007*, 2007, pp.272-275.

22. Prochaska, O., and DiClemente, C., "Stages of change in the modification of problem behaviors," In: Hersen, M., Eisler, M., and Miller, M., eds. *Progress in Behavior Modification. Sycamore, IL: Sycamore Publishing Company*, 1992, pp.184-214.

23. Prochaska, O., Velicer, F., Rossi, S., Goldstein, G., Marcus, H., Rakowski, W., Fiore, C., Harlow, L., Redding, A., Rosenbloom, D. and Rossi, R., "Stages of change and decisional balance for 12 problem behaviors," *Health Psychology*, Vol.13, No.1, 1994, pp.39-46.

24. Pekkanen J., Marti B., Nissinen A., Tuomilehto J., Punsar S. and Karvonen J., "Reduction of premature mortality by high physical activity : A 20-year follow up of middle-aged Finnish men," , *Lancet I*, 1987, pp.1473-1477.

Research Introduction

Yutaka Moriya

Kameyama Lab

Global Information and Telecommunication Studies

Waseda University

Research on Digital Archive Management

Agenda

- About Myself
- Previous Research during Undergraduate Study

  Research on compiling Tourism Thesaurus and Linguistic Comparison of Tourism
- Current Research in GITS

  Construction of a Digital Archive for "Nippon News" and Considerations for Archive Management

  - Research Background
    - Archival Science
    - Joint Research with National Museum of Japanese History
  - Architecture / System Design
  - Experiment & Result
  - Conclusion & Future Works

Research During Undergraduate Study

Research on compiling Tourism Thesaurus
and
Linguistic Comparison of Tourism

- presented in IADIS
- International Association for Development of the Information Society 2008

Research Background

- The experiences of tourists are very important.
- Tourist will write their experiences and publish it somewhere like their blog, and tourism information site.
- To effectively use these data, we believe that a specialized thesaurus of tourism is needed.
- Therefore, we applied the method in LIS (Library Information Science), to analyze the relationship among the words to construct the thesaurus.

Methodology

- Extract data about Paris from "4-travel":written by Japanese people, and from "travel blog" written by English speaking people
- Apply text mining method on each data, and compared them for creating a thesaurus.
- Finally, we analysis is made changed out to see whether linguistic expressions for Paris according to the cultural difference of visitors.

TravelBlog

http://www.travelblog.org/

Analysis of Keyword Frequency

Comparison of Japanese and English Keywords from Tourism Blog

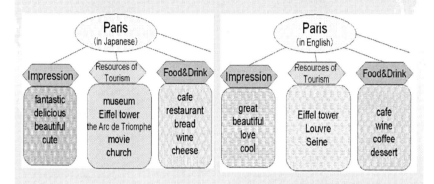

Figure 1. Japanese Thesaurus made from "Travel Blog"

Figure 2. English Thesaurus made from "4travel"

Comparison of Frequency of Words on the Blogs

Code(in Japanese)	41
Code	10
Louvre (in Japanese)	228
Louvre	241
pyramids(in Japanese)	93
Pyramids	14
Movie, movies(in Japanese)	111
movie, movies	43

Another Experiment

- "KWIC Concordance for Windows" 5]
  - Word extraction
  - Estimation of word frequency

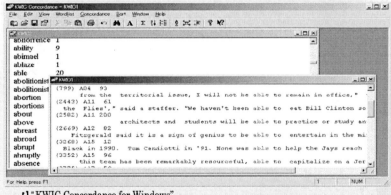

5] "KWIC Concordance for Windows"
(http://www.chs.nihon-u.ac.jp/eng_dpt/tukamoto/kwic.html) 2008年3月21日確認

The Appearance Frequency of Keywords in Tokyo and Kyoto Tourism Reviews

	KWIC1 Tokyo 2006	Appearance Frequency		KWIC1 Kyoto 2006	Appearance Frequency
1	the	13456		the	6712
2	and	8662		and	3841
3	to	8460		to	3788
4	a	7311		a	3491
⋮	⋮	⋮		⋮	⋮
300	should	118		away	52

Analysis Result

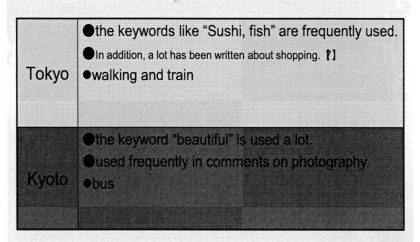

Tokyo	●the keywords like "Sushi, fish" are frequently used. ●In addition, a lot has been written about shopping. ?] ●walking and train
Kyoto	●the keyword "beautiful" is used a lot. ●used frequently in comments on photography ●bus

(http://www.jnto.go.jp/jpn/tourism_data/survey_material_details.html)
（2008年4月24日確認）

For the review on Kyoto, the appearance frequency of keyword "Tofu" and its related words is only 9
※. (Appearance Frequency: 0.054, Appearance Frequency of "Hospital":

Conclusion

- ◆Tourism Information is analyzed from the viewpoint of Keyword appearance frequency.
- ◆The advance in Computer and Text Analysis Technique has enabled us to analysis opinion of many people.
- ◆Although the results for this study can not be used directly in marketing, However, without curiosity, the characteristic can not be easily found.
- ◆Therefore, these results might be important for supplier in the market.

Research During Master Study

Construction of a Digital Archive for "Nippon News" and Considerations for Archive Management

presented in
IPSJ EIP -44
(Electronic Intellectual Property)
9 June 2009

Research Background

- Joint research project "Using News Movies for Historical Study"
- The project is conducted with National Museum of Japanese History (NMJH) in cooperation with Kawasaki City Museum
- (Kawasaki City: A city south west to Tokyo)
- In this research, NMJH is transcribing the narration from "Nippon News" (from 1946 to 1951 and numbered 1 through 312)

National Museum of Japanese History

Kawasaki City Museum

Research Background

- ◆ We are particularly exploring ways to transform the films into a database
- ◆ Additionally, we have historians using the completed prototype system in order to take into consideration their actual needs for future improvements

System Requirement

- ◆ Systematic management of the narration text, so that it is easily viewable
- ◆ A System to edit the narration text
- ◆ Link to the multimedia content from the narration text

Architecture

◆ Metadata

  ◆ System will be used extensively in future

  ◆ Therefore, the metadata schema which is based on international standard is needed

  ◆ The "TV-Anytime Forum" metadata scheme, which the most appropriate in our case, is used

Metadata

◆ First, the required fields of the metadata schema are extracted

Title	<tva:Title type="seriesTitle">
Sub-Title	<tva:Title type="main">
narration	<tva:Synopsis>
Keyword	<tva:Keyword>

Raw Narration Text Data
(example)

NO1　第1号

音楽/文字 ニュースタイトル
音楽/文字
『日本ニュース　映日製作　日本映画社』
音楽/文字
『日本ニュースが生れ變わりました』
『旧い殻を脱きすてるべく　我々は　昨年の十月　社團法人日本映画社を解散し』
　　『新しき年とともに　新しき陣容と　新しき思想を以て　株式會社　日本映画
　　社を創立しました』
　　『そして　ここに　働く皆様の　眼となり声となり　民主日本の　建設に力を
　　盡す　新生日本ニュース第一号を送ります』
『NO.1 1946』
音楽/文字
『45』
音楽/文字
『民主革命の旋風』
【公職追放令で揺れる幣原内閣】
音楽/アナウンサー
「連合軍最高司令部は、昭和21年1月4日軍国主義指導者の官公職よりの追放及び右
翼団体結社禁止の画期的指令を発し新春の政界朝野を一大旋風の中に巻き込みまし
た。閣僚中に該当者を含む政府では総辞職か改造かの岐路に立ち、四日に引き続き
五日も協議を続行しました。慌しい五日の首相官邸。」

Raw Narration Text Data
(example)

NO1　第1号

音楽/文字 ニュースタイトル
音楽/文字
『日本ニュース　映日製作　日本映画社』
音楽/文字
『日本ニュースが生れ變わりました』
『旧い殻を脱きすてるべく　我々は　昨年の十月　社團法人日本映画社を解散し』
　　『新しき年とともに　新しき陣容と　新しき思想を以て　株式會社　日本映画
　　社を創立しました』
　　『そして　ここに　働く皆様の　眼となり声となり　民主日本の　建設に力を
　　盡す　新生日本ニュース第一号を送ります』
『NO.1 1946』
音楽/文字
『45』
音楽/文字
『民主革命の旋風』
【公職追放令で揺れる幣原内閣】
音楽/アナウンサー
「連合軍最高司令部は、昭和21年1月4日軍国主義指導者の官公職よりの追放及び右
翼団体結社禁止の画期的指令を発し新春の政界朝野を一大旋風の中に巻き込みまし
た。閣僚中に該当者を含む政府では総辞職か改造かの岐路に立ち、四日に引き続き
五日も協議を続行しました。慌しい五日の首相官邸。」

XML Instance
(Example)【1/2】

```
<?xml version="1.0" encoding="UTF-8" ?>
- <tva:TVAMain xmlns:tva="urn:tva:metadata:2002" xmlns:mpeg7="urn:mpeg:mpeg7:schema:2001"
   xmlns:xsi="http://www.w3.org/2001/XMLSchema-instance" xsi:schemaLocation="urn:tva:metadata:2002
   C:\www\tva_metadata_v13.xsd urn:mpeg:mpeg7:schema:2001 C:\www\mpeg7_tva.xsd">
 - <tva:ProgramDescription>
  - <tva:ProgramInformationTable>
   - <tva:ProgramInformation programId="crid://www.km.gits.waseda.ac.jp/RKK/news1">
    - <tva:BasicDescription>
       <tva:Title>1</tva:Title>
      - <tva:Genre href="urn:tva:metadata:cs:ContentCS:2002:3.1.1">
         <tva:Name xml:lang="jp">ニュース</tva:Name>
        </tva:Genre>
        <tva:CaptionLanguage>JP</tva:CaptionLanguage>
      - <tva:CreditsList>
         <tva:CreditsItem role="urn:mpeg:mpeg7:cs:RoleCS:2001:V103" />
        - <tva:CreditsItem role="urn:mpeg:mpeg7:cs:RoleCS:2001:V97">
         - <tva:PersonName>
            <mpeg7:GivenName xml:lang="jp">顕治</mpeg7:GivenName>
            <mpeg7:FamilyName xml:lang="jp">宮本</mpeg7:FamilyName>
           </tva:PersonName>
         </tva:CreditsItem>
        - <tva:CreditsItem role="urn:mpeg:mpeg7:cs:RoleCS:2001:V97">
         - <tva:PersonName>
            <mpeg7:FamilyName xml:lang="jp">山本</mpeg7:FamilyName>
            <mpeg7:GivenName xml:lang="jp">安英</mpeg7:GivenName>
           </tva:PersonName>
         </tva:CreditsItem>
        </tva:CreditsList>
```

XML Instance
(Example)【2/2】

```
 - <tva:SegmentInformationTable>
  - <tva:SegmentList xmlns:mpeg7="urn:mpeg:mpeg7:schema:2001">
   - <tva:SegmentInformation segmentId="1-1-1">
      <tva:ProgramRef crid="crid://www.km.gits.waseda.ac.jp/RKK/news1/1-1-1" />
    - <tva:Description>
       <tva:Title type="seriesTitle">民主革命の旋風</tva:Title>
       <tva:Title type="main">公職追放令で揺れる幣原内閣</tva:Title>
       <tva:Synopsis>連合軍最高司令部は、昭和21年1月4日軍国主義指導者の官公職よりの追放及び右翼団体結社禁止の画期的指令を発
       し新春の政界朝野を一大旋風の中に巻き込みました。閣僚中に該当者を含む政府では総辞職か改造かの岐路に立ち、四日に引き続き五
       日も協議を続行しました。懐い五日の首相官邸。</tva:Synopsis>
       <tva:Keyword>連合軍最高司令部</tva:Keyword>
       <tva:Keyword>右翼団体結社</tva:Keyword>
       <tva:Keyword>総辞職</tva:Keyword>
      - <tva:RelatedMaterial>
       - <tva:MediaLocator>
          <mpeg7:MediaUri>http://localhost:8080/dwr/Contents/1-1-1/1-1-1.avi</mpeg7:MediaUri>
         </tva:MediaLocator>
        </tva:RelatedMaterial>
       </tva:Description>
     - <tva:SegmentLocator>
        <mpeg7:MediaTimePoint />
       </tva:SegmentLocator>
      </tva:SegmentInformation>
    - <tva:SegmentInformation segmentId="1-1-2">
       <tva:ProgramRef crid="crid://www.km.gits.waseda.ac.jp/RKK/news1/1-1-2" />
     - <tva:Description>
        <tva:Title type="seriesTitle">民主革命の旋風</tva:Title>
```

Architecture

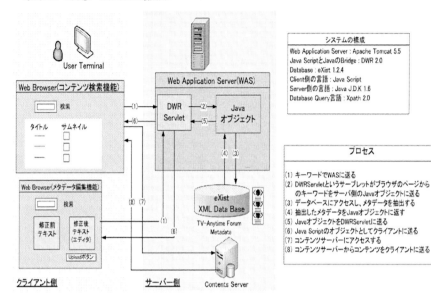

Content Retrieval System

Editing of the Narration Text System

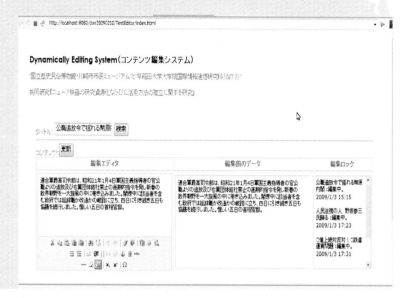

Experiment & Result

◆ We invited the historians from the museum to test the prototype, and obtain their opinion,

Feedback

◆ Regarding the interface

- ◆ For the search result interface, it is better to show the title, thumbnail, together with the narration text.
- ◆ highlight or apply bold text to the keyword in the search result interface.

Experiment & Result

◆ Regarding the system
  ◆ The search should include AND and OR logical function.
  ◆ In Japanese, there are a lot of words or phrases, which are same in meaning, but written in different way.
    For example, 「子供」and 「子ども」both means kids, but are written differently.
    It is desirable that our system could response similarly to these situations.

Consideration for Improvement(1/2)

◆ For the interface, after the feedback from historians and experts, we have a deeper understanding on their requirement.
◆ There are still rooms for improvement for the prototype that we have developed.
◆ For the retrieval function, the prototype was designed for single keyword.
◆ After the feedback, we think that we should include functions like multiple keywords search, logical function like AND/OR, and etc.
◆ Therefore, we are proposing to modify XPath in our second prototype.

Consideration for improvement(4/4)

- For the problem of multiple phrases with same meaning, we would like to implement the statistic approach in text mining technology to improve the performance.
- First, is to reduce the redundancy by utilizing the Japanese Thesaurus.
- Then, if the word or phrase is not recorded in the thesaurus, the new word will be compiled into dictionary.
- The word will be added to the vocabulary list, then is used to improve the performance of retrieval in future.

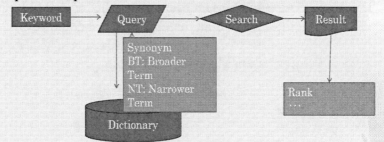

Conclusion(1/2)

- Based on the requirements and needs from the museum, and after taking consideration from engineering point of view, a Multimedia Archive Management System is proposed.

- For the first prototype, we have obtained the feedback from historians and museum experts. In future, we will obtain questionnaire result in parallel, in order to achieve a multifaceted feedback of the system usability.

Conclusion(2/2)

♦ There are many types of approaches in historical study. To satisfy the needs of these historical studies, we think that we should further the research in supplying more efficient tools for the historians.

♦ From the research, we feel that the engineering support plays an important role towards historical study. In addition, we think that our proposal could help to solve one of the existing problems in Japanese Museum Information Management System.

REFERENCES

♦ **Conference paper or contributed volume**
♦ Chang,Choi. et al. 2006 Travel Ontology for Recommendation System based on Semantic WebAdvanced Communication Technology. *ICACT 2006. The 8th International ConferenceVolume 1*, Seoul, Korea ,pp.624-627
♦ Lobna,Karoui. Et al. 2006 Context-based Hierarchical Clustering for the Ontology Learning Web Intelligence archive *Proceedings of the 2006 IEEE/WIC/ACM International Conference on Web Intelligence*, Hong Kong, China, pp.420-427
♦ **Web Site**
♦ "4travel" (http://4travel.jp/) (see 19.Sept, 2007)
♦ "ChaSen"(http://chasen.naist.jp/hiki/ChaSen/) (see 19.Sept, 2007)
♦ "travelblog"(http://www.travelblog.org/) (see 19.Sept, 2007)
♦ "KWIC Concordance for Windows" (http://www.chs.nihon-u.ac.jp/eng_dpt/tukamoto/) (see 19.Sept, 2007)

A Study on Distance Language Education System based on Corpus Linguistics
--Research and Evaluation--

Song LIU[1]

Yoshiyori URANO[2]

[12]Graduate School of Global Information and Telecommunication Studies,
Waseda University, Tokyo, JAPAN
[1] liusong@aoni.waseda.jp   [2] urano@waseda.jp

Abstract:

Nowadays, more and more students in Japan have begun studying Chinese language. Due to the limitation of resource, most of the students can only study syntax in the classroom, but with little chance to communicate with native speakers. A lot of ways have been tried to resolve this problem. In this research, we have introduced a new language education mode named Tutorial Chinese: small class consists of native speaker tutors and 4 students, supported by the tools as video conference, corpus based CAI tools and support platform. In this research, corpus linguistics based curriculum analysis and design method has been tried to utilize. Reasonable corpus has been used to construct distance education system functions more effective for the language education. Functions that can collect and analyze corpus generated in the real classroom has also been designed and constructed. The research is part of a project named CCDL (Cross-Cultural Distance Learning), which is carried out by Waseda University.

Keywords: Corpus, Chinese Language Education, CCDL Project, Tutorial Chinese

Outline

- Research Background
    - – CCDL project and Tutorial Chinese
    - – Corpus based language education
    - – Mobile phone situation in Japan
- Corpus based Chinese language education support system sample
    - – Corpus based listening CAI system
    - – Mobile learning system
- Future works

1 Introduction-Research Background

1.1 CCDL project and Tutorial Chinese

CCDL is a project of Waseda University. The aim of this project is, in the first place, to construct mutual understanding and good ties of friendship between students of Waseda University and those of its overseas (particularly Asian) sister universities. Secondly, it aims to develop an effective method for the acquisition of English as a common language and other foreign languages. For the attainment of these aims, the latest multimedia and Internet technologies such as video conferencing, chat and e-mail systems are fully utilized. Up to now, there are 60 participating universities from 21 countries all over the world. More than 800 courses are carried out through the year. The table below shows the development status of CCDL and the figure below shows the distribution of CCDL participating universities

CCDL Cross-Culture Distance Learning
- Participating Universities

Korea University (Korea)
Kangwon National University (...)
De...e Salle University (Philippines)
Uni...ty of Malaya (Malaysia)
Nat...l University of Singapore (Singapore)
SEAMEO RELC (Singapore)
Thammasat University (Thailand)
University of Peking (China)
Hong Kong Baptist University (China)
Capital Normal University (China)
Tamkang University (Taiwan)
National Taiwan Normal University (Tai...)
University of Brunei (Brunei)
Zaid University (UAE)

Nottinngham Trent University (U.K.)
University of Edinburgh (U.K.)
University of Essex (U.K.)
University of Kiel (German)
University of U...) (U.S.A.)
University of Hawaii at Hilo (U.S.A.)
University of Hawaii at Manoa (U.S.A.)
University of Colorado (U.S.A.)
Syracuse University (U.S.A.)
Laffayatte University (U.S.A.)
Far Eastern State University (Russia)
Japan Foundation (Australia)
Monash University (Australia)
University of New South Wale (Australia)
University of Auckland (New Zealand)

Figure 1   Participating universities of CCDL

Distance Tutorial Chinese

Face-to-Face Tutorial Chinese

Figure2 Two Tutorial Chinese Modes

Table 1 Tutorial Chinese

TUTORIAL CHINESE	
Object	All students in Waseda University
Subjects Name	Chinese Conversation Practice
Class Style	Tutor 1 – Students 4
Class Quantity	10 weeks (twice a week, 20 lessons in total)
Curriculum	1.5 hour for one class + Self study
Credit	4 credits
Teacher and Tutor	2 teachers in JP, 4 teachers outside of JP 5 tutors from University of Peking 5 tutors from Capital Normal University 10 tutors from National Taiwan Normal University 15 tutors from Waseda University

Compare with the traditional normal Chinese education, Tutorial Chinese has the following features:

● The small class style provides sufficient time for conversation and study.

● The native speaker Tutors will teach students the most practical and alive Chinese directly.

● The students are main speakers instead of teacher, better to practice their speaking and listening ability.

● Grammar, vocabulary and conversation are integrated around topics, and the practice near to real situation will be set.

The following figure shows the contrast between traditional education and Tutorial Chinese.

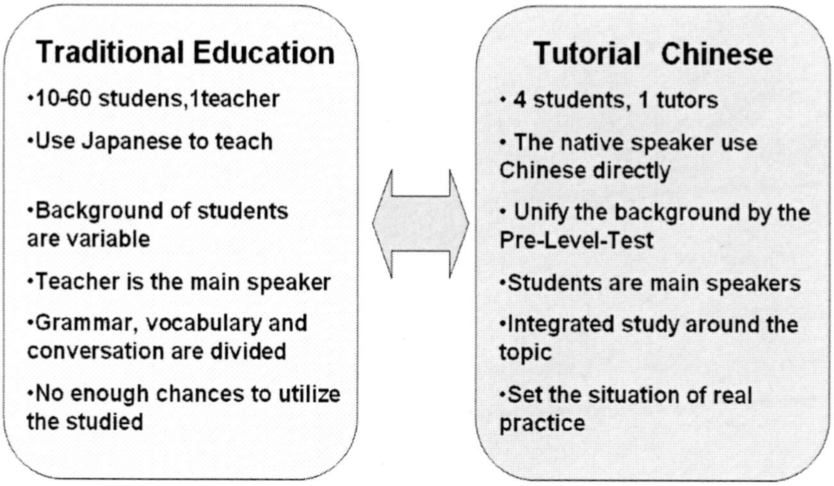

Traditional Education	Tutorial Chinese
•10-60 studens,1teacher	• 4 students, 1 tutors
•Use Japanese to teach	• The native speaker use Chinese directly
•Background of students are variable	• Unify the background by the Pre-Level-Test
•Teacher is the main speaker	•Students are main speakers
•Grammar, vocabulary and conversation are divided	•Integrated study around the topic
•No enough chances to utilize the studied	•Set the situation of real practice

Figure3 Contrast between traditional education and Tutorial Chinese

In order to support this new language education mode, we developed a Tutorial Chinese Platform (TCP) in 2003. The main education management server is located on the Waseda campus and manages all the classes that stretch over multiple countries. Unlike other distance education platforms, which are based on normal static classes, The Tutorial Chinese Platform is based on interactive dynamic conversation lessons. Through this platform, results of the lesson are fed back to the teacher and students by the tutors soon after the lesson. Functions such as report submission, homework correction, study log recording, BBS, web test and web questionnaire, etc have already been developed previous to the CALL-drill and Web-test tool on which this paper is based

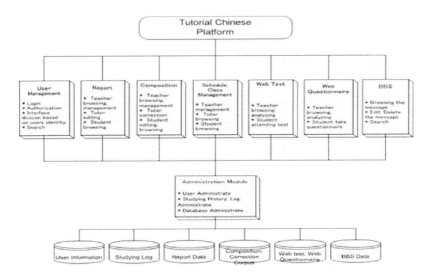

Fig. 4 TCP Module Structure

Tutorial Chinese Screenshot

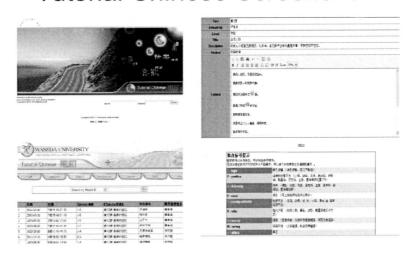

Fig. 5 TCP Module Structure

1.2 Corpus based language education

(1)   What is a Corpus?

- the term 'corpus' is simply the Latin for 'body'

- In modern Linguistics this term is used to refer to large collections of texts which represent a sample of a particular variety or use of languages that are presented in machine readable form.

- Multimedia corpus and enriched data

Tony McEnery, Andrew Wilson, *Corpus Linguistic*, Edinburgh University

(2)   Research Areas about corpus

Nowadays, the common research areas where corpora can be and have been used are listed below:

- Computational Linguistics

- Cultural Studies

- Discourse Analysis and Pragmatics

- Grammar/Syntax

- Historical Linguistics

- Language Acquisition

- Language Teaching

- Language Variation

- Lexicography

- Linguistics

- Machine Translation

- Natural Language Processing (NLP)

- Psycholinguistics

- Semantics

- Social Psychology

- Sociolinguistics

- Speech

(3) How Can We Use Corpus into Language Education?

- Corpus examples are important in language education as they expose students to the kinds of sentences that they will encounter in real life situations.

- Corpus can be used to look critically at existing language teaching materials

- A further application of corpus in this field is their role in computer-assisted language education.

(4) WTCC (Waseda Tutorial Chinese Corpus)

A Chinese Corpus named WTCC (Waseda Tutorial Chinese Corpus) is based on three sources: The Grammatical Knowledge-base of Contemporary Chinese corpus by Beijing University (approx. 10000 words), HSK (Hanyu Shuiping Kaoshi, approx. 8000 words) and Japanese Basic University Educational Vocabulary corpus (approx. 3000 words). We have added translations in Japanese, pronunciation signs in Pinyin and difficulty level tags to these basic corpus sources and listed it on the class website as a Vocabulary Corpus. Students take computerized achievement tests based on this Vocabulary Corpus. Furthermore, we have added 8000 vocabulary words from the class textbook to this Vocabulary Corpus information to make CALL drills to evaluate the daily improvement of the students.

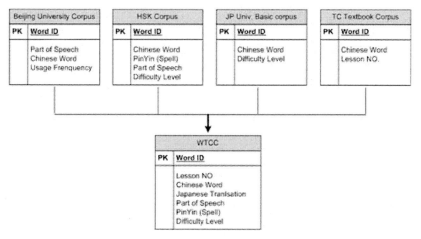

Fig. 6 WTCC Construction

The construction process consists of 5 steps:

A) Split sentences of TC textbook into words and morpheme.

B) Extract the POS, Pinyin spell and difficulty level information or each word by searching the Beijing University Corpus, HSK corpus and Japanese Basic University Educational Vocabulary corpus.

C) Select the target word from polyphonic or multi-meaning words based on the TC textbook.

D) Find the Japanese meaning of words using auto translation tools and manual confirmation.

E) Construct the corpus into an Internet based database.

Table 2 Corpus example of WTCC

ID		CN	JP	POS	Spell	Diff.
618		大	大きい	adj	da4	1
729		…过	…したことがある	pre.	guo4	1
730		参加	参加する	v	can1 jia1	1
731		多大	どのくらい、いくつ	num	duo1 da4	1
732		房间	部屋	n	fang2 jian1	1

7 33		高兴	喜ぶ	v	gao1 xing4	1
7 34		高兴	うれしい	a dj	gao1 xing4	1
7 35		功课	授業	n	gong1 ke4	3
7 36		号码	番号	n	hao4 ma3	2
7 37		机会	チャンス	n	ji1 hui4	1

1.3 Mobile phone situation in Japan

• From 2001, the 3-G Mobile Phone have been utilized. High speed communication has been supplied, which support multimedia file format, such as music, animation, television, and so on.

• In the year 2007, 3-G Mobile Phone user has been up to 88,100,000 in Japan.

• From 2003. 11 , AU has begun to supply Packet flat-rate system. It saved end users' money of packet communication. Nowadays all of mobile communication careers have utilized this kind of system.

Fig. 7 Japanese mobile phone situation

2. Corpus based Chinese language education support system sample

2.1 Sample 1—Corpus based listening CAI System

- Computer-assisted instruction system for self-teaching of discriminating Chinese four tones.
- Based on the analysis results of the characteristics of mistakes and errors made by Japanese students
- Gives more direct perception about Chinese four tones visually through illustrations and gives an effective guidance of four tones listening.
- Possible to carry out massive data analysis.

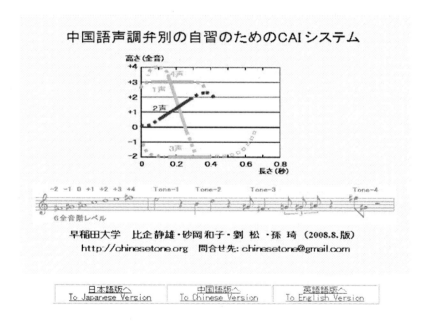

Fig. 8 listening CAI System

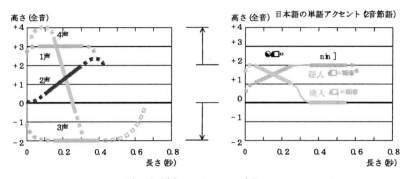

Fig. 9 Chinese tone and Japanese accent

3 modes—Screening Mode

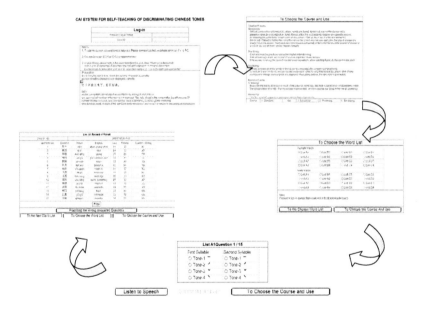

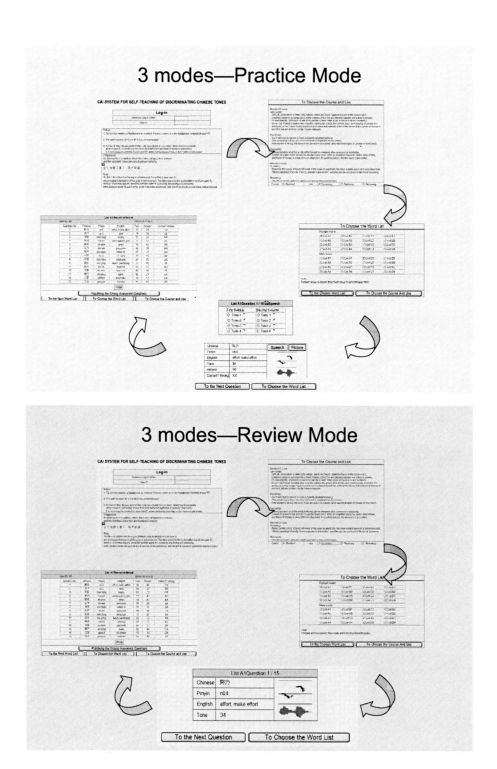

Fig. 10.3 Modes of CAI System

Experiment

- Participants: freshmen and sophomore students

- Period: 2 times in 2007. 12

- Number: 86 students took the first test
             104 students took the second test
             55 students took both tests.

- Contents: 4 tables of 15 bi-syllabic words
               During the two tests, part of students
               took online practice

Result of two syllable words

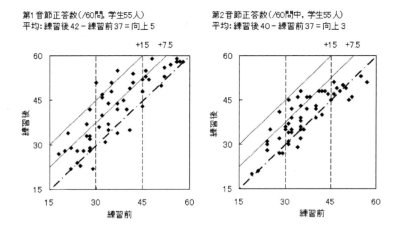

Fig. 11 Result of two syllable words

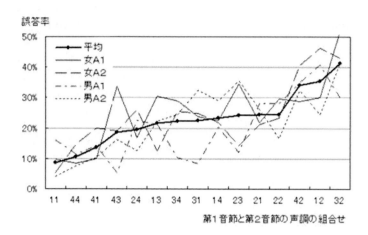

Fig. 12 Error rate of all combination of two-syllable tones.

Ongoing work

- Difficulty calculation of Tone discrimination

- Add the difficulty perimeter to Listening CAI System to enhance system efficiency and performance

2.2 Sample 2—Mobile Learning System

We have used B/S (Browser/Server) structure in this system. On the server side, a web server has been used as the bridge between the user and the database server. User requests are sent to the database server through forms from client interaction and the results returned. On the client side, no special software is required to ensure that most standard computers are ready to use the system.

The LAMP (Linux, Apache, MYSQL, PHP) mode has been used as the development environment in this system, which has many advantages: (a) the entire technology stack is available through open-source; (b) it works fine for most applications; (c) it is easy to learn; (d) it allows one to build a web application quickly; and (e) there are many open source code examples available that make creating an entire web application even easier. The combination of Linux, Apache, PHP and MYSQL has formed an ideal network database environment.

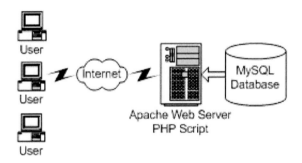

Fig.13 Development Environment

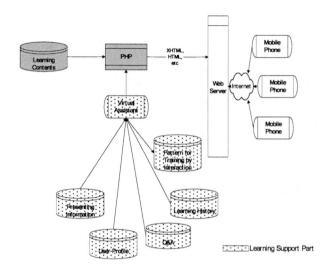

Fig.14 System Architecture

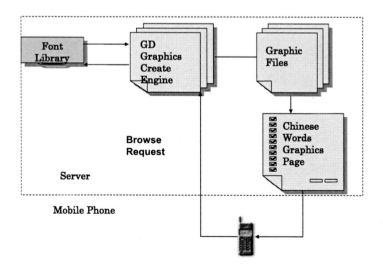

Fig.15 Scheme of font display

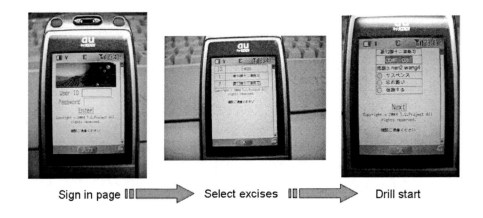

Sign in page → Select excises → Drill start

Fig.16 Screenshot of system

The mobile CALL-Drill and Web-Test tool has many advantages which distinguish it from conventional software. Among these advantages are: (a) a web-based user interface for students and teachers to facilitate system access, (b) a layer architecture to make authoring flexible, (c)a textbook based corpus to make drills more effective, (d)a ubiquitous environment to make drills accessible whenever, wherever users are.

3. Future Works

3.1 Corpus based listening CAI system

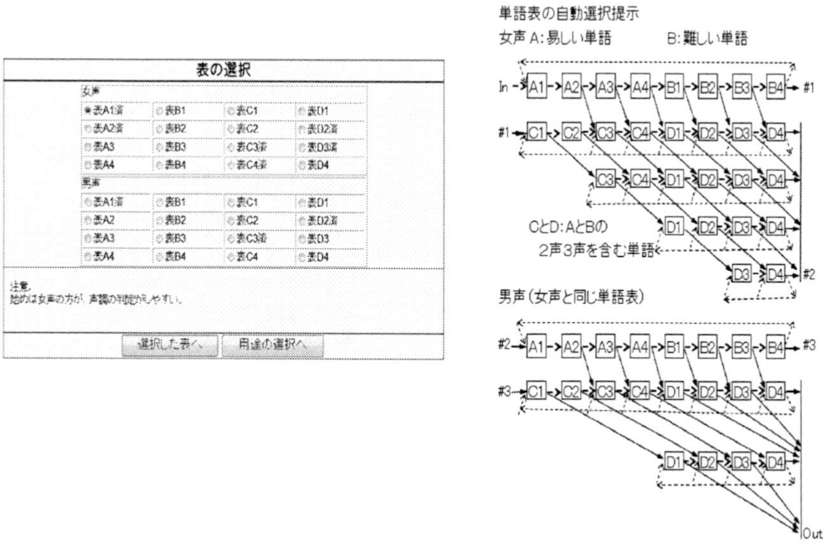

単語表の自動選択提示
女声 A：易しい単語　　　　　B：難しい単語

表の選択

女声
* 表A1番　　○表B1　　○表C1　　○表D1
○表A2番　　○表B2　　○表C2　　○表D2番
○表A3　　　○表B3　　○表C3番　○表D3番
○表A4　　　○表B4　　○表C4番　○表D4

男声
○表A1番　　○表B1　　○表C1　　○表D1
○表A2　　　○表B2　　○表C2　　○表D2番
○表A3　　　○表B3　　○表C3番　○表D3
○表A4　　　○表B4　　○表C4　　○表D4

注意。
始めは女声の方が、声調の判定がしやすい。

選択した表へ　　用途の選択へ

In → A1 → A2 → A3 → A4 → B1 → B2 → B3 → B4 → #1
#1 → C1 → C2 → C3 → C4 → D1 → D2 → D3 → D4
C3 → C4 → D1 → D2 → D3 → D4

CとD：AとBの
2声3声を含む単語　D1 → D2 → D3 → D4
D3 → D4 → #2

男声（女声と同じ単語表）

#2 → A1 → A2 → A3 → A4 → B1 → B2 → B3 → B4 → #3
#3 → C1 → C2 → C3 → C4 → D1 → D2 → D3 → D4
D1 → D2 → D3 → D4
Out

Fig.17 Automatic table selection for CAI system

In the next step, we plan to enhance the CAI system by Predicting rules of difficulty in discriminating bi-syllabic Chinese tones. The possible rules of predicting the observed data will include
1) Properties of confusion among voice pitch patterns in bi-syllabic tones,
2) Ill effects of kinds of consonants and vowels involved in each syllable,
3) Unclearness of the utterance of speech presented in the system, and
4) Degree of unfamiliarity of the words.
By applying these rules to the linear multi-regression model, the accuracy of predicting need to be confirmed.
Then, this rule will be utilized in any words to enhance our system's corpus. In future, the automatic table selection based on the difficulty predicted by the rule will also be planed to realize.

3.2 Mobile learning system

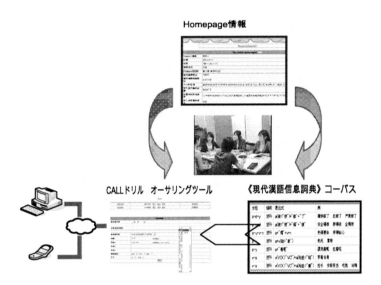

Fig.18 Future mobile learning system structure

In future versions, we plan to develop new functions as follows: an automatic registry system that adds new vocabulary used in the live tutorial lessons into the Corpus automatically. New vocabulary will be reported by the tutors after each class and will be registered in the server database. The server will refer to the WTCC Corpus database and if the word is already registered, the server will provide the educational data for further study. If the word is not yet registered, the server will acknowledge it as a new entry and make an additional entry. This additional information will be circulated among the students through their computers and mobile phones. The whole process will be automated to greater enhance learning for all users.

The Evaluation of Mobile Collaborative Systems

Valeria Herskovic [1], Sergio F. Ochoa [1], José A. Pino [1], Pedro Antunes[2]

[1] Department of Computer Science, University of Chile, Santiago, Chile

[2] Department of Informatics, University of Lisbon, Portugal

Abstract

This paper presents work continuing the research presented at the 2008 Summer Academy. Our focus is the evaluation of collaborative systems, particularly in scenarios involving mobile users. In the previous Academy, we presented a survey of existing evaluation methods and an initial proposal for mobile collaborative systems evaluation. In this paper, we propose an evaluation framework to organize the evaluation process, as well as our progress in the evaluation method for mobile collaborative systems.

The paper starts with a general setting: introducing collaborative work and why its evaluation presents many challenges. Some previous work in this area is summarized, and the main contributions are highlighted.

A second part deals with our proposal for an evaluation framework, i.e., a macro strategy that can be used to organize an evaluation process, and which can include several evaluation methods and tools. Its features are presented and discussed. Furthermore, the framework is used in two case studies.

The third and final part contains our specialized study of the evaluation of mobile collaborative work: its distinctive features and how to address evaluation. Our proposal, which is based on modeling collaborative work processes through MCM graphs, is also presented. Finally, an example of this evaluation is presented.

1   Introduction to Groupware

- Software designed to help people involved in a common task achieve their goals
- Basis for Computer Supported Collaborative Work (CSCW)
- Small groups – large groups
- Human factors are important
- People and MIS: "People must help the system perform well" (entering data…)
- People and CSCW: "The system helps people achieve their goals" (supporting needs…)
- Much software oriented to support individual tasks
- However, little support for group work or team work

2   The 3-C model

- Communication
- Collaboration
- Coordination

Varying degrees of each ingredient

3   Groupware systems classification
   [Ellis et al., 1991]

Time Space	Synchronous	Asynchronous
Co-located		
Distributed		

4   Why do we need to evaluate Groupware?

- Few groupware systems are evaluated
- Causes
  - Single user evaluation is not applicable
  - Expensive
  - Unavailable resources
  - Long-term

Which method to use?

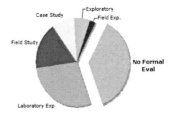

[Pinelle and Gutwin, 2002]

5 Motivation: How to evaluate?

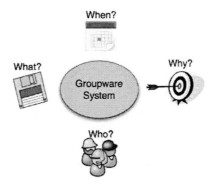

6 Evaluation methods: Requirements

- Individual realm: positive/negative contributions to individual goals, tasks and aspirations
- Group realm: communication, information sharing, interdependency, mutual adjustment and efficiency and effectiveness of the group
- Organizational domain: individuals and groups as perceived as contributing to a major endeavor set up by a common vision, mission and goals

7 No such method exists...

- Individuals' information is usually gathered at the cognitive level, focusing on events occurring on a time frame in the order of minutes or seconds;
- Group information is gathered at the interaction/communication level: activities in the range of several minutes and hours
- Information regarding organizational impact concerns much longer time frames, usually in the orders of days, months or years

8 Domains...

- One domain may be emphasized over the others
- E.g., organizational impact may be considered the most important one
- (In military aviation: organizational objectives overcome usability issues)

9   Further complexity...

- Results must be weighted by certainty, which depends on maturity of what is being evaluated
- At analysis: concepts only generate high uncertainty
- In implementation and deployment: having an actual system means higher certainty and precise results

10   Incremental evaluation

- Throughout the development cycle, from conception of the system, through its analysis, design, implementation, deployment and later lifetime
- At several stages, measures should be conducted to assess the system's current state, to correct deficiencies and improve design
- Variables with appropriate methods, e.g. satisfaction: analysis (focus groups), deployment (questionn.)

11   Incremental evaluation

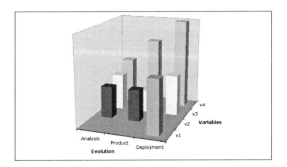

12   Evaluation strategy

- Incremental evaluation is conceptualized and probably idealized
- It assumes high level of control over the design and the evaluation
- In practice: design problems, change in context and ideas implies focus of evaluation may change in unexpected ways
- Methods themselves must evolve in time according to the evaluators' perceptions and goals

13 Pragmatic evaluation

- Multiple occurrences: evaluation may occur frequently, at any point in time
- Multiple forces: various stakeholders may have different impacts and be in conflict with the evaluation tasks
- Cost: repeated evaluations are expensive and time-consuming. Resources may be scarce or unavailable

14 How to evaluate? Mc-Grath's goals

- Field strategies: observations of realistic work
- Experimental strategies: artificial experiments aiming to study few activities with high precision
- Respondent strategies: sampling a large and representative population
- Theoretical strategies: theory to identify variables

15 What to evaluate? Pinsonneault & Kraemer's framework

- Contextual variables: personal, situational, group structure, task characteristics and technology characteristics
- Group process: decisional, communicational and interpersonal characteristics
- Outcomes: task-related outcomes and group-related outcomes
- Group process vs. Outcomes are very different:
- Group process: ethnography, analytical methods
- Outcomes: experiments (value creation)

16 What to evaluate? Neale et al.'s simplified framework

- Contextual variables
- Level of work coupling attained by the work group, which combines technology characteristics with group process characteristics

17 What to evaluate? Araujo et al.'s simplified framework

- Group Context
- System usability
- Level of collaboration
- Cultural impact

18 When to evaluate?

- Timing of evaluation parallels the maturity of the target system
- Formative evaluation: feedback (design ideas, usability problems, perceived satisfaction with the technology, possible focal points for innovation and alternative solutions)
- Summative evaluation: complete information on the developed groupware and its impact on users, group and organization.

19 Some selected methods

- 12 representative methods
- They have been used in practice
- Groupware Heuristic Evaluation (GHE)
- Groupware Walkthrough (GWA)
- Collaboration Usability Analysis (CUA)
- Groupware Observational User Testing (GOT)
- Human-Performance Models (HPM)
- "Quick-and-dirty" Ethnography (QDE)
- Performance Analysis (PAN)
- Perceived Value (PVA)
- Scenario-Based Evaluation (SBE)
- Cooperation Scenarios (COS)
- E-MAGINE (EMA)
- Knowledge Management Approach (KMA)
- Other techniques: Logging, Questionnaires, Interviews, Focus Groups, video recordings

20 Evaluation framework

- Macro strategy used to organize the evaluation process. Several methods and tools
- Method: procedure to apply evaluation tools
- Tool: single instrument

21 Variables (1)

- Generalization
- Precision
- Realism

(McGrath)

22 Variables (2)

- System detail: depth or granularity
- Scope: breadth

23 Variables (3)

- Invested time

Variables may be correlated
Practical approach: efficiency
Other variables?

24 Radar graph of evaluation variables

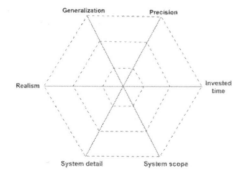

25 Performance levels (Reason)

Human performance:
- Situation
- Control

26 Situation dimension

- Routine: well-known activities

- Planned: plans and procedures
- Novel: problem analysis and decision-making activities

27 Control dimension

- Mechanical: predefined sequence imposed by the technology
- Human: technology does not impose any predefined action sequence
- Mixed: control opportunistically flows between the humans and the technology

28 Performance levels

- Role-based: routine tasks performed with mechanical control at the individual level
- Rule-based: tasks with some latitude of decision from humans but with constraints of a specific plan imposed by technology
- Knowledge-based: interdependent tasks performed by humans

29 Performance levels

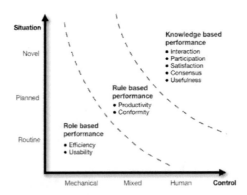

30 Role-based Scenario

- Data gathered at the individuals' cognitive level
- Events occurring during a time frame of minutes or seconds
- Laboratorial settings and considerable instrumentation
- System detail is high but scope is low

- High precision and generalizability

31 Role-based evaluation

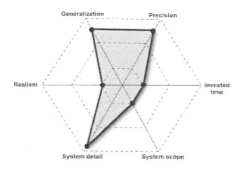

32 Rule-based scenario

- Data concerns several subjects who must coordinate themselves to accomplish a set of tasks
- Events occur between several minutes and hours
- System details being considered have large granularity (e.g., exchanged messages)
- Laboratorial settings using less instrumentation
- Invested time in this evaluation is higher

33 Rule-based evaluation

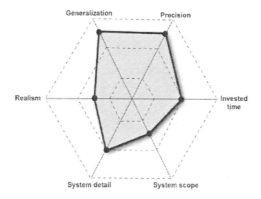

34 Knowledge-based scenario

- Data focused on the organizational impact
- Time frames usually in the orders of days, months or years
- Knowledge management, creativity and decision-making abilities
- System detail has coarse granularity
- Wide scope
- Qualitative settings
- Ex.: case studies, ethnographic studies

35 Knowledge-based evaluation

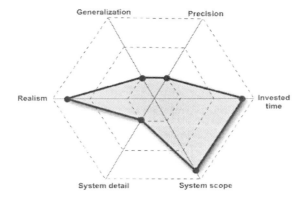

36 Evaluation lifecycle

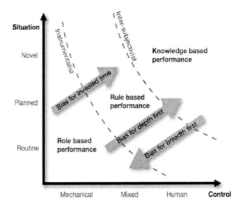

37 Evaluation lifecycle

- Instrumentalist strategy is mostly focused on accumulating knowledge through experimentation
- Inter-subjectivist strategy is concerned with interpreting the influences of technology on the individuals, groups and organization
- Implications on Level of Risk

38 Evaluation guidelines: Knowledge-based

- Variables pertaining to the organization and group
- Metrics:
Interaction
Consensus
Participation
Usefulness
Cost reduction

39 Evaluation guidelines: Role-based

- Variables pertaining to the individual
- Metrics:
Efficiency
Usability

40 Evaluation guidelines: Rule-based

- Variables in the middle of the extremes
- Metrics:
Organizational goals
(conformance to
regulations)
Group performance
(productivity)

41 Selected Methods

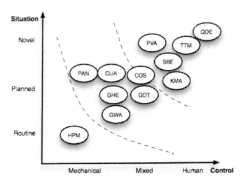

42 Guidelines

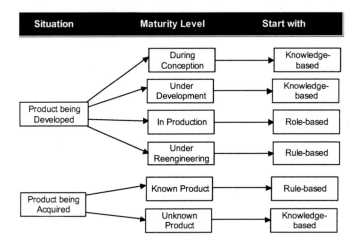

43 Case studies

- Two examples taken from real applications
- Both are products under development
- A: collaborative software requirements inspection tool
- B: mobile collaborative application to support construction examination activities

44 Case A: Software requirements inspection

- Synchronously complete a matrix with perceived correlations between software requirements and specifications
- Identify areas where software development has been underachieving
- Define priorities for further developing technical specifications
- A tool to support this activity

45 Case A: Knowledge-based evaluation

- Matrix of correlations: qualitative task. New pension system
- Complex: several reviewers involved who may have different perspectives about the software application, interpretations of what is involved in application development, hidden agendas, etc.
- 8x24 matrix and 192 potential correlations to evaluate
- COS: Cooperation Scenarios

46 Case A: Knowledge-based evaluation

- Two experiments. Afterwards: questionnaire with open questions about most positive and negative aspects
- Functionality
- Usability
- Negative aspects:
  - o Difficult to use by inexperienced users
  - o Bad performance
  - o Absence of graphical information
  - o Difficulties for obtaining a summary view of the negotiation

47 Case A: Role-based evaluation

- Optimize the shared workspace use
- Analytically devise different options for shared workspace use and predict their performance
- Keystroke-Level Model (KLM)
- Each user interaction may be converted into a sequence of mental and motor operators
- Individual execution times have been empirically established and validated by psychological experiments
- Three low-level functions were modeled:
  - o Locating correlations

- o Selecting correlations
- o Negotiating correlation values
- Alternative designs
- Comparison criterion based on execution time

48 Case A: Role-based evaluation

Design conditions	Design A	Design B
a) 3 users		9.8 s.
a.1) no scroll (75% probability)	5 s. MMPKKPKK	5 s. MMPKKPKK
a.2) scroll (25% probability)		11.3 s. MPKKMPKKPKKMMPKKPKK
b) 6 users		9.8 s.
b.1) no scroll (75% probability)	8.6 s. MPKPKMMPKKPKK	5 s. MMPKKPKK
b.2) scroll (25% probability)		11.3 s. MPKKMPKKPKKMMPKKPKK

49 Case A: Conclusions

- First evaluation: low precision and generalizability
- Perceive the value attributed by the Organization to the tool
- Second evaluation: fine-grained details
- Functionality offering the best performance
- Both cases: time invested was low
- System detail: low and high
- System scope: high and low

50 Case B: Construction Examinations

- Construction Contractor and sub-contracts
- Examinations to diagnose the progress to approve, reject or ask changes to built elements
- Inspectors are on the move and record the contingency issues
- Traditional way: paper blueprints

51 Case B: Construction Examinations

- Mobile shared workspace named COIN
- Digital blueprints

- Tablet PC
- Mobile collaboration among the users
- Sharing data between two mobile computing devices
- Two evaluations

52 Case B: Knowledge-based evaluation

- Scenario-based evaluation (SBE)
- During the software conception phase and during the design phase
- Two steps: (1) individual interviews to construction inspectors and (2) a focus group to validate the interview results

53 Case B: Knowledge-based evaluation

- During Conception phase:
- Three experienced construction inspectors
- Characterize work scenarios, specify and prioritize the functionalities
- Consensus on the types and features of the scenarios to be supported
- No consensus on the tool functionalities
- After interviews: results written and given to inspectors

54 Case B: Knowledge-based evaluation

- A week later: focus group (3 hr.)
- Most perceptions changed
- Functionalities:
- (1) transparent communication among inspectors
- (2) selective visualization of digital annotations
- (3) annotation filtering by several criteria
- (4) unattended and on-demand annotations synchronization
- (5) awareness of users availability and location

55 Case B: Knowledge-based evaluation

- During design process: a preliminary prototype
- SBE
- Interviews after training and use
- Identify functionalities…
- Long list of specific and detailed comments

- Issues were written and given back to the participants

56 Case B: Knowledge-based evaluation

- After a week: focus group session
- Categorize the inspectors' comments
- Critical features (12)
- Recommendable (17)
- Optional (8)
- Developers: key to match functionalities to needs
- Evaluation effort: double than on the first eval.

57 Case B: Rule-based evaluation

- After first version: COS evaluation
- Experience involved an area of 2000 mt2 approximately, deployed in two floors
- Two civil engineers: first with COIN, later without COIN. Observers.
- Interviews

58 Case B: Rule-based evaluation

Experience	Labels Found	Inspection - Elapsed Time	Annotations Review - Elapsed Time	Total Elapsed Time
With COIN	37	23 minutes	6 minutes	29 minutes
Without COIN	38	35 minutes	9 minutes	44 minutes

59 Case B: Rule-based evaluation

Experience	Time for Retrieving Blueprints	Time to Integrate Annotations	Time for Reporting Annotations	Tasks Creation - Elapsed Time	Contingencies Report - Creation Time
With COIN	< 2 minutes	< 1 minutes	< 2 minutes	35 minutes	< 2 minutes
Without COIN	Go to the main contractor's office	1 hour (*)	Go to the main contractor's office	40 minutes (*)	1 - 2 hours (*)

60 Case B: Discussion

- SBE evaluation: Evaluation effort <-> number of participants <-> degree of realism
- COS evaluation: Effort also increases with the number of participants. It could be reduced using agents
- COS: Realism? Testing scenario similar to real scenario

61 Conclusions on why groupware evaluation is so difficult

- Difficulties:
  1. Practical
  2. Theoretical
  3. Methodological
- Tradeoffs
- Variables
- Complex evaluation framework
- Performance levels
- Straightforward decision making process
- Maturity of the prototype being developed
- Development lifecycle
- Time available to evaluate the prototype

62 Mobile Collaborative Work

- Usually involves loosely coupled work:
  - o Autonomous work
  - o Sporadic on-demand collaboration

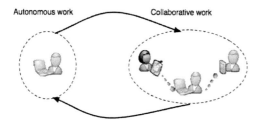

- Difficulties to analyze/model this type of work
- Importance of time and communication

63 Mobile Collaborative Work Characterization

- Characterization Criteria: Time
  - o Simultaneous: available to work synchronously
  - o Non-simultaneous: asynchronous work

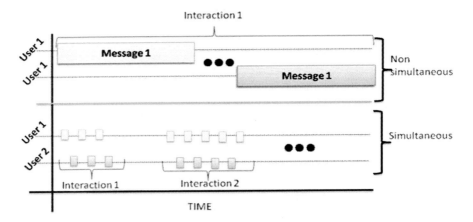

- Characterization Criteria: Reachability
  - o Reachable: communication channel + availability
  - o Unreachable: no communication channel, unavailability, or both

64 Classification of Collaboration Scenarios

- Using these two dimensions, four possible scenarios are created:

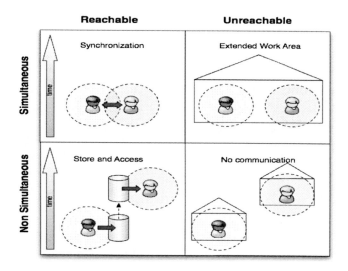

65 Transitions

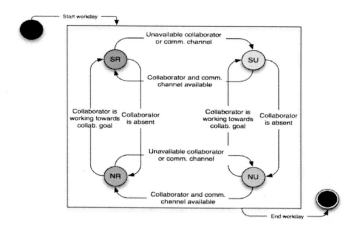

66 Mobile Collaboration Modeling (MCM) Language

Modeling elements in the MCM language

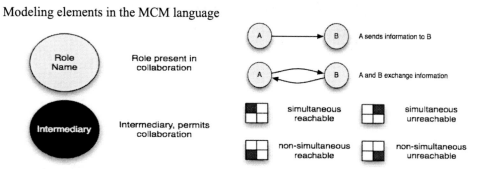

67 Constructing an MCM graph

Step	Goal	Variables
1	Identification of roles	System users, se ;
2	Role characterization	Location, Devic Working hou network
3	Identification of relationships	Information flows (inputs and outputs for each user)

68 Example: Application Scenario

- Urban search and rescue
  - Groups of firefighters
  - Goal: rescue victims as fast as possible
  - Tasks: search and rescue, rubble removal, build support for damaged infrastructure, assignment of resources, etc.

69 Identification of Roles

- We identify all the roles that participate in a search and rescue scenario

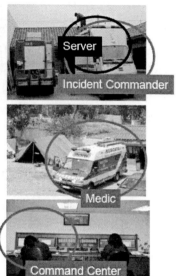

70 Role Characterization

- We characterize each of the identified roles
- Logistics, Team Captain, Entry Control, Medic, Incident Commander:
    - o Location: emergency and support area
    - o Devices: PDAs
    - o Network type: MANET
    - o Working hours: during emergency
- Dispatch Center Operator:
    - o Location: dispatch center
    - o Devices: Desktop computers
    - o Network type: Wired
    - o Working hours: 24/7

71 Identification of Relationships

- We identify information flow between actors. For example, the team captain:
  - Coordinates effort with other teams.
  - Reports progress.
  - Requests resources and receives replies from logistics.

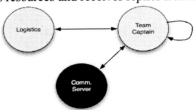

72 MCM Graph

- With this information, we can build a MCM graph for the situation

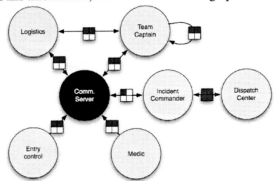

73 Mobile Application Requirements

- Flexibility
- Consistency and Availability
- Automatic connection
- Heterogeneity and Interoperability
- Communication
- Awareness
- Protection

74 Mobile Application Requirements

- Categorized according to each scenario and transition

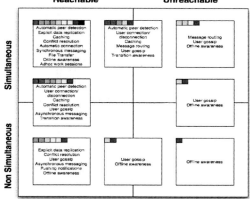

75 MCM Evaluation Method

Step	Goal	Actions
1	Create MCM graph	Observation, interviews, modeling
2	Determine general requirements	Specify which general requirements do not apply.
3	Generate test list	Software automatically generates checklist.
4	Conduct evaluation	Evaluate and mark which tests were successful, which weren't and any additional comments.

76 Graph Modeling & Analysis Tool

- Create and edit MCM Graphs
- Automatic verification to detect errors in analysis or construction
- Automatic generation of requirements checklist

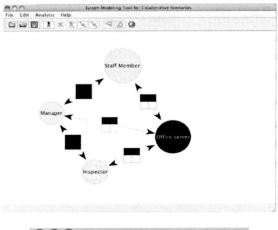

77 Evaluation

- MobileMap: tool to support firefighters at medium-sized emergencies
- 3 stages of development (so far)

78 Goal: PDA application to manage cartographical information in the field, support decision making

- Goal: PDA application to manage cartographical information in the field, support decision making
- One type of user was considered

- Collaborative capabilities
  - o Information exchange, points of interest
  - o File transfer

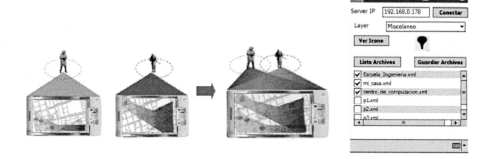

79 MobileMap v1: Analysis

ROLES	Location	Devices	Working Hours	Network Access
User	Emergency area	PDA	During emergency	Ad-hoc

RELATIONSHIPS	User
User	Yes; bidirectional information synchronization

User

80   MobileMap v1: Requirements

Requirements: User/User	Required?	Done?
Ad-hoc work sessions	X	No
Asynchronous Messaging		
Automatic Connection	X	No
Automatic peer detection	X	No
Caching	X	No
Conflict resolution	X	Yes
Explicit data replication	X	Yes
File transfer	X	Yes
Message routing	X	No
Pushing notifications		
Offline awareness	X	No
Online awareness	X	No
Synchronous messaging	X	No
Transition awareness	X	No
User connection/disconnection	X	No
User gossip	X	No

81   MobileMap v2: Overview

- Goals: usability, collaboration, support firefighters in decision making, add GPS support
- Still one user

82 MobileMap v2: Requirements

Requirements: User/User	Required?	Done?
Ad-hoc work sessions	X	No
Asynchronous Messaging		
Automatic Connection	X	No
Automatic peer detection	X	No
Caching	X	No
Conflict resolution	X	Yes
Explicit data replication	X	Yes
File transfer	X	No
Message routing	X	No
Pushing notifications		
Offline awareness	X	No
Online awareness	X	No
Synchronous messaging	X	No
Transition awareness	X	No
User connection/disconnection	X	No
User gossip	X	No

83 MobileMap v3: Analysis

- Goal: more collaborative features, major usability improvements

ROLES	Location	Devices	Working Hours	Network Access
Firefighter	Any	PDA	Any	GPRS, MANET
Operator	Alarms Ctr	PC	Continuous	Internet
Fire Truck	Any	PDA	During driving	GPRS
Server	Alarms Ctr	Server	Continuous	Internet

A to B RELATIONSHIPS	Firefighter	Operator	B Fire Truck	Server
Firefighter	X		X	X
Operator				X
Fire Truck	X		X	X
Server	X		X	

84 MobileMap v3: Analysis

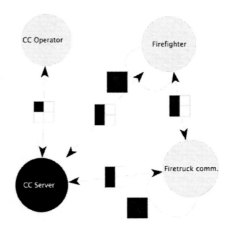

85 MobileMap v3: Requirements

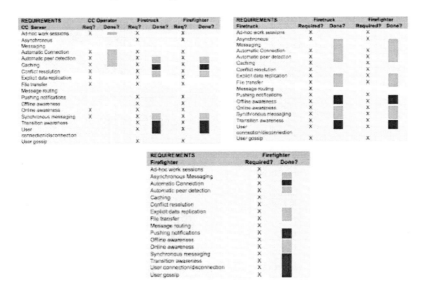

86 Current Work

- Applying evaluation method to hospital settings (positive results so far)
- Analyzing requirements for SU scenarios in depth

87 Future Work

- Evaluation of MobileMap
- Design of application for search and rescue
- Usability evaluation of MCM Language

88 Conclusions

- Help developers to clarify, analyze and design mobile groupware systems.
- Address coupling, work, collaboration patterns.
- Evaluation method
  o May use app in development at any phase (analysis, design, prototype, etc)
  o Low cost
- Limitations

Acknowledgments

This work was partially supported by grant No. 1080352 from Fondecyt (Chile) and grant No. R0308LAC004 from LACCIR.

Bibliography

- C.A. Ellis, S.J. Gibbs, G.L. Rein: Groupware – some issues and experiences. *Communications of the ACM* 34(1), 1991, 39-58.
- V. Herskovic, J.A. Pino, S.F. Ochoa, P. Antunes: Evaluation methods for Groupware. *Lecture Notes in Computer Science* 4715, 2007, 328-336.
- P. Antunes, V. Herskovic, S.F. Ochoa, J.A. Pino: Structuring Dimensions for Groupware Evaluation. *Unpublished manuscript-submitted for evaluation* 2009.
- J.A. Pino, V. Herskovic: Evaluating Collaborative Work. In N. Baloian, W. Luther, D. Söffker, Y. Urano (eds.): Multimodal Human-Machine Interaction in Different Application Scenarios. Logos Verlag, Berlin, Germany, 2008, pp. 1-30.

Seamless integration of formal and informal learning

Nelson Baloian
Department of Computer Science – Universidad de Chile
Blanco Encalada 2120, Santiago, Chile
nbaloian@dcc.uchile.cl

Gustavo Zurita
Department of Management and Information Systems – Universidad de Chile
Diagonal Paraguay 257, Santiago, Chile
gnzurita@fen.uchile.cl

Many computer systems have been developed in order to support various types of learning. Some systems support individual learning process, (Carbonell, 1970), while others support collaborative learning processes (Baloian, 2008). Recently, the wide-spread availability of mobile devices has led to an increased interest in the use of mobile computing to support formal and informal as well as individual and collaborative learning (Guerrero, 2003).

Despite initial success in the development and use of mobile applications, there is still the problem of integrating them more completely and seamlessly with a range of learning activities --whether they are in the classroom, in the field, or at home. The learning material created and/or used while working with one system cannot be easily transferred to another. Technology-supported learning takes place as an isolated event or a special occasion, rather than being integrated with a range of technology-supported activities, follow-ups or content. Because switching from one technology-supported learning system to another is either impossible or takes too much time, teacher-centered models, and those relying on "chalk and talk" often end up prevailing. As a consequence, the computer is still used by students mainly as an archive for electronic documents, and by teachers as a means to present multimedia documents instead of using it as a tool for enabling more advanced and involved forms of learning and collaborating.

This work proposes a set of common frameworks and approaches as a first step for integrating computer supported learning activities performed on various scenarios and settings.

Systems developed on this framework will certainly have more possibilities for integrating with each other and will be used in a more integrated and comprehensive way than most systems developed so far. In this way we are going to try to overcome a problem still faced by computer-based learning support systems: although they are very successfully supporting a certain, often isolated learning activities they can seldom be combined with other systems to enable more consistent and comprehensive support. This rises the costs of using more specialized computer support for all the different learning modes, inside and outside the classroom, since data generated with one system might not be usable in another and both teachers and learners have to work to adapt to a range of systems, interfaces and ways of interacting. In fact, according to the model of technology adoption of Briggs (1998), an integrated approach may also positively influence adoption of computer support for teaching/learning activities since users will have to learn just one user interface for many situations/scenarios, resulting in a greater comparative technological advantage.

Motivation

- Fragmentation of learning experiences with different tools in different contexts create a need for integration of classroom activities (structures) & learning "in the wild" (unstructures)

- Different interaction rules in each application

- Briggs' Technology Transition Model assumptions apply: potential users will adapt technology if its benefits outweigh its disadvantages (notably, the cost of learning how to use it), adjusted by the frequency of use.

- Lack of common data platform to exchange data

Workflow: PDA → Desktop → Whiteboard

Figure 1: The workflow nowadays includes dynamical changing of scenarios

Different Scenarios: does it necessarily mean different platforms?

During learning many different scenarios can occur (See Figure 2): One such scenario occurs inside the classroom while the teacher is presenting the learning material or the students are working individually or cooperatively. Another scenario arises outside the classroom when the students are working "in the field;" and a third occurs when students are working at their homes. Figure 2 illustrates the cycle of technologically-supported learning scenarios that are key to this project as follows:

A)   The teacher creates and/or shows the learning material to the students using an electronic blackboard; this can also be done collaboratively with the students. Students can receive this material and work with it on their PCs, Tablet PCs or handhelds and work individually or collaboratively.

B)   The students go "in the field" to collect data and/or to undertake other field-related learning tasks. They are able to do this using their mobile devices either individually or collaboratively, and are supported in their activities with an ad-hoc network

C)   Students work on the material, preparing a presentation or homework on their computer at home. Then they present this material to the rest of class in the classroom (thus returning to the first scenario A).

This integration will be done at several levels, including the Data level, for which a common data model for learning materials based on LOM and XML will be applied, at the communication level, for which we will adapt a framework for easily and robustly communicating software running on different type of devices (PCs, PDAs, Tablet PCs, smart phones) and human-computer interaction level, for which we will develop a consistent set of interfaces based on gestures for touch sensitive input devices of various characteristics and different sizes

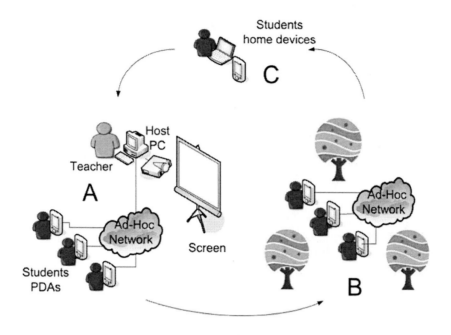

Figure 2: The cycle of technologically-supported learning scenarios

Research Questions

- Is it possible to develop an integrated interaction model across platforms?

- Widgets? Gestures? Both?

- Which type of learning activities can be modeled in this way?

- Can we describe them with a pattern language?

Research Proposal

1. Identify learning scenarios which can be supported by this type of learning activities

2. Describe it formally (find the right language to describe them)

3. Chose 2-3 specific example to develop

4. Evaluate the scenarios

Requirements: A Technical platform

- To adopt/adapt or developed a platform which offers:
    - o a learner-centered design based on patterns for interaction design of educational technologies (PDAs, pen-tablets & whiteboards),
    - o a collaborative environment for learning and teaching,
    - o a seamless integration of interaction design inside and outside of formal learning environments.

Learning with patterns and Learning patterns

- A good scenario?
    - o Teacher explains a pattern: (for example, columns of neo-classical architecture)
    - o Students go „out" to collect examples of instantiations of this pattern (congress palace, national library, this may also include geographical information)
    - o They process the gathered material in their homes
    - o They show their findings to the class, share.
- The Software: Creating a pattern

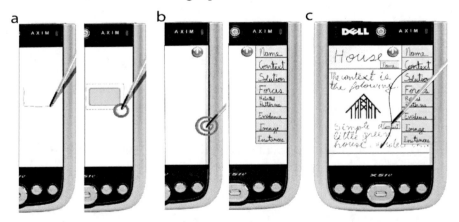

Figure 3: Creating patterns

Using PDAs or Tablet-PCs, the teacher creates a first a list of the components a pattern will have, defining a template in order to pass to the students. In order to create a pattern, a user draws two lines of a rectangle in one stroke. This gesture is recognized by the system and a complete rectangle will appear on that place representing the new pattern (see figure 3a). Double-clicking on the rectangle the system enters into the mode where the components of the pattern are defined. The ways to specify the content of a component are: a) hand-written text 3b) sketching, 3c) images (or icons) from a file, d) typed text entered with the virtual keyboard or the built-in text recognizer of PDA or Tablet-PC). For ending the addition of the component a horizontal line should be drawn at the bottom. Before starting the addition of the next component the name of the already created should be selected from the list the teacher has provided. For this, the user has to double-click on the grey line on the right border of the screen (see figure 3b). This will show the list of the components labels already created. One of them should be selected (Figure 3c).

- Actions on patterns

    o **Browse and modify the pattern:** A pattern is a column of (graphic) elements separated by horizontal lines. Elements can be browsed with a scrolling function. An icon containing the name of the element is displayed at the bottom-right corner. By clicking on this icon the element can be modified. A pattern can be modified by its author or group of authors. Patterns created by the teacher can be browsed, but not edited by the students.

    o **"Cloning" patterns:** Students record their findings and create new patterns which are modified "clones" of them which will inherit the structure. They can add or modify descriptions of its components.

    o **Instantiating patterns:** Instantiations of certain pattern will consist of photographs or handmade sketches of a certain object found which complies with the pattern definition. The nodes corresponding to the instantiations or clones can be browsed and edited.

    o **Linking patterns:** An essential aspect of working with patterns is to understand and to manage relations between them. The system supports this by allowing the definition of relations between two or more patterns. This is done by handwriting a line from a node identifying a pattern to the node of another. This relation will be "understood" by the system, creating a logical link between them for easing the navigation among linked node.

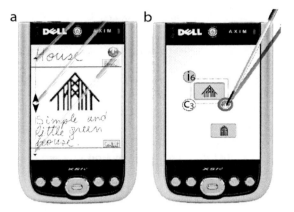

Figure 4: Instantiating and Linking patterns

- Synchronizing patterns

  o Teacher can distribute an initial pattern to the students so that they can search for instantiations and/or generate new ones based on them. Since each pattern is saved as separate file, this can be done by usual means over any available network.

  o Students will additively synchronize the set of patterns they have if the patterns, instantiations and clones correspond to the ones distributed by the teacher as a single set. This will happen automatically every time two students' PDAs get connected by a wireless ad-hoc network (see Figure 5a, 5b and 5c).

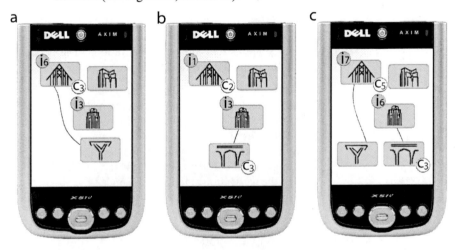

Figure 5: additive synchronizing of patterns, a) and b) show the content of two users before synchronizing, c) the content of both after the synchronization.

o   Students may also exchange patterns selectively and work collaboratively on the same pattern by synchronously editing it. This can be
achieved by putting together the students' PDAs and activating the
IRDA communication feature between them. This will create a
common working area where they can edit the pattern synchronously.

- Comparing patterns

   o   Teacher can distribute an initial pattern to the students so that they
   can search for instantiations and/or generate new ones based on
   them. Since each pattern is saved as separate file, this can be done
   by usual means over any available network.

   o   Students will additively synchronize the set of patterns they have if
   the patterns, instantiations and clones correspond to the ones distributed by the teacher as a single set. This will happen automatically
   every time two students' PDAs get connected by a wireless ad-hoc
   network

   o   Students may also exchange patterns selectively and work collaboratively on the same pattern by synchronously editing it. This can be
   achieved by putting together the students' PDAs and activating the
   IRDA communication feature between them. This will create a
   common working area where they can edit the pattern synchronously.

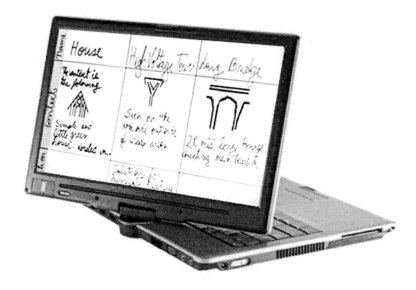

Figure 6: Comparing patterns

UML Diagram with System Overview

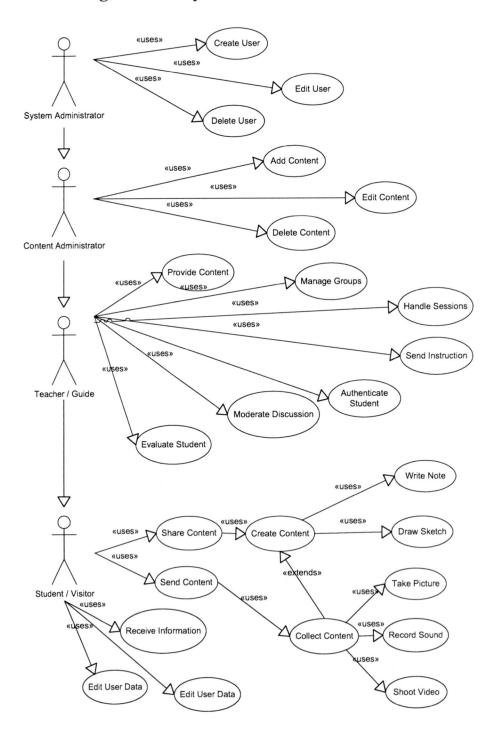

Actors:

> » System & Content Administrator
>
> » Teacher / Guide
>
> » Student
>
> » Student Group (in Shared Screen Mode)

Main functionalities:

> » Create written and graphics content
> (take notes, draw sketches)
>
> » Collect audiovisual materials or content
> (take pictures, shoot movie, interview people)
>
> » Exchange content with teacher & peers:
> synchronous, addressed to an individual,
> a group or the whole group on a distributed,
> but shared screen (shared screen mode)
>
> » Receive instructions (may be asynchronous,
> prepared before outdoors activities)

System Architecture:

> » Decentralized architecture with MANET, no central
> server, dynamic participants list
>
> » Replicated architecture : All users have their own copy
> of the data and the application
>
> » State-based synchronization: The current state of the ob-
> ject (and not event) is used for synchronization
>
> » Trans-Platform : Object exchange between java and
> .NET using XML
>
> » Support for gesture-based interaction: Providing a reus-
> able library for gesture recognition

- Current Supported Gestures (Easily extensible)

  » **Flipping to next/previous slide:** By moving the stylus from one vertical edge of the PDA screen to the other, the user flips between different pages on the same level.

  » **Creating a node:** By drawing half a rectangle, the user creates a node. Handwritten or other content within the rectangle will be included and stored within that node. These nodes are by default private but may be shared with other students' PDAs or shown on the interactive whiteboard.

  » **Deleting a node:** A node may be deleted by drawing an "x" in one stroke across the boundaries of the node on the screen.

  » **Sharing a node:** The content of a node may be shared with other students or the teacher. This is done by dragging the node to the icon of a single participant or a group of participants. Dragging the node to an icon of the whiteboard sends the node to the whiteboard.

  » **Linking nodes:** Two nodes may be linked by drawing a straight line from one node to another. In this way, a network of nodes may be created.

  » **Saving structured content:** By moving the stylus from the top edge of the PDA screen to the bottom edge, the network of nodes is saved. The content of the generated documents is organized as a concept map, providing flexibility to organize & merge individual nodes.

Interaction Design Patterns

- First in architecture (Alexander 1977)
    - » Communicate design problems & solutions
    - » Not too general & not too specific, to use "a million times over, not doing it the same way twice"
- Software engineering (Gamma 1997)
    - » Proxy: surrogate for an object to control access
    - » Observer: when one object changes state, its dependents are notified

- Interaction Design Patterns
    - » Reusable standard solutions to common problems in interaction design
    - » Components simplify the development of consistent and ergonomic multiple user interfaces
    - » Developed for desktop GUI and web design, mobile applications, only few on learning environments

Conclusions

- Based on theoretical learning concerns and the need to provide a consistent framework to support learning activities in formal and informal settings, we have developed a software prototype for PDAs and interactive whiteboards.
- PATTERNS may play an interesting role in Computer Supported Learning:
    - » Learning with patterns,
    - » Patterns for learning

References

- N. Baloian, J. A. Pino, H. U. Hoppe, (2008) Dealing with the Students' Attention Problem in Computer Supported Face-to-Face Lecturing, Educational Technology & Society, 11(2), pp. 192-205

- Briggs, R., Adkins, M., Mittleman, D., Kruse, J., Miller, S., Nunamaker, J.F. (1998), A technology transition model derived from field invesitigation of GSS use aboard the U.S.S. Coronado. Journal of Management Information Systems 15, (3), pp. 151-195.

- Carbonell, J.R; (1970), AI in CAI: An artificial intelligence approach to computer-assisted instruction. IEEE Transactions on Man-Machine Systems, 11, (4), pp. 190-202.

- Guerrero, L.A., Pino, J.A., Collazos, C., Inostroza, A., Ochoa, S. (2004), Mobile Support for Collaborative Work". 10th. International Workshop on Groupware (CRIWG'2004), San Carlos, Costa Rica. Sept. 5-9, pp. 363-375. Springer LNCS 3198, Berlin Heidelberg, Germany.

Geocollaboration in Learning Scenarios

Gustavo Zurita

Department of Management and Information Systems – Universidad de Chile

Diagonal Paraguay 257, Santiago, Chile

gnzurita@fen.uchile.cl

Nelson Baloian

Department of Computer Science – Universidad de Chile

Blanco Encalada 2120, Santiago, Chile

nbaloian@dcc.uchile.cl

ABSTRACT: Research increasingly indicates that the inability of students to apply the concepts and content learned inside the classroom in real situations is, in many cases, because teaching activities have been taken out of context. Therefore, learning can be reinforced, supplemented, instantiated or understood through concrete activities conducted in contexts and real scenarios outside the classroom. Localization is relevant in association with learning activities. Current developments, improvements and enhancements (integrated cameras, Bluetooth, GPS, Wi-Fi, IRDA) in mobile devices, combined with contextual and locational support computing, are contributing to the recent development of new mobile learning applications for learning outside of the classroom: situated learning. Several investigations of informal learning and mobile learning support applications for learning outside the classroom without the benefits of localization have had diverse positive outcomes. Nonetheless, only a few investigations include the use of location–based services using GPS and map visualization in students' mobile devices that contain functionalities to use localization to associate, reinforce and achieve innovative teaching practices. However, there is no investigation in literature proposing situated learning applications: (a) that instantiate university educational content; (b) or propose methodologies or conceptual frameworks to help identify which university educative content can be better supported; (c) or what benefits localization through geographic information systems offers in the different modes of collaboration in time and space (geocollaboration); (d) or what devices contextualize and localize georeferenced content that must be used in different pedagogical practices (problem-solving, feedback, assessment, reflection, etc.) that combine activities in and outside of the classroom to generate and create knowledge and learning.

The goals of this research are: To design a conceptual framework to identify types and characteristics of university educational content that can be better supported by situated-learning activities (contextualization and localization of learning activities), collaborative activities (using geo-collaborative tools) and constructivist activities. To identify and evaluate the different modes of geocollaboration in time and space that may be applicable to teaching activities and practices among students, the professor and the students-professor.

The teaching activities and practices will be associated with educational considerations that require contextualization and physical localization of places, the geo-referencing of data and information by students outside the classroom (situated learning supported by mobile devices), supported by the professor inside the classroom using a system that displays the georeferenced information of students on a map on a screen. The state of the art in situated learning applications is expected to be conceptualized and analyze all variants and possibilities of geocollaborative systems providing support to collaborative and constructivist educational activities to be performed in real contexts while the data and information necessary are georeferenced. This conceptualization will be specified in a conceptual framework that will lead to diverse activities being conducted outside of the classroom, inside the classroom and a combination of both.

1 Situated learning supported by Mobile Devices

- GPS combined with contextual computing contribute to the development of new mobile learning applications: mobile situated learning

  - o new possibilities into the real learning scenarios
  - o location and context information brings important features to the tasks and activities learning of the students
  - o location and/or can determine his or her activity/task
  - o Many collaboration modes enhanced the learning activities

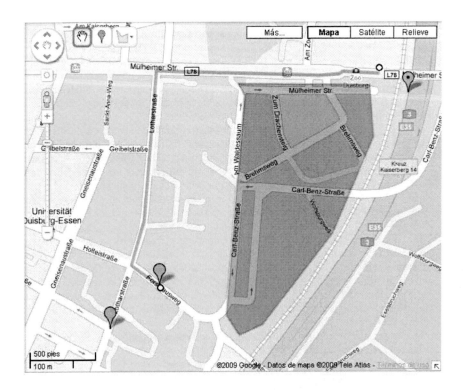

2 Advantages of georeferencing in learning

- Data and information georeferenced in learning scenarios would potentially offer advantages:

  - tailoring educational content to a specific location
  - content generation and adaptation resulting in a more personalized learning experience.

This is a video of MIT's Enviromental Detectives game extracted from:
http://www.youtube.com/watch?v=goPTuUMu_oc

- The features of georeferenced data and information have been recently explored in learning activities and mainly in educational games. Categorized in two types:

  - using tracking devices to support collaboration,
  - using the location as event triggers

  - Some research includes the use of GPS through visual maps in the mobile devices of students, enabling them to use localization in associating, strengthening and achieving innovative learning practices

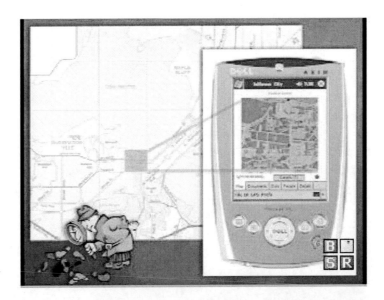

○ The professor can simultaneously track the movement of students on a map in real time, displayed visually on screens, later analyze the movements by students during the activity

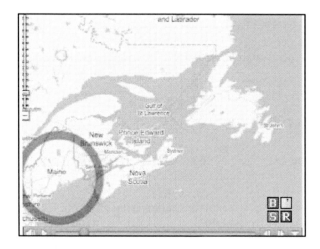

3. Example

Citation from:

Supporting Mobile Language Learning outside Classrooms

Hiroaki Ogata, Chengjiu Yin, Rosa G. Paredes, *Yasuko Oishi and Takahito Ueda*
J., Nobuji A. Saito, and Yoneo Yano *International Students Center,*
Dept. of Information Science and Intelligent *Tokushima University*
Systems, Tokushima University *oishi@cue.tokushima-u.ac.jp*
ogata@is.tokushima-u.ac.jp *ueda@pm.tokushima-u.ac.jp*

Proceedings of the Sixth International Conference on Advanced Learning Technologies (ICALT'06) 2006, cp. p. 169.

- At the beginning of the class, teachers are giving some tasks to overseas students
- The student is asking the direction for the destination at a convenience store.
- The student arrived at the final destination and carries out the task by interview.
- During the trip, the teacher gets the location of each student and gives an instruction.
- After the trip, the teachers reflect on their results and learn lessons.

4. Benefits of Georeferentation in Learning

- Generally, the results of these investigations indicated that the georeferenced data and information help contextualize the learning activities conducted in real physical locations:

  - real experience on learning activities
  - association of the space with the creation of knowledge
  - more enriching in knowledge creation than what occurs inside the classroom, attain high levels of motivation, association of concepts, etc..

5. Opportunities of research

- However, these investigations do not account for several relevant aspects that must be taken into consideration in situated learning:

  - previous research largely dealing with the basic and high school educational content, to instantiate games and the capacity for solving general problems in real contexts

    ○   Learning content. University educational content will be used Geology, Architecture, Social sciences. (anthropology, psychology, sociology), Management, Computer Science, …

- There are not any conceptual framework which associated georeferenced data and information in situated learning scenarios

- **Conceptual framework of situated learning applications.** The analysis of the different modalities and advantages of the contextualization and localization of georeferenced data and information in collaborative situated learning applications and complementary activities inside the classroom will be conceptualized in a conceptual framework

- The situated learning application does not use the advantage of GIS and collaboration: geocollaboration

- **Advantages of using geographic information systems (GIS):** Georeferencing data and information in association with real maps which are represented visually:

    ○   the association of diverse data and information: texts, images, files, etc.
    ○   recording the history of routes
    ○   making notes on real geographic zones
    ○   determining routes
    ○   comparing different notes made in different locations

- **The advantages of collaborative data georeferencing (geocollaboration).** The methods of collaboration that can be used in situated learning applications include two important participants: the students and the professor.

The students may work collaboratively

Time/ Space	Same Time	Different Time
Same Place	*	*
Different Place	*	*

The professor may work collaboratively with students:

Time/ Space	Same Time	Different Time
Same Place		Analyzing activities performed by students
Different Place	feedback, tracking, giving intrucctions	

- Interfaces must use visually, gestures and sketches metaphors based on touch-screen mobile devices
  - o The applications or prototypes proposed by the different situated learning activities include the construction of interfaces based on menus, buttons, scrolls, etc
  - o Use the advantages of using touch-screen gestures and sketches of mobile devices (Tablet-PC, PDAs). Using gestures and sketches considerably fosters human-computer interaction and they have not been included in any of the applications reviewed in the literature

6. Visually Human-Computer Interface based on gestures

- Assigning participants to working sessions: The facilitator assign participants to working sessions, which are represented in the user-interface by rectangles (Group 1 and Group 2). These rectangles are easily created and managed by gestures based on the touch-screen system of the devices. Participants are visually represented by a visual icon labeled with his/her name.

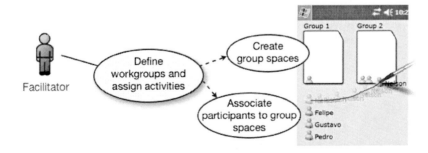

- Setting the participants' focus of attention. All participants can be re-arranged on real time at any working session by dragging them to the corres-pondent space: Group 1 or Group 2 working on the design of a house nd car respectively.

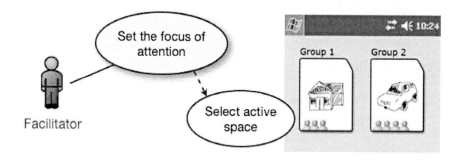

- Participants' restricted self- organization, working together in the only active space georeferencing data and information collaboratively. A label-pont is created by a double click over the map in order to add more information about it.

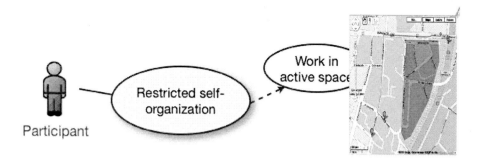

- Pen-based gestures; Editing, deleting, rotating, resizing and sketching over a previously taken photograph used as background for the sketches.

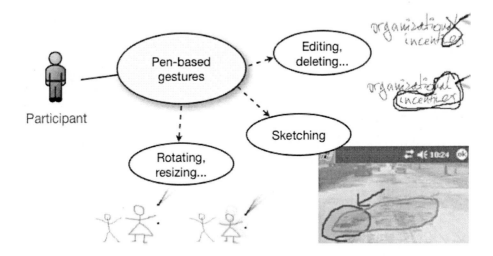

Social Impact of IT: examples in Public Participation, Strategic Alignment and Open Source|

Jens Hardings[1], Alejandro Cataldo[1], Ana Fernández[1]

[1] Pontificia Universidad Católica de Chile
{jhp, ajcatald, asfernand}@ing.puc.cl

Abstract. In this work we show three examples of social impact of Information Technology. The first one proposes the usage of trust and reputation models in public participation, allowing a change from a, possibly wide-scale, top-down tradition, to a truly participative and meritocratic approach based on the usage of information systems gathering direct and indirect information related to trust and reputation. The second example shows a prototype of a simple model to obtain feedback about the strategic alignment of IT in SMEs, using a fast and lightweight process. A final example uses an open source based approach to technology transfer in a governmental IT planning.

Keywords: public participation, strategic alignment, open source, social impact, information technology

AGENDA

- Motivation
- Reputation Systems
- Reputation Metric
- Application Case
- Conclusions

MOTIVATION

- Citizen participation is essential in democracy.
- It is very important to generate spaces for participation.
- Citizens do not have a direct relationship with their authorities.
- Citizens can not express their opinions.
- Good ideas loose the chance to be used as future policies.

A Collaborative System Based on Reputation for Wide-Scale Public Participation

Ana Fernández Ontiveros, Jens Hardings
Pontificia Universidad Católica de Chile

AGENDA

- Motivation
- Reputation Systems
- Reputation Metric
- Application Case
- Conclusions

INTERNET TODAY

- Globalization and the Internet.
- Crescent popularity of virtual communities.
- Decentralised information systems.
- Interaction with unknown people.

REPUTATION SYSTEMS

- Help establish mutual trust between agents by assigning reputation.
- Use past transaction feedback.
- Assumption: Past behaviour is an indicator of future behaviour.
- High reputation ⇧ trustworthy agent

OPPORTUNITY

- The promise of IT in politics is to:
  - Allow every citizen to express his opinion in every topic relevant to him.
  - Make a close interaction between citizens and elected politicians.

I've said!

The one who rules here is

Politics is based on **toleranc e**, **dialogue** and **consens**

AGENDA

- Motivation
- Reputation Systems
- Reputation Metric
- Application Case
- Conclusions

REPUTATION SYSTEMS

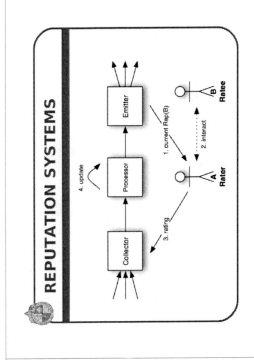

REPUTATION SYSTEMS

- Register the behaviour of participants.
- Make such information available for other users.

REPUTATION SYSTEMS

- Example

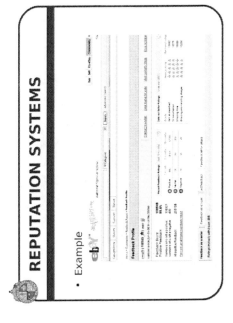

REPUTATION SYSTEMS

- Example

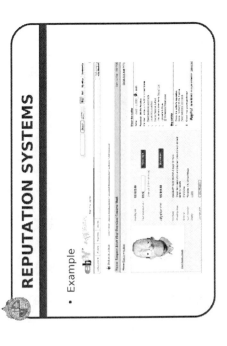

REPUTATION METRIC

- The metric of a reputation system is the way the reputation of an agent is calculated.

- The proposed metric is based in:
  - Level of recent activity
  - Ratings from others

REPUTATION METRIC

- Level of recent activity:
  - Participating Reputation (R_P):
    - Whenever a user participates in the system he should be rewarded
    - A good way to measure the participation is by the relative contribution factor
    - C_i^P as the relative contribution factor for participation for $0 \leq C_i^P \leq 1$ $i = \{1,...,m\}$ and

$$R_P(a) = \sum_{i=1}^{m} \beta_i C_i^P(a)$$

AGENDA

- Motivation
- Reputation Systems
- **Reputation Metric**
- Application Case
- Conclusions

REPUTATION METRIC

- Level of recent activity

  - $R_P(a)$ is the participating reputation of agent a
  - $R_L(a)$ is the leadership reputation of agent a
  - $T(a)$ is the residential time of agent a in the system
  - k is a discount factor between 0 and 1

$$F(a) = R_P(a) \cdot R_L(a) \cdot k^{T(a)}$$

REPUTATION METRIC

- Ratings from others:
  - Peer Reputation (R_Q)
    - Users in the system can be qualified by others for a performed activity
    - An agent will be rated and given a positive or negative qualification $Q = \{1, 0\}$ respectively
    - Each user will have an ordered list to store his last h qualifications
    - Q_a is the time-sorted list of qualifications assigned by others where $Q_a[1]$ is the oldest rate and $Q_a[h]$ is the most recent

REPUTATION METRIC

- The trust of user a is then defined as:

$$Trust(a) = \frac{R_Q(a)^{1+F(a)} - 1}{R_Q(a) - 1}$$

REPUTATION METRIC

- Level of recent activity:
  - Leadership Reputation (R_L)
    - Certain users have the ability to generate participation in others and such ability should be rewarded
    - C_i^L as the relative contribution factor for leadership for $0 \le C_i^L \le 1$ $i = \{1, ..., n\}$ and

$$R_L(a) = \sum_{i=1}^{n} \delta_i C_i^L(a)$$

REPUTATION METRIC

- Ratings from others:
  - Peer Reputation (R_Q)
    - Agents will behave more probably like they did in last transactions
    - Therefore we chose a metric that computes a weighted sum of all ratings
    - The older a rating is, the less it influences the current reputation

$$R_Q(a) = \sum_{j=1}^{h} \frac{Q_a[j]}{(h-j+1)^2}$$

AGENDA

* Motivation
* Reputation Systems
* Reputation Metric
* Application Case
* Conclusions

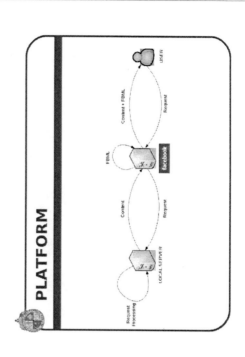

REPUTATION METRIC

Evolution of trust for different users

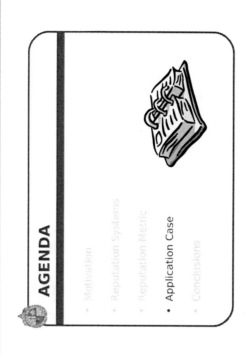

PLATFORM

PLATFORM

* Using a well-known social network has the advantage of a fast and massive distribution.

* We built the application in the popular social network Facebook.

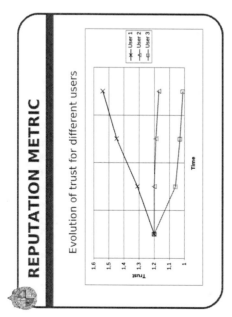

APPLICATION CASE

APPLICATION CASE

- The experiment was developed in the student union of the Engineering School at my university.
- An instance of participation for students with its representative entity.
- Purpose:
  - Identification of good ideas from students to become future projects.
- Application link
  - http://apps.facebook.com/participacai

Agenda

- Motivation
- Test development
- Test application
- Conclusions

Diagnosis of IT usage in SMEs - Alignment

- Alejandro Cataldo
- Jens Hardings

Biggest investment item for SMEs is IT

Item	Industrial	Comercial	Servicios	Otros
Terrenos y propiedades	14,9	14,8	10,7	18,7
Construcciones	33,4	27,7	26,4	36,8
Maquinarias y Equipos	46,2	27,5	35,5	45,8
Vehículos	41,5	28,3	14,6	44,6
Licencias	4,2	5	10,4	10
Computadores - software	45,8	44,9	63,6	58,7
Capital de trabajo	17	24,5	30,6	24,2
Capacitación	20,8	20,5	41	29,9

Fuente: Cuarta Encuesta Longitudinal de PyME, noviembre 2007 - junio 2008, CIP/UAI

Evidence shows that SMEs do not achieve optimal use of IT

Smaller organizations often implement IS in a less than optimal way

Milind Kumar Sharma and Rajat Bhagwat (2006)

Good alignment is important for good enterprise performance

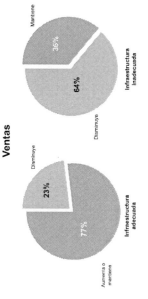

Ventas

77% / 23%

Infraestructura adecuada

Aumenta o mantiene

Disminuye

64% / 36%

Infraestructura inadecuada

Mantiene

Disminuye

Alignment is achieved when IT supports the strategy

Biggest investment item for SMEs is IT

Item de inversión	Sector			
	Industria	Comercio	Serv.Financ.	Otros
1. Terrenos	9.7%	7.6%	12.5%	13.1%
2. Construcciones / Ampliaciones	24.3%	18.0%	24.3%	24.0%
3. Maquinarias / Equipos no computacionales	37.5%	24.9%	10.3%	36.4%
4. Vehiculos	37.3%	32.9%	12.3%	30.2%
5. Licencias / Royalty	5.1%	3.2%	0.4%	3.3%
6. Computadores / Software	33.3%	34.4%	53.1%	38.5%
7. Capital de Trabajo	21.2%	24.4%	22.4%	21.9%
8. Capacitación	14.4%	14.3%	26.7%	18.7%
9. Otro	1.5%	2.1%	2.7%	0.2%
10. Ninguno	28.0%	36.7%	29.0%	23.6%

Fuente: Bravo & Lima. Informe final: Primera encuesta longitudinal A pequeñas y medianas empresas. 2008.

Problem: SMEs need to align their IT *but does not know how to do it*

"SMEs are therefore under increasing pressure to employ IT/IS effectively in order not only to maintain their competitive positions but also simply to survive"

Reza, 2006

Proposed Solutions

Diagnostics
- Measurement
  - Matching
    - Simpler
    - Operatier problems and less information
  - Moderation
- Check-Up
  - ISCUM
  - Tagliavini
  - Ravarini
    - More complete
    - Have little support and incomplete bibliography

SISP
- Designed for big enterprises

Procedimiento: Alineamiento del Perfil Estratégico

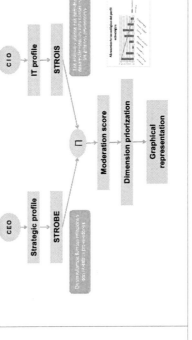

CEO — Strategic profile — STROBE

CIO — IT profile — STROIS

∏

Moderation score

Dimension priorization

Graphical representation

Integrating existing methods into a new test

Test outcomes

- Strategic profile alignment (8 Dimensions)
  - Strategic priorities
  - Profile alignment
- Process analysis through moderation (12 Processes)
  - Process priority
  - Process alignment
- Process analysis Tagliavini (12 Processes)
  - Diagnosticos x Procesos
  - Terapias para procesos

Graphical representation

Matrix representation

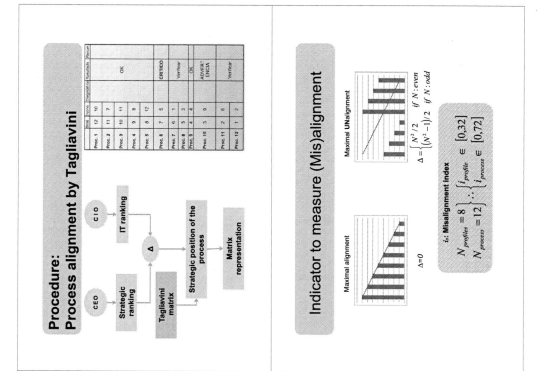

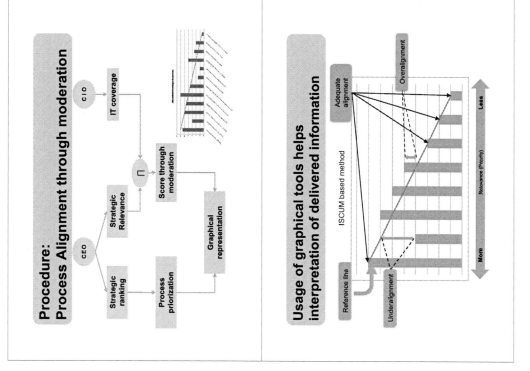

SMEs show less alignment at a process level

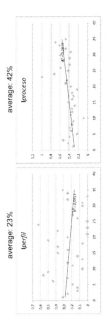

average: 23%

Iperfil

average: 42%

Iproceso

El test fue aplicado a un grupo de 35 PYME

* Periodo: Noviembre 2008 – Mayo 2009
* Clasificación:
  — Por trabajadores : 5(Mi), 13(P), 16(Me), 1(G)
  — Por Región   : 15(II), 3(III), 1(VIII), 16(M)
* Tipo de respondientes
  — Dueños/Gerentes : 27
  — Otros   : 8
* Tipo de entrevista
  — Personal   : 22
  — Por correo   : 13

Process alignment: Santiago better than Antofagasta

Process profile

Antofagasta (27%)   Santiago (26%)

Strategic profile alignment: Antofagasta better than Santiago

Strategic alignment profile

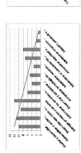

Antofagasta (19%)   Santiago (38%)

SMEs in Antofagasta are more defensive than in Santiago

Social Impact of IT: examples in Public Participation, Strategic Alignment and Open Source

Jens Hardings Perl <jhp@ing.puc.cl>

Departamento de Ciencia de la Computación
Pontificia Universidad Católica de Chile

Agenda

1. Open Source

2. Imparcialidad Tecnológica Informada

3. Study
   - Recommendations

Agenda

1. Open Source

2. Imparcialidad Tecnológica Informada

3. Study
   - Recommendations

Motivación

- Chile "official" policy of technological neutrality ("neutralidad tecnológica").
- defined late on
- Decisiones on technology have important access implications
  - Use of specific office software to fill out application forms
  - Use of a specific browser to access PSU scores

Motivación

- Chile "official" policy of technological neutrality ("neutralidad tecnológica").
- defined late on
- Decisiones on technology have important access implications
  - Use of specific office software to fill out application forms
  - Use of a specific browser to access PSU scores
  - ...

Motivación

- Chile "official" policy of technological neutrality ("neutralidad tecnológica").
- defined late on
- Decisiones on technology have important access implications
  - Use of specific office software to fill out application forms
  - Use of a specific browser to access PSU scores
  - ...

¿What is Technological Neutrality? I

- Multiple definitions
  - applies to laws (not applicable to policy technology)
  - "evaluation of cost over benefits" (José Antonio Barriga)
  - "objective factors" (Proyecto de Acuerdo 433, cámara de diputados)
  - "not to be inclined or favoring a particular technology over another at the time to decide the acquisition of a good or service" (José Francisco Salas)
  - "freedom of people, institutions, organizations and enterprises related to the state to choose what type of technology is to be implemented" (Hernán Orellana)
- Late "official" definition: (febrero de 2008, Directiva de Contratación Pública No. 8):

¿What is Technological Neutrality? II

- "Technology neutrality principle: The chilean government adheres to the principle of technological neutrality, implying no technology should be prefered over another, seeking the best available technlogy in the market at each time. However, justified reasons might exist in some circumstances to prefer certain type of technology, in which case, the justifications have to be clearly specified in the terms."

Neutrality in IT policies

Definition: "neutral" (source: Oxford Enlish Dictionary)
- {adj.} orig. Sc. Esp. of persons: not taking sides in a controversy, dispute, disagreement, etc.; not inclining toward any party, view, etc.; impartial, unbiased.
- ...
- By definition: in order to be neutral we should not use any technology
  - or we might use them all ¿¿??
- When using a particular technology, we loose neutrality (lock-in)
  - Migration costs
  - Initial investments already made
  - Mid-term plans

Neutrality is not always desirable

- SII: 97,3% personal tax reports made online (Abril 2007). 98,45% in 2009.
  - It is not achieved by being neutral
  - 1 technological system (HTTP, HTML, SSL, PKI based on X.509)
  - other systems are discouraged (SMTP instead of HTTP, PGP instead of SSL, PDF instead of HTML, ¿paper + pencil?)

Agenda

- Open Source
- Imparcialidad Tecnológica Informada
- Study
  - Recommendations

Informed Technological Imparciality

Principles
- No prior preference
- Usage of general criteria
  - sustainability
  - interoperability
  - ...(as simple and objective as possible)
- Mandatory enquiry
- Transparency: decisions publicly available
- Specific criteria
  - Particular exceptions o clarifications
- Does not avoid opting for a particular technology

Agenda

- Open Source
- Imparcialidad Tecnológica informada
- Study
  - Recommendations

Study to evaluate the use of Free Software in the State

- Review of diverse realities
  - Germany
  - Brasil
  - Venezuela
- Survey in Chilean State
- Interviews
  - Biblioteca del Congreso Nacional
  - Servicio Nacional de Aduanas
  - Superintendencia de Pensiones
- subject is wider that usage of FLOSS (Free / Libre / Open Source Software)
  - "sovereignty": no dependence or lock-in from providers, specific systems and hardware
  - open standards and interoperability

General Conclusions

- Objetive has not to be "subsidizing" FLOSS (Free / Libre / Open Source Software)
  - Not necessary, unless anticompetitive practices arise
  - On the contrary: el state should take advantage of FLOSS
- ¿How do we evaluate IT projects in order to maximize the benefit for the country?
- Much wider question thatn "¿use FLOSS or not?"

Support public entities

- Most have SME problems
  - small scale, staff with multiple roles
  - little training in IT specific areas
- Require support to enquire information and consider general criteria (sustainability and interoperability)
- Government entity to inform and correct possible mistakes
  - economies of scale
  - serious, up to date and available studies
  - best practices generation

Agenda

 Open Source

 Imparcialidad Tecnológica Informada

● Study
  ● Recommendations

Recommended strategic lines of action

● Keep chilean public sector policy
● Keep policy of respecting criteria of protecting:
  ● interoperability and data persistence
  ● respect public standards
  ● incorporating good security practices
  ● use of Open Systems
● Informed technological impartiality
● Evaluation of IT projects following TCO models
● Incorporate criteria of specificity, disgregation and replication

Criteria in acquisitions I

Specificity
  ● resulting developments from the existing base are (at least) property of the public entity
  ● avoidance of "lock-in" situations and allow mantainability
  ● apply open source model: better competition and usage of previous investments

Criteria in acquisitions II

Disgregation
  ● advantages of separating goods and services associated to FLOSS solutions, separating roles of Development, Deployment and Exploitation, and Support
  ● turnkey procurement model makes competition hard for smaller incumbents

Criteria in acquisitions III

Replicability
- licensing of custom developments and customizations published in a public repository under FLOSS licensing model
- reusability by public and private agents
- BSD type license
- internal and external developments

Results and Challenges

- Use of GobForge platform
- Incentives: PMG (Programa de Mejoramiento de la Gestión / Management improvement program)
- "MOP Manifest" on evaluating IT projects by Ministry of Public Works
  - to be published 28th of july 2009
- Challenges
  - How to generate successful collaboration
  - Generation of internal capabilities
  - Evolution of partly proprietary, partly open source solutions

Social Impact of IT: examples in Public Participation, Strategic Alignment and Open Source

Jens Hardings Perl <jhp@ing.puc.cl>

Departamento de Ciencia de la Computación
Pontificia Universidad Católica de Chile

Agenda

- Open Source
- Imparcialidad Tecnológica Informada
- Study
  - Recommendations